Speculations of War

Speculations of War

*Essays on Conflict in Science Fiction,
Fantasy and Utopian Literature*

Edited by ANNETTE M. MAGID

McFarland & Company, Inc., Publishers

Jefferson, North Carolina

This book has undergone peer review.

ISBN (print) 978-1-4766-7279-3
ISBN (ebook) 978-1-4766-4082-2

LIBRARY OF CONGRESS AND BRITISH LIBRARY
CATALOGUING DATA ARE AVAILABLE

Library of Congress Control Number 2021000373

Front cover illustration © 2021 T Studio/Shutterstock

Printed in the United States of America

*McFarland & Company, Inc., Publishers
Box 611, Jefferson, North Carolina 28640
www.mcfarlandpub.com*

For Hillel, Suzie, Elie, Jonathan, Tamar,
Yaakov, Ayelet, Shira, Ike, Devora, Jeremy, Dov, Sam, Ella,
Emuna Bella, Boaz Yididya, Oriyah Chava,
Aharon Yisrael, Moshe, Shmuel Simcha and Yehuda Meir

With hope for a peaceful future
for generations to come

Table of Contents

Part III. Cold War and Post–9/11

Preface

The intersection of war and science fiction has been a topic of fascination for me throughout my adolescent and adult life. A childhood trip to Gettysburg, a guided walk through the battle grounds, a digital map of battles fought, a diorama of uniformed boys and men aiming muskets with bayonets, blue against gray, all captured my imagination, as did Ambrose Bierce's most famous speculative science fiction Civil War story, "An Occurrence at Owl Creek Bridge" (1890). My interest in the interface of various wars and science fiction (SF) led to my panel at the Northeast Modern Language Association conference, where other scholars shared their unique approaches to the influences of war and SF. Those presentations turned into the essays that are included in this volume.

One unique element of this volume is its focus on how the approach to the SF war genre has changed over the years. Late 19th-century tales and utopian treatises such as Edward Bellamy's *Looking Backward*, for instance, predominantly focused on moral and social attitudes and were replete with lengthy lectures supporting economic, sociological and Marxian issues. Nearly 100 years later, SF such as *Star Wars: Episode V—The Empire Strikes Back* (1980) depicts inherent dangers of capitalism and imperialism, rendering planets as battlefields in space. Other books featuring similar studies of the interface of war and SF—such as Keith Booker's *Monsters, Mushroom Clouds and the Cold War* (2001), David Seed's *American Science Fiction and the Cold War: Literature and Film* (2013), and Steffen Hantke's *Monster in the Machine: Science Fiction Film and the Militarization of America After World War II*—focus on a singular period of time. This volume uniquely examines not only a variety of conflicts spanning the decades from the Civil War to 9/11 and the years that followed, it also includes theories of philosophers, such as Kenneth Burke, who seek reasons and offer rhetorical examples depicting the warring nature of mankind.

This volume uniquely examines conflicts from a philosophical introspection as well as with a futuristic forecasting. The inclusion of a variety of wars, correlating SF, fantasy and utopia, in literature and film allows

1

this volume to serve as a forum which bridges a variety of disciplines for a multiplicity of scholarly approaches such as through Kenneth Burke's literary analysis, historical, philosophical, psychological, sociological and film analyses. *Speculations of War: Essays on Conflict in Science Fiction, Fantasy and Utopian Literature* reveals the place of SF, fantasy and utopian literature within the conflicts throughout history, as an adept predictor and a thoughtful resolutionistic text.

The study of SF presented here is highly significant, not only for the understanding of the purpose of literature and film beyond their value as entertainment, but also for its seeming prescience in projecting issues and outcomes which may serve as guidelines to understanding the role of SF, fantasy and utopian literature in the assessment of highly volatile events. During a time of warring conflicts, individuals, who might be penalized for speaking out against a regime, might use another means of conversation to assess and possibly criticize their government. Science fiction, fantasy and utopian literatures approach issues that might be interpreted as inflammatory, but are often shrouded in the disguise of phenomenology, which may soften the message. One example of the employment of the SF genre to offer alternatives to reality can be witnessed in Miyazaki's SF films, which became part of the national debate in Japan during the 1970s through the 1990s regarding what it means to be Japanese in an increasingly global world.

In essays related to global wars, this volume speculates on the significance of cloaked references as well as the overt messages woven into the literature and films of SF, fantasy and utopias. At times, SF is used to allude to possibilities of alternative imagined political and social systems, as can be seen in Zülfü Livaneli's *Son Ada (The Last Island)*. As Asimov postulates, the basis for a good SF story is the inclusion of society; in addition, Darko Suvin's definition requires provisions for a feeling of alienation, estrangement (within) society. This approach allows for an exploration involving a variety of paths leading or blocking the protagonist's self-actualization as described in Maslow's hierarchy of needs. An exploration of three SF novels concerning the Algerian War of Independence reveals the various authors' skills at producing scenarios suggesting a semblance of truth, which promotes a reader's willingness to suspend disbelief. Such a study also reveals authors' focuses on SF alternative outcomes for what seems to be inevitable warfare.

Even in a time of seemingly irrefutable war, such as the 1904 Russo-Japanese war, journalist Jack London (who was on assignment in Japan) used reality as a springboard for the creation of his SF parable, "The Unparalleled Invasion," a futuristic historian's account of potential Chinese aggression. The story highlighted, among other simplistic reasons for their race-based fears, the irredeemable differences between Chinese people and white Americans of European descent. Those were (and still seem to be) genuine fears related to immigration, but they were cloaked in the guise of SF.

Another essay in this volume focuses on the War on Women. For more than a century, the utopian genre has functioned as a means for women to imagine futures in which women are the equals of men and recognized as fully human. It is documented, however, that feminist dystopian and utopian writers' responses to the War on Women are most frequently portrayed as metaphorical warfare on misogynist cultures. Male writers, on the other hand, depict futuristic male-dominated societies that reproduced, sometimes viciously, kyriarchal norms. In another essay, atomic cyborg love stories reveal the focus of Hollywood films during the Cold War period.

The variety of approaches related to the interface of global warfare and SF has not, until now, been covered in a single volume. Even though John J. Pierce's *Great Themes of Science Fiction: A Study in Imagination and Evolution* (1987) includes a variety of wars from early conflicts to the Revolutionary and Civil Wars through World Wars I and II, to support his argument regarding the strong interface between SF and war; Pierce devotes only one chapter within his three volume treatise. Utilizing a more comprehensive approach, *Speculations of War: Essays on Conflict in Science Fiction, Fantasy and Utopian Literature* offers the reader a unique opportunity to explore scholarly studies in one volume. The essays included herein yield an in-depth analysis of motivations related to the potential of war and the possibility of SF conjectured resolutions.

Introduction

Speculations of War: Essays on Conflict in Science Fiction, Fantasy and Utopian Literature is a multifaceted collection of essays written by scholars in a multiplicity of areas, including literature, history, philosophy, psychology, sociology and film, with each essay providing a unique perspective from the author's area of expertise. It is unique in that it approaches war and science fiction (SF) through the in-depth knowledge of a variety experts and a thorough analysis of the literature under discussion. The collection aims to present SF, fantasy and utopian literature as a platform for analyzing the myriad complexities of interfacing literature and film and as entities reflecting the impact of various wars on humanity. The result is a carefully compiled collection of literary studies which fits into the realms of SF, categorized, not as the traditional mechanical, hard SF, but into the rubric of what Ursula K. Le Guin described as speculative fiction, fantasy and utopia. Science fiction is often thought of as having "a concern with the future within the place of technology and nature: both causing and remedying future catastrophe" (Gadpaille 2018, 17). The volume's focus on speculative SF can be viewed as "a safe preference, given that all fiction engages in speculation" (Keeley 2015, 169); nonetheless, while a preponderance of SF, fantasy and utopian literatures have been identified through various surveys as "still a 'guy' thing" (Barron 2004, 499), with a readership of 74 percent male and 26 percent female, this volume aims to present a more balanced ratio of both male and female scholars who are also SF, fantasy and utopia enthusiasts.

Part I, "Fomenting War," begins with an in-depth analysis of a landmark publication by philosopher Kenneth Burke, *A Grammar of Motives*, a meditation on the "drama of human relations." In "*Ad Bellum Purificandum*: Kenneth Burke's Rhetoric of Fiction Between the Wars," AmyLea Clemons analyzes Burke's theories of language, motives, and drama which are infused with a preoccupation (what he would call an "occupational psychosis") with how human communication both creates conflict and can "purify" war through reaching consensus. Clemons argues that Burke's concepts of "purification," "entelechy," and "form" speak directly to the mid-century SF genre's occupational psychosis. Burke's work illuminates the unique rhetorical properties of SF as symbolic action—as "equipment for living" toward war's purification and termination.

"Speculations on the Interconnectedness of Edward Bellamy, His Utopian Writing and the Civil War" offers a utopian viewpoint embracing the termination of war. My (Annette M. Magid's) essay examines Bellamy's quest to create a perfect society, free of conflict, war and strife. The essay reveals the profound effect *Looking Backward* and *Equality* had on nearly 1 million readers in the late 19th century and the influence of Bellamy's philosophy into the 21st century. Furthermore, I argue that Bellamy's political focus was a possible reaction to the devastation he witnessed when soldiers returned home, physically and emotionally scarred following the Civil War.

Erin M. Roll's "Clouds Over the Valley: Images of War and Peace in the Films of Hayao Miyazaki" concentrates on three films: *Nausicaä and the Valley of the Wind* (1984); *Laputa: Castle in the Sky* (1986); and *Howl's Moving Castle* (2004). Roll explores Miyazaki's childhood in post–World War II Japan, which Roll asserts influences his vision as a filmmaker. Roll argues that Miyazaki's views on war, spirituality and pacifism found their way into Miyazaki's films; however, Roll observes that good and evil are not clearly defined. This essay also explores the persistent fear of rage, and what it will lead people to do, if left unchecked; near the end of each film, rage comes to its head in the form of a massive, almost apocalyptic, battle.

In Part II, "World Conflicts," Emrah Atasoy asserts in "Epistemological Warfare(s) in Dystopian Narrative: Zülfü Livaneli's *Son Ada* and Anthony Burgess' The Wanting Seed" that philosophy of the knowledge of warfare plays a crucial role in utopian thought, stipulating that whoever holds the mainstream episteme at hand determines the means of social engineering and of regulation. Atasoy asserts that although the literary dystopia presents a dark, pessimistic vision, the utopian impulse does not vanish completely. The utopian hope is maintained at the end of dystopian narrative despite the dystopian impositions as the reader is guided through the lens/perspective of the protagonist. Atasoy's study analyzes epistemological war within a narrative which reveals the problematic nature of identity politics in dystopian narratives. Warfare becomes a tool through which the unique individual identity of the protagonist is reinforced.

Ruy Burgos-Lovece's "Three Options and Three Science Fiction Novels Concerning the Algerian War of Independence" analyzes the textual world of SF where completely new societies are built to inform existing ones from different points of view. Burgos-Lovece explores three speculative French SF texts that portray, intentionally or not, possible French societies issuing from the end result of the Algerian War of Independence. In addition to mere societal resonance, the three novels portray a pattern of progressive decline in France's expectations for the end result of the Algerian War: from the heights of optimism as a united nation that consolidates its world preeminence to a consolation-prize solution as a mutually helpful federation to the depths of despair, depicted as a nation turned to cattle by its former pets.

Jack London's service as a war correspondent in Manchuria on a mission to cover the Russo-Japanese War is the background for Julie Hugonny's "Napoleonic Conquest and Chinese Absorption: Dialectics of Territorial Expansion in Jack London's 'The Unparalleled Invasion.'" Hugonny illustrates that London's story showcases different approaches to conquest and offers a prime example of early 20th century fear of the "yellow peril." By telling the story of extermination of the Chinese people within the safe confines of SF, a genre defined by its powers of extrapolation, its firm grounding on historical facts, and its provable science, Hugonny illustrates that London offers a reflection on the state of modern war, and the consequences of refusing to play by its rules.

Part III, "Cold War and Post–9/11" begins with Naomi R. Mercer's "Waging Metaphorical Warfare in Feminist Dystopian and Utopian Writing," which examines 1970s feminist utopian texts in which many authors carried the Cold War and its threat of nuclear annihilation to its logical conclusion by depicting post-apocalyptic societies that seized the opportunity to build egalitarian communities. Mercer also discusses some of the dystopian novels of the 1980s and beyond which reproduced traditional gender roles in extremis. Mercer analyzes texts from both the utopian genre during the Second Wave feminist movement and from the dystopian turn that occurred during the backlash against feminist gains. In addition, Mercer focuses on novels depicting a metaphorical war against pervasive kyriarchal systems of oppression—most recently manifested in the current political climate as the "War on Women," which Mercer stipulates is just as insidious and catastrophic as nuclear holocaust—and has been ever-present in American culture from the post–World War II era.

In "A Call to Arms: *Star Wars, Star Trek* and the Science Fiction of the German Democratic Republic," Thomas P. David assesses Horst Ansorge's novel *Raumkundschafter Katman* [*Space Scout Katman*] (1987) and Wolfgang Kellner's short story "Tödlicher Irrtum" [Fatal Mistake] (1985), which depict hostile confrontations with alien civilizations, necessitating armed and ready vigilance in the face of an existential threat. David suggests that violently aggressive aliens are the antithesis of the commonly accepted trope of Anglo-American SF. David refutes this violent SF approach since there were to be no bloody clashes of SF civilizations in the pages of the German Democratic Republic (GDR) and stipulates that SF civilizations would necessarily represent a higher stage of development and would accordingly be inherently peaceful. Juxtaposing reality with SF, David asserts that with Ronald Reagan's "Address to the Nation on Defense and National Security" also known as the "Star Wars Speech" on March 23, 1983, revealed that such a violent confrontation could became a really-existing possibility. David stipulates that in the context of the renewed arms race of the Reagan era and the development of the Strategic Defense Initiative, the GDR literary works are a warning of the clear and present danger of a colonization of the world (and the space around it) by the U.S.

In the final essay, "Love and Death in Two Nuclear Defense Films," Doug Davis explores post-human romance stories *Strategic Air Command* (1955), and Stanley Kubrick's black comedy, *Dr. Strangelove: Or, How I Learned to Stop Worrying and Love the Bomb* (1964). Some of Hollywood's most celebrated films about the bomb aren't really about the bomb at all. Instead, what they are really about is love. Davis argues that the Cold War impacted the war film genre by forcing a revision of Hollywood's long-established codes of personal melodrama to include the non-human. These films condense their era's debates over nuclear war into stories about the intimate and even erotic relationship men have with their war machines, resulting in a kind of kinky "atomic cyborg love story" within the Cold War SF mini-genre.

In this volume, the multiplicity of approaches to SF, fantasy and utopia, spanning countries, cultures, philosophers, scientists and creative thinkers is intended to provide a more in-depth conversation related to the dynamics of various wars as well as impending conflicts. Scholarship continues to reinforce the various approaches to understanding the influence of war embedded in SF, fantasy and utopian literature and film, offering postulations which in turn suggest possibilities for the existence and continuation of life in general and humankind specifically. It is through the speculation of possibilities that resolutions to worldwide encounters may be realized.

PART I

Fomenting War

Ad Bellum Purificandum

Kenneth Burke's Rhetoric
of Fiction Between the Wars

AmyLea Clemons

At first glance, the relationship between SF and war might seem obvious: the tropes of SF fiction seem to almost rely on space battles, laser guns, fantastic explosions, and a lingering taste of the (particularly American) military structures. While we could spend time here listing the tropes and moral claims made by SF texts about war, a more productive essay would reconsider how the genre's rhetorical and cultural actions are always rooted in a rhetoric—and a rhetorical theory—of war and conflict. Wayne Booth's *The Rhetoric of Fiction* is often the first resource for connecting literature and rhetoric, but SF scholarship could better be served by an examination of the theories that informed much of Booth's project: Kenneth Burke's network of theories that link rhetoric, war, and literature. But more than just an application of Burke's ideas is warranted here: this essay seeks to do as Carl Freedman does in *Critical Theory and Science Fiction* (Freedman 2000, xvi)[1]: to find the ways that SF texts are themselves theoretical utterances. In fact, SF texts reflect and enact Burke's theories about conflict and cooperation in explicit, visible ways *because* Burke created his theories while engaging with the culture that produced both "literary" SF like *1984* and long forgotten pulp SF, and an extended exploration of the intersections of Burke's rhetoric, symbolic explorations of war, and the SF genre is long overdue.

For the sake of coherency, I limit this discussion to Burke's rhetorical theories developed from the 1930s to the late 1950s. In particular, this essay argues that the social-epistemic "New Rhetoric" founded[2] by Burke is not just a set of alternate terms that scholars might use to analyze wartime SF, but that the period's SF texts and the New Rhetoric present parallel theories of the role of communication in conflict that come to the same conclusion: Without cooperative, critical, and creative language use, humanity has little hope for survival. In this light, Burke's early and mid-career work becomes a useful reference for SF scholars wishing to consider the science fiction of this time as not only *impacted* by war, but as performing and creating their own theories of communication, war, and symbolic conflict.

This essay serves as a mediating space to consider Burke, rhetoric, and literature in the period roughly from 1930 to 1950; it attempts to use Burke's theoretical tools—which are themselves best understood as responses to ongoing global conflicts of that time—to suggest ways SF scholars might reread the era's science fiction as attempts to not just reflect cultural tensions, but to actively shape to those concerns, by "purifying" the major terms in conflict during that time—the terms associated with nationalism, racism, scapegoating, and conquest that would, eventually, lead to a Second World War we often associate with terms also connected to science fiction: progress, technology, computing, futurism. First, this essay sets the boundaries for this discussion, outlining the field of science fiction scholarship's basic assumptions about the texts of this era and their themes, representations, and attitudes. Next, Kenneth Burke's basic principles of rhetoric and literature are reviewed and re-read as an argument for creating literature with a particularly self-aware brand of rhetorical expression in order to purify war. This essay ends, as Burke liked to do, with a kind of cheat sheet recommending future studies that acknowledge the complex theories of communication already present in wartime SF literature, perhaps *because of* its position in history.

SF in the Early 20th Century

This essay seeks to discuss "wartime" SF, with a special focus on the period leading up to the Second World War. In SF scholarship, this particular period is difficult to characterize simply, since period definition trails only genre definition as a major preoccupation of the field. To begin with, Adam Roberts initial definition of the SF genre as a whole notes that defining SF is at times "tedious debate" (Roberts 2016, 4), we might even argue, based on the topics of SF theories that defining SF is a major preoccupation of the field, perhaps in part due to the perception of the genre as somehow less than literary. Those who seek to describe SF as a set of features often omit subgenres like dystopian and utopian fiction in order to create cohesive portraits of various eras in the history of the genre. Roberts constructs a cohesive history of the genre based on its emergence as an alternate epistemology after the Western crisis of religion; despite (or perhaps because of) his social-constructivist approach to the genre, he divides the periods of SF history in conventional ways for the field: after decades (or centuries) of proto–SF works, the technological revolutions of the late 19th century led to a genre that emphasizes the "wonder" of the scientific world and the possibilities for human progress therein (Roberts 2016, 3–4). Like most others, Roberts only obliquely considers war—the conflict that drives the formation of SF for him is more personal, an epistemic crisis for the new reading masses following the Enlightenment and Reformation (Roberts 2016, 4–5).

Roberts separates the early 20th century into two parallel tracks for SF: the "high modernist" end (Roberts 2016, 228) in which he includes the more philosophical and socially conscious SF and the "pulp" side of the genre. While the high modernist texts sought to help audiences work through the political upheavals after World War I, and to "come to terms with what those changes meant" (Roberts 2016, 229), the pulp side was "by and large, a puerile and aesthetically limited literature, aimed at the lowest denominator" (Roberts 2016, 259). Between the wars, these two lines of SF came to codify the genre at large: containing, as the pulps did, "a particular emphasis on excitement, wonder, sexual arousal and self-satisfaction, mediating the emotional response of their readers through technology and science" (Roberts 2016, 259) but also fully invested in questioning and exploring possible outcomes for the human race.

Most define the World War II era SF as a "Golden Age" brought on by John Campbell's editorship at the magazine *Amazing Stories* (Attebery 2003, 37). Pinning a specific date range proves difficult, though, beyond Campbell's start date in 1938, and like the genre itself, the end point for the Golden Age remains hotly contested. In the period just prior to World War II up through the 1950s, though, a few generalizations can be made, with or without the idea of a "golden age": the work in this time reflects the excitement and wonder appeal of the pulps, but does so with some social consciousness. The glitter and glam of "the future" was never far from the aesthetics of the magazines and novels, but this period also included Isaac Asimov's musings on ethics and humanism and Robert Heinlein's narratives of social revolutions The SF between the wars and at the beginning of the Golden Age was "an especially social fiction," concerned with the issues of "science, modernity, and progress" (Cheng 2012, 7).

In short, what this essay calls "wartime SF texts" were responsible for characterizing the genre as a space for cultural exploration, fueled by not just the real world science and technology of that era, but the discussions that logically followed such changes.

Because of SF's multiple purposes and its role as a way audiences understood their own worlds as major changes occurred, SF scholars have not been wanting for literary theories or methodologies of interpretation. The narrative scholars have built to explain this is necessarily founded on a mixture of cultural analysis (wide ranging studies focusing on the religious, socio-economic, and educational influences on SF developing in United States, Russia, and other regions that pioneered the first SF works), the history of publishing trends (to account for the move from pulp books to more serious "literary" SF), genre theory (or theories—perhaps the most hotly debated research question), biographical research (identifying specific big name figures in the establishment of SF as a genre), and, of course the philosophy of/history of/sociology of science (or other iterations, which provide metacritical studies of how "science" came to be a fictional subject in the first place). And these studies are certainly valuable for their insights into specific generic qualities that we have identified as SF. They are also at times inadequate for considering SF's specific rhetorical actions during World War II.

World War II SF

While scholars disagree in how they categorize the relevant dates involved, and the term "golden" itself, it is clear that the post–World War II era allowed the genre to settle and become a major force in social construction. Genre is, as Carolyn Miller argues, a social action: It emerges as a standard response to repeated rhetorical situations, and thus is a major cultural influence, reifying the social positions involved in those situations. Through genre study, critics can determine dominant ideologies and relationships among readers, writers, and texts for the repeated (conventional) situation at hand (Miller 1984, 154–60). Here, the situation in question would be not just global war, but the anxieties experienced by an educated, reading public in a highly mediated era—a far different rhetorical situation than the global conflicts of the past. World War II necessarily, then, left its mark on the SF of the age, even if the conventional understanding of the Golden Age omits war and its effects as a theme.

Darko Suvin's characterization of SF as "cognitive estrangement" hints at the genre's extra-textual effects, but the particular impact of that kind of defamiliarization on the wartime literature has not been a strong focus (Suvin 2014).[3] In fact, in 2014, a reprint of the cornerstone chapter of Suvin's landmark book *Metamorphoses of Science Fiction* includes a Postscript in which the theorist laments that his original theory failed to account for issues of class and power, in what he considers to be a naive attempt to "freeze out history" and excise it from his aesthetic reading of the genre. And while Fredric Jameson's work on SF as a genre specifically designed to enlighten audiences to their social positions and masked ideologies ends with his claims in *Archaeologies of the Future* about humanity's essential utopian desire (Jameson 2005, 3),[4] how specific fictional texts make that argument and feed that drive during war time in general and the particular situations of World War II has been less thoroughly explored than it could be.

Most scholars studying the Golden Age do reference the war as a cultural influence on the topics the genre focused its energies on, but the ensuing discussion stays at the level of theme and representation. For example, John Cheng's introduction to what he calls "interwar" SF literature focuses on the idea of "science" as the driving force behind the creative scientific fictions of that era just prior to World War II (Cheng 2012, 6–8). In Cheng's reading, this period between the wars established "figures and ideas that have come to characterize the genre as we know it today," including the "tropes [that] organized both science fiction's literary tradition and its larger social discourse" (Cheng 2012, 9). Cheng concludes that those tropes emerged in large part due to the figure of "Science" itself as the era's epistemological and cultural foundation, leading to a generally optimistic attitude about technology, art, and human progress. While Cheng notes the genre's ability to negotiate audience fears of invasion by racial Others his focus on the participatory nature of science fiction during this era and not the rhetorical potential those stories carry to direct cultural attitudes toward war.

Of course, some critics do attempt to track the cultural impacts of/on SF literature in general; if we extend their theses, it is clear that any analysis of SF in the 20th century requires some accounting for the reciprocal relationship between the war and the texts that influenced it/were influenced by it. For example, Suvin's work does attempt—however much he criticizes himself—to explain how dystopia, utopia, and science fiction texts require audiences to imagine "utopian horizons" and constitute Possible Worlds (PWs) in their imaginations by positioning their own "empirical" (experienced) worlds against the fictional constructs in SF texts (Suvin 2010, 124–25). While Suvin's later work rightly critiques his initial erasure of class, race, gender and other alterities possible in this imagining audience, his model does have room for that kind of historicizing and rhetorical analysis of the relationships between audience interpretation of SF and their own social positions. In fact, by suggesting that the "openness" of a utopian text in particular is formed by a readerly action, and that action is, logically, determined by the reader's position, Suvin could be seen as recommending an analysis the localized, historicized meaning of a text that would *necessitate* explorations of the War.

Scholarly work on the early and mid–20th century has become so rooted in the narrative of the boisterous, romanticized joy of the pulps and the Golden Age that the impacts of the two wars and the period of turmoil between them has been oddly excised. It is, of course, important to see how the technological drives and sense of futurity created an optimistic sense of science and exploration. But if we extend Jameson beyond his assertion of a human drive associated with "wish fulfillment" we see that the desire to create ideal socio-economic situations beyond our lived experience is an echo of wartime conquest, globalization, and even Jameson's own concept of late capitalism as a divisive system (Jameson 2005, 55). The utopian end of SF is always political for Jameson because it is a cognitive model on which to build new versions of those system; it is not a giant leap to suggest that the rhetorical expression of these drives might also involve managing the idea of war itself.

These cultural reading do allow us to, for example, discuss how changes to the means of production (pulp fiction) worked in concert with changes to the expectations and experiences of the reading audience, or let us reveal the cultural tensions that defined the ideologies behind the war to give us the golden age of SF, as Freedman argues, the criticism tends to be unidirectional in its assumption about how SF interacts with the world—theories exist to be applied to text. While Jameson separates utopian impulses from utopian projects then (Jameson 2005, 4), he still fails to account for the *literariness* of the texts he uses as examples. And searching for a literary-cultural answer through mixtures of historicism, post–Marxist theory (as Jameson, for example), and strictly Formalist readings, such studies often lead critics around the edges of the social-epistemic dimension of rhetoric without actually engaging rhetorical theory as an explanatory model or considering that the texts themselves may be.

For example, a text like the *Cambridge Companion to Science Fiction*, with all the constitutive power such academic field guides perform, includes as principal methods and theories such as historical criticism; genre theory; critical lenses like Marxist, feminist, structuralist, and postmodern theories; and reviews of major themes and figures in the field. As editors Edward James and Farah Mendlesohn write in their Foreword to the *Cambridge Companion*, science fiction scholarship has emerged in nontraditional ways, leading to an odd array of critical methods: "[M]ost of the tools of scholarship, like the postwar publication of science fiction in books, was provided by amateurs, by dedicated fans, some of them ascending to scholarly objectivity" like the big names the *Companion* reviews (James and Mendlesohn 2003, xvii). And so despite the strong theoretical ties that Freeman argues for, science fiction scholarship, a major theoretical lens has been left largely unexamined: the rhetorical. And if we are so concerned about give and take, and if we are to argue that SF has had serious, fundamental impacts on our understanding of the world, our technology, and our communication, then it is equally worth thinking about the ways that theories of rhetoric are themselves already embedded in and part of the discourse of science fiction.

The Literary Burke

Kenneth Burke has long been recognized as a major figure in the fields of rhetoric, communication, and literary criticism. His prolific career, spanning six decades of the 20th century provides scholars with a wide range of tools, approaches, and definitions; from his initial career as a literary critic and editor of the *Dial* to his midcareer shift to rhetoric, to his later work with religion and the rituals of the scapegoat mechanism, Burke's ideas are representative of the range of possible approaches to the humanities in general. His broad field of knowledge in literature, history, science, and philosophy results in texts some have difficulty reading; and his theories tend to build on his previous work, expanding and jumping off, requiring the audience to remember his previous iterations of the ideas to keep up.[5] An eclectic figure, Burke is difficult to place in a single literary or rhetorical school, and his life-long avoidance of attaching himself to a specific university, or even field of study, means that those who use Burke find themselves more involved in Burke Studies than any single theoretical lens; he is, as Ed Appel suggests, an "intellectual guerrilla fighter" (Appel 2004).

Literary concerns took up much of Burke's early career. His first book, *Counter-Statement* (1931), argues for literature as both a separate aesthetically defined text and as socially-aware rhetorics. *Permanence and Change* (1934) focused on language's role in creating the conditions for change (with literature as Burke's key examples). *Attitudes Toward History* (1937) continued that discussion, and began to introduce material that Burke would focus his master trilogy: *A Grammar of Motives* (1945), *A Rhetoric of Motives* (1950), and the incomplete *A Symbolic of Motives*—all of which attempted to explain not just what motivates us but how we communicate those motives, framing and reframing our realities in symbolic action. In this period, Burke also attempted a cohesive literary theory in *The Philosophy of Literary Form* (1941), which can and should be read in parallel with his other work to point to the specifically *literary* nature of language that leads to social change.

Despite the density and—admittedly—scattered presentation of his writings, Burke's ideas are easily borrowed as tools for critics of all kinds of human interactions and they provide a literary scholar a way into rhetoric and vice versa. For example, Burke's claim that literature is "equipment for living" is easily borrowed by those engaging in cultural studies, linking the act of reading to social acts (Burke 1974, 293).[6] But Burke also claims that works of literature are "strategic answers, stylized answers" to the conflicts that form the basis for war (Burke 1974, 1)[7]; the techniques of that styling and strategizing and the logical structures that form the argument for the answers become the basis of what we might call "genre." Therefore, instead of divorcing Burke's literary scholarship from his attempts to describe how rhetoric can help us move beyond war we should be more closely linking the two, paying attention to how Burke's historical location, writing between the wars and during the Great Depression, comes to bear on his ideas about communication in general and literature in particular (Weiser 2008, 21).[8]

It is not surprising that Burke's comments also refer to the literature of his time, including texts we would now call SF and dystopian fiction. When Burke writes to his friend Malcolm Cowley just after the unleashing of the second atomic bomb on Japan that "[t]he era of the Mad Scientist of the B movie now seems with us in a big way," and that "[t]here seems now no logical thing to do but go on tinkering with this damned thing until they have blown up the whole damned world," he uses both a science fiction trope and a dystopian rhetoric of hyperbolic extrapolation to critique his surroundings (Burke 1988, 268). While his literary reviews do not seem to include science fiction texts, he is clearly aware of the genre as a shorthand, and scattered references to SF tropes and themes—particularly utopianist thought and hyperbolic extrapolations—appear throughout even his more traditional reviews. In one book review from the 1950s, Burke ends his critique quite bleakly: "All the year round, mankind is an open season. And may the experiments of the physicist, as modified by the military, permit the experiments of the humanist to continue.... Spare us the effects of a 'progress' from the fall of Adam to the atomic fall-out" (Burke 2010, 409). Burke's play on words in this last phrase hints at his solution of purification: the ambiguity and play of language that all rhetoric, but literature in particular, can provide.

In his very first book *Counter-Statement* (1931) Burke struggles to prove that art can be both "aesthetic" and have a social purpose. In the very first section he poses a question that appears in his work for the next 30 years: How can literature act as a preventative measure, interfering in what Burke sees as our destructive tendency to "perfect" our conditions into a state of decay? Elizabeth Weiser argues that Burke's initial struggle to find a way to "fall on the bias" and "cut across" the arguments between those who would see literature as pure aesthetics and those 1930s revolutionaries who wanted to employ literature as propaganda eventually lead Burke to his broad theories of communication, conflict, and resolution (Weiser 2008, 8); that attempt to rhetoricize literature without losing its aesthetic complexity drives the theories found in the first half of Burke's career. Burke's work up through A Rhetoric of Motives in 1950 constitutes a rhetorical theory of literature that is always inherently preoccupied with war and infused with what we might call a "dystopian imagination" that mirrors the prevalent speculative fiction of the mid–20th century in the U.S. Therefore, to understand the literature of that period means uncovering the rhetorical strategies that form and inform texts—a task for which Burke's theories are well-suited.

Likewise, though, Burke scholars—who tend to limit themselves to either Burke's social-rhetorical work or his literary criticism—should pay attention to the ways SF literature (and particularly dystopianist thought) is involved in much of Burke's early theories. The themes and theses of the literature of World War II and the period between the wars inflect Burke's social theories about war just as much as the wartime concerns filter into his literary criticism. In fact, Burke's central idea of rhetoric as a means of purifying war is inextricable from his position as a wartime scholar and his literary theories.

Burke's Rhetoric of Literature

Burke's A Rhetoric of Motives outlines a new approach for modern critics analyzing how texts work. Early in A Rhetoric of Motives, Burke makes the startling claim that rhetoric is *not* about persuasion—a top-down, author-controlled action—but about what he calls *identification*: "A is not identical with his colleague, B. But insofar as their interests are joined, A is identified with B. Or he may identify himself with B even when their interests are not joined, if he assumes that they are, or is persuaded to believe so" (Burke 1969, 20). Exactly how A convinces B (or vice versa) that "their interests are joined" and what ultimate effect this joining creates becomes Burke's preoccupation. In this revision of what Burke calls the "traditional approach" (Burke 1969, xiv)[9] to rhetoric, identification serves as "an accessory to the standard lore." By revising and adding to what was the standard view of persuasion at that time, Burke is able "to show how rhetorical analysis throws light on literary texts and human relations generally" (Burke 1969, xv). Burke's phrasing here implies that the literary is a special case of "human relations" and that both are in need of rhetorical criticism.

In Burke's New Rhetoric, rhetorical discourse is not just an explicitly persuasive speech or written treatise; rhetoric happens when identification enables what Burke calls the "ambiguities of substance" (Burke 1969, 21). Individuals are not necessarily separate from one another (the differences that divide them are bridged) once they are engaged in the symbolic act of identification: "In being identified with B, A is 'substantially one' with a person other than himself. Yet at the same time he remains unique, an individual locus of motives. Thus he is both joined and separate, at once a distinct substance and consubstantial with another" (Burke 1969, 21).[10] In other words, rhetoric, once the province of pure persuasion, is now a matter of being, identity, and ethics. Instead of wielding textual weapons designed to hammer the audience into submission, the rhetor's main job, for Burke, is to create a merger of identities—to show that the listener's *interest* is the same as the rhetor's. Both this discussion and Burke's essay "Rhetoric—Old and New" from 1951 clearly asks scholars to readjust their view of rhetoric—and, importantly, he does so in both texts by starting his inquiries with literary criticism and explication (Burke 1951, 202–9).

Burke's insistence on a "new" rhetoric that is founded on cooperation emerged directly as a result of his fears that emerged during World War II (Clark 1997). Gregory Clark defines Burke's project as utopian in its desire to end conflict through a process of identification, even if "the nature of language as well as human nature makes the cooperative utopia he envisions not possible" (Clark 1997). Identification is not just, then, a persuasive tool, but a critical component of cooperation. Identification may be Burke's most important tool in examining how we might go about "purifying" war to prevent the events of the world wars from repeating themselves: If we are able to see ourselves in the Other through the use of linguistic identifiers, we can eliminate the impulse to engage in violent conflict.

The role of literature in the identification process first becomes important when we consider Burke's assertion that all rhetoric (identification) is first dependent on a prior division—a separation of self and other: "Identification is compensatory to division. If men were not apart from one another, there would be no need for the rhetorician to proclaim their unity. If men were wholly and truly of one substance, absolute communication would be of man's very essence" (Burke 1969, 22). While Burke scholars have argued about the ontological implications for this claim at the practical level, it means that *speaking* is dependent initially on an already-established *conflict*: a conflict of interest, identity, or simply *being* separated from each other by nature of having unique bodies.[11]

This primary division is, for Burke, necessary for the acting-together to occur; if we were wholly identified, without some kind of conflict, there is "no reason for strife" because none of our terms or situations can come into conflict. Division is necessary to create new ideas and move human history, or we risk "becoming too hopelessly ourselves" (Blakesley 2002, 17).[12] Rhetoric is the way we balance identification and division; by enacting "symbolic action" to blur the lines between Self and Other, rhetors can ease the tensions caused by that primary division. Or, more simply put, by showing the "sameness" of opposing sides, rhetors can mediate—with words, images, sounds—the space between bodies in conflict to suggest that we are all in this together. Rhetoric is not, then, manipulation or trickery, but a cooperation that emerges from a shared sense of identity and purpose through a transformation of the terms we use to create and maintain those identities.

It is important to note that Burke's discussion of rhetoric intertwined with the literary; in fact, *A Rhetoric of Motives* uses Milton's *Samson* as its opening example of the transformative power of language and rhetoric's ability to define terms that lead to merger and division. As Reuckert reminds us, when speaking of rhetoric as identification, Burke consistently uses *literary* examples to demonstrate ways consubstantiality is achieved and conflict managed, and the whole of dramatism is built from the pieces of Burke's literary theories (Reuckert 1982, xiv).[13] But rhetorical scholars tend to brush aside the literariness of Burke's foundational term, considering Burke's key move as an erasure of the line between rhetoric and literature, a kind of flattening of literature and speech into a singular idea of communication (Burke, A., Jensen, and Selzer 2018).[14] And Burke himself does at times seem to espouse this belief, particularly when he talks about literature as "equipment for living" and poetry as a kind of "stylized answer, strategic answer." But if we take Burke at his word that literature is, indeed, "strategic," then we need to ask what strategies particularly "literary" texts—poetry, myth, narratives, novels—offer that enticed Burke to use primarily literary references in his introduction to his most important ideas: identification, war, and motivation.

Literature is Burke's key metaphor for all of his work; his theory of "dramatism" or the "drama of human relations" is what ultimately threads together his interdisciplinary work in literature, history, rhetoric, philosophy, linguistics, religion, sociology, and economics. The language of the drama—with its agents, acts, and scenes—as a metalinguistic model of analysis lets Burke approach—as cultural studies theorists would later insist upon—everything as a text, in particular, a staged narrative. Considering the theater of war that was his backdrop, Burke's insistence on the poetic as not just a reflection of the world but a critical tool for reading the world makes sense; how else could he, in his favorite phrase, "come to terms" with the chaos that was the Second World War and its aftermath?

Burke's literary reviews alone justify his implications that literature might serve as a critical method for explaining conflict's linguistic roots—and therefore how war might be purified through the symbolic mediation of our tensions. In addition to his own reading, Burke remained deeply entrenched in the literary circles of that time. Robert Wess and Selzer's *Kenneth Burke and His Circles* and Selzer's *Kenneth Burke in Greenwich Village* highlight the philosopher's continued literary presence from the

1920s and 1930s among major modernist literary figures and critics, and as Anthony Burke, Kyle Jenson, and Zelzer point out in their introduction to Burke's unfinished manuscript titled *War of Words*, Burke's "regularly irregular" teaching positions at universities around the United States allowed him to interact with many major literary figures of the time—both critics and authors (Burke, A., Jensen, and Selzer 2018, "Introduction"). Burke's interlocutors during this period included both poets: notably, William Carlos Williams and Robert Penn Warren; and critics: Stanley Edgar Hyman and Richard McKeon (Burke, A., Jensen, and Selzer 2018, "Introduction"). From Burke's correspondence, it is clear that he was not alone in trying to furiously work out a theory of language, literature, and war that would help him understand the events unfolding around him.

With his foundational texts drafted between the wars and during World War II, Burke seeks to understand what literature is for, and he comes up with the only answer that could have been satisfying to a voracious reader like himself: more reading. For Burke, rhetoric, war, and literature cannot be untangled from each other—and for those of us looking backward at the SF literature of this time, Burke's comments on war and what writing does for readers and writers negotiating the terms of conflict provide a look into philosophies (and the terms that comprise them) that appear regularly through the dystopian and SF works of this period.

Purifying World War

What does it mean to use literature to "purify" war? Burke scholars offer different answers, depending on which of Burke's texts they emphasize, but in the broadest sense, Burke's entire theory of dramatism might be seen as his attempt to work out just what that purification looks like. Ultimately we might say along with Weiser, Blakesley, and James Zappen and that "purification" is the use of a dialectical process to transcend the terms we use that create our sense of order, since order and hierarchy are found the categories needed to justify war (Zappen 2009, 279–301). More simply, purifying war through literature requires the rhetor and the audience to agree to alter the terms surrounding the conflict—and hopefully with that, remove the impetus for violence to the Other.

Another way to consider purification is through "dramatism." Weiser argues that Burke's theory of dramatism, while intended to be used "beyond its immediate scene," is a product of Burke's wartime fears as much as his literary theories (Weiser 2008, xii). Dramatism as a theory "explores and encourages dialectic (the celebration of differing perspectives) and transcendence (the search for points of merger) in a parliamentary debate that is the opposite of the stance of monolithic certainty mandated by total war" (Weiser 2008, xiv). Weiser's linkage between war and language revolves around that key word *certainty*; instead of a monologic voice, Burke argued for a "babel" of voices or a "parliament" that parallels poetic strategies of ambiguity (Weiser 2008, 63). Instead of the kind of "dialectical transcendence" available in the Hegelian synthesis model, Burke argued for a "poetic transcendence" of terms that would avoid certainty (Weiser 2008, 106–7).

This ambiguity through poetics can be achieved in many ways; what makes literature so important to Burke's theory of purification is not so much its privileged status as an aesthetic artifact—if that were the case, then the purification would be *limited to* poetics and would be a rare occurrence. Instead, literature might be seen as an exemplar of what language can do: offer new choices (new terminologies) for how to perceive our own situations. By strategically employing the ambiguities of language humans can "manage the conflicts within [their] original perspective or choose new linguistic principles" to describe reality and thus prescribe action (Weiser 2008, 130). Fiction—particularly science fiction—gives voice to those new perspectives and linguistic choices by playing out the "what ifs" of those changes and providing for the audience those linguistic tools to make the changes themselves.

Creating this theory was Burke's "obsession." Anthony Burke, Jenson, and Selzer's recent archival work to recover the incomplete *War of Words* manuscript suggests that for much of Burke's drafting of *A Rhetoric of Motives,* poetics remained a key term, and it was only late in the production of that text, that a major section on poetics was excised, leaving the book still heavily influenced by literature but without a clear statement of *why* Burke felt it important (Burke, A., Jensen, and Selzer 2018, "Introduction"). Re-linking the literary to Burke's project of purifying war, though, is what ultimately betrays Burke as a writer deeply influenced by—if not specific SF texts—the themes and theses of the SF literature of his time.

Burke as Dystopian Theorist

While we might take time to tease out Burke's relationship to Golden Age SF in general, it is far easier to see Burke's thinking on war as directly influenced by both the philosophy and literary genre we today call "dystopian." Burke has often been accused of "utopian" tendencies; Clark and Zappen both use that term as a descriptor of Burke's optimistic view for rhetoric. But others have identified Burke as primarily pessimistic about humanity's tendencies: have discussed at length Burke's general utopianist—or not—position as he attempts to purify war. Burke's own introduction to *A Rhetoric of Motives* seems ambiguous at best as to his belief in whether his efforts will prevent a disastrous future: "We do not flatter ourselves that any one book can contribute much to counteract the torrents of ill will into which so many of our contemporaries have so avidly and sanctimoniously plunged" (Burke 1969, xv).

While dystopian literature's place among science fiction might be contended, the SF elements of the genre in its formative years cannot be denied: From Zamyatin's *We* in 1920 to Orwell's post-war *1984,* early dystopian thinking and texts were read as and coded as science fiction, and the genre flourished during the period now known as the Golden Age. Although not all science fiction of that era was specifically dystopian, Jameson's utopian desire is evident in much of the work that became canon for the scifi—and, eventually, speculative fiction—genre. It is worth noting, then, that Burke's reasoning and explanations during this period are marked by a dystopian logical structure; in fact, we might argue that his declaration of *ad bellum purificandum* would not exist without those dystopian threads throughout his work.

In Burke's first book *Counter-Statement,* written at the beginning of the Great Depression, the philosopher attempts to reconcile the idea of "art for art's sake" with the political literature of the time. Early in the book, he seemingly wanders into a discussion of Capek's *R.U.R.* While his resulting comments about the play's lack of "eloquence" seem to be an odd aside and barely connected to the topic at hand: "psychology and form," this kind of move becomes Burke's signature in his monographs (Burke 1968, 38). Such a distracted paragraph is not there to derail Burke's comments on the propagandization of art, but to first show us what texts have influenced his conclusions and then to use the reference to color our reading of the more on-topic discussion that follows. Even though Burke does not summarize the play in any helpful way, his drive-by review—admittedly negative—amid this explication of art's social function reminds us that such texts are part of the discourse to which he is responding; he has more than a passing familiarity, then, with the didactic fictions of the era.

In *Counter-Statement*, Burke shows a particular attention to that kind of writing in his opening statements on "pamphleteering" and its relationship to "pure" art and "proletariat" literature can easily be applied to utopian and the emerging genre of dystopian fiction. In discussing censorship (always a "dystopian" issue), Burke compares Plato's *Republic* to Aristotle's *Poetics*, declaring that the censorship in The Republic requires a "one-to-one ratio between art and society"—a direct correlation between what is imagined and what comes to be (Burke 1968, xii). Burke, unsurprisingly, links this Platonic fear of mimesis to the totalitarianism of the 20th century. Burke continues down this dystopian path as he describes how "liberal" art, acting as a lightning rod (as Aristotle suggests in the Poetics) can quell the fears of the day, becoming a release valve. The fear he describes is recognizably dystopian: "The sort of fear I had in mind, for example, concerned the attitude toward the 'promises' of applied science. More and more people, in recent years, are coming to realize that technology can be as ominous as it is promising. Such fear, if properly rationalized, is but the kind of discretion a society should have with regard to all new powers" (Burke 1968, xiii). Burke's dystopianism appears here, as he first applauds those rational enough to fear, then warns us to pay attention to the fears, all the while assuming reason will prevail against both mass panic and blind scientific pursuit.

Later in *Counter-Statement*, Burke gives the first hint of his idea of purification when he argues that:

> society might well be benefited from a disintegrating art, which converts each simplicity into a complexity, which ruins the possibility of ready hierarchies, which concerns itself with the problematical, the experimental, and thus by implication, works corrosively upon those expansionistic certainties preparing the way for our social cataclysms. An art may be of value purely through preventing a society from becoming too assertively, too hopelessly, itself [Burke 1968, 105].

Many dystopian fictions situate their logic in this structure of hyperbolic extension: They seek to demonstrate what happens when a culture becomes too capitalist, too egalitarian, too controlled, too masculine, too religious, and so on. Burke aligns art with its ability to quell this extension, but his inclusion of that as a reason why art is not merely aesthetic shows how deeply invested he and those around him were at this time—as Europe continued its way to a new war—in showing literature's potential.

Counter-Statement serves as more than just a rationale for viewing art as a strategy for rhetoric. The book's section titled "Lexicon Rhetoricae" gives us a hermeneutic for analyzing the rhetoric of literature. Even here, we see Burke's concern for identification and reader participation—both of which are essential to seeing art as an intervening force in war. In describing the Symbol and the emotions or associations it may arouse in a reader, Burke notes that "[o]ften, to 'charge' his work Symbolically, a writer strains to imagine some excessive horror, not because he is especially addicted to such imaginings, but because the prevalence of similar but less extreme symbols has impaired their effectiveness" (Burke 1968, 164). Why, Burke asks, are our fictions filled with graphic horrors? His answer is that fiction must be extreme to have the desired impact. His following discussion of the proletariat novel utilizes the terms of the Lexicon to show the relationship between "aesthetic" devices and rhetorical ones, connecting again reading, action, and social change.

Further evidence for Burke as an essentially dystopian thinker appears later in his career, but is no less important to understanding his early work as inflected by utopian wishes and SF tropes. Written amid the Vietnam War, Burke's essay "Toward Helhaven" might be the most revealing justification for including the rhetorician as a key SF thinker. "Helhaven" is based on a similar essay Burke completed just before the stock market crash in 1929 (Burke 2003, 55), and despite its subtitle "Three Stages of a Vision," it is actually divided into six parts: The introduction describes the context and exigence of the essay, Part I imagines the eventual impact of computers on the labor force, Part II satirizes the "residual problem" behind technology, Part III parodies a travel brochure for the titular "Helhaven" community, a short poem follows, and the essay ends by revisiting and revising Parts I and II, looping back to a satirical call for us all to move "ONWARD, OUT-WARD, AND UP!" toward "HELHAVEN" (Burke 2003, 65).[15]

The structure of the "vision" in "three parts" (or six) shows Burke's progression through the various rhetorical strategies for both imagining Suvin's Potential Worlds and for inviting the audience to take on specific attitudes toward their own. In the introduction, Burke shows us the problem with social criticism *without* literature: "I have, for several months, been compulsively clipping news stories about pollution, in the long run any kind of complaining becomes a damned bore" (Burke 2003, 56). While he has plenty of logical, scientific evidence, then, that our industrial advancement is destroying the planet, Burke knows that newspapers are not the best way to convey an argument for conservation. Instead, Parts I and II take on a semi-narrative structure, declaring that "[s]ome give a decent life on Earth ten years, some thirty, some at most a hundred" (Burke 2003, 62)—a sentiment common in SF and its various subgenres since its inception.

In Part II, to avoid "boring" his readers, Burke offers his own dystopian vision of ecological collapse, overwhelming technological presence, and constant surveillance. Not known for his narrative prowess (Burke's failed attempts at novel-writing are, apocryphally, why he started studying literature in the first place), Burke produces a "fiction" that is more of an outline of a dystopian landscape than a coherent story following his own rules for the logic of purification and identification: "When you find that, within forty years, a great and almost miraculously handsome lake has been transformed into a cesspool, don't ask how such destruction might be undone. That would be to turn back—and we must fare ever forward" (Burke 2003, 61). The forward motion that Burke sarcastically recommends would be to "end up by using the rotted waters as a new fuel. Or, even better, they might be made to serve as raw material for some new kind of poison, usable either as a pesticide or to protect against unwholesome political ideas" (Burke 2003, 61). For Burke, a poisoned environment means truly poisoned environs, politics and all. The impulse to move "ever forward," lauded by Jameson as a utopian wish fulfillment, is here seen as the root not just of dystopia, but of technology itself: our insistence on calling technology "progress" presents us with a set of terms we cannot escape until death.

Burke further extends this into a full blown dystopian landscape in Part II—one which reads much like descriptions we would find in Golden Age SF, but in the style of Swift's *Modest Proposal*: "Buy shares for yourself or your family in Helhaven, the greatest apocalyptic project this side of Mars.... Also, in one compartment of the bubble, there will be an actual manmade shoreline, with waves, and breakers, splendid for surfing, and the best white sand for luxuriating on the beach (though protected from the sun and exposed only to a scientifically designed substitute)" (Burke 2003, 62). In his advertisement for the fictional Helhaven, Burke teases out his main social concerns: surveillance culture, technology's dehumanizing effects, and ecological disaster. Left at that, the essay would have been an effective, if a bit preachy, damnation of the United States' practices in the 1970s.

But Burke's writing is performative, and he would not leave us with only satire, which leaves little room for the ambiguities of language he celebrates as the way to transcend war. Instead, he moves to a poem titled "Envoi: Nocturne with Noise":

> Spring springs among us, on this sod,
> Spring vs. Total Fall
> And may there be some kind of God,
> that He have mercy on us technologic all [Burke 2003, 64].

This short verse brings the entirety of his war-time literary theory into focus: In four lines, Burke provides a prayer for redemption; the prayer *form* acts, as Burke argued back in *The Philosophy of Literary Form*, as a *chart* of desires brought forth into language (Burke 1974, 5–6). By moving from satire to prayer Burke implies that the appropriate response to conflict, war, and the tensions brought about by technological progress is not just to imagine the probable outcome, but to include in that imagining an appeal to transcendence—a God figure or "god term" that can purify those conflicts through the merger and division of terms available in the poetic mode. The play on "Fall" as both seasonal and a metaphor for humanity's faults points to Burke's faith in language's ambiguity; given Burke's own atheism this final poem is a call not to a deity but *to poetry,* with all of its heteroglossia and polysemy, as the solution to technology's rigid construction of terms that will cause further war. In other words, we might say that Burke's theory of war and literature actually calls for SF as an ethical response to the rigid certainties in which science alone might result.

These few examples of Burke's dystopian thinking show that his theories might be helpful for teasing out more of the metarhetorical work of the SF between the wars: in other words, Burke's rhetorical theory, inflected with popular science fiction ideas, might show us ways that the SF of the 1930s, 40s, and 50s was *already* theorizing the rhetorical work of literature as a means to prevent war.

A Lexicon for Science Fiction

At the end of his first work, Burke offers a "lexicon rhetoricae"—a handbook of terms he wants to use to analyze how literature works on its audience to invite what he would later call identification. This section offers a set of key Burke ideas that scholars studying the rhetoric of wartime SF might want to review; I summarize the Burkeian concept, but I have also reframed the term to demonstrate its applicability to and particular use in SF studies for the literature between the wars and the Golden Age. This "lexicon" of Burke's ideas deserves detailed application to Golden Age SF literature *because* are already infused with and informed by what Burke might call the "motives" of the SF genre. Like Burke's original Lexicon Rhetoricae, I do not want to provide a rigid, prescriptive framework for analysis, but instead, I want to point to paths scholars might take in relation to canonical and less canonical SF texts of that time period, always with an eye on what that genre does to mediate, rationalize, and prevent conflict through rhetoric.

In order to create a more sustained example of theory application, I've used Aldous Huxley's 1931 *Brave New World* as an exemplar. Huxley's dystopian novel is recognized by most as a work of science fiction, and, as Wayne Booth said, didactic fiction is often almost too obvious in its rhetorical construction. Since *Brave New World* is one of the most commented-upon SF texts in the canon, this brief application will highlight ways that rhetorical theory can add to the discussion we have been having since its release.

Trained Incapacity

This essay begins with Freeman's thesis that SF is inherently theoretical, for a given kind of theory. Structuralist and formalist theory, though, only shows the internal workings of a text, not the *impact* of its logic of its audience. Burke's work attempts to correct that. In *Permanence and Change* Burke emphasizes, particularly in Part I, the relationship between interpretation and action—that *reading* is an action that calls into being other re-actions. It is not, he argues, simply that societies change or, in a more

Marxist screen, that conflicting classes eventually lead to a synthesis of two opposing groups. For Burke, there must be a critical moment when the situation is interpreted—when, to continue Burke's opening metaphor, a trout in a stream recognizes the bait *as bait* and swims the other direction. Unlike the simple yet noble trout, however, "We not only interpret the character of events (manifesting in our responses all the gradations of fear, apprehension, misgiving, expectation, assurance for which there are rough behavioristic counterparts in animals)—we may also interpret our interpretations" (Burke 1984, 6).

A dystopian trout would write about the horrors of bait, and other trout would respond in kind—the more horrific that bait-story, the more likely other trout are to avoid shiny lures. Burke continues to expect the (albeit flawed) human mind to first recognize, then interpret, criticize, and finally act. While there may be some jumping around between the interpretive and critical stages, the form remains basically stable, with "any educated action" being one that has been "abstracted," that is, put into a schema of interpretation (Burke 1984, 105). What is worrisome to Burke is that "trained incapacity" (a term he steals from Veblen) will prevent us from completing these steps, and, by implication, prevent us from amelioration. The more we are educated to respond in predictable ways to situations around us, the more likely we are to take the bait. Recognizing bait as bait and recognizing our patterns of behavior as a kind of negative education takes work on the part of a critical animal. How can we possibly avoid becoming Pavlov's dog—or worse, the chickens who are trained to come running at the sound of a dinner bell, but who end up in that final time running to the butcher block? (Burke 1984, 10).

Burke does not provide a singular answer in *PC*, but his other work points directly to the literary as a way through or beyond. In *Brave New World*—as with most 20th century dystopian novels—characters have been quite literally brainwashed with hegemonic axioms like the pro-capitalist "Ending is better than mending" (Huxley 1998, 52) and the caste system affirming liturgies like "Alpha children wear gray. They work much harder than we do, because they're so frightfully clever. I'm really awfully glad I'm a Beta, because I don't work so hard. And then we are much better than Gammas and Deltas" (Huxley 1998, 27). When this training to always define self against Other becomes a teaching on par with religion (as "Fordism" is presented in the novel), such training can incapacitate the actors who enter into conflict. A critical reader of *Brave New World* would want to first point to the ways characters are *represented* as helpless, even child-like. Then, to consider this text as an attempt to purify the conflicts just prior to World War II, a critic should note the places Huxley and his characters attempt to transmute the terms that divide them—and hope that a parallel move will be made by a reader experiencing Suvin's "cognition."

Technological Psychosis

In *Permanence and Change*, Burke notes a growing dependence on technology; this dependence is not just an addiction to the physical technology itself, but to mechanization as a metaphor for all aspects of human interaction. The "psychosis" is reflected in the way we now filter the world first through the idea of technological processes. This psychosis is most visible, of course, in the tradition of technological dystopias such as Orwell's *1984*, Zamyatin's *We*, and Kurt Vonnegut's *Player Piano*. Like most of the technological dystopias, Burke's fears seem centered on the man/machine divide, and he asserts that "man is essentially human, however earnestly he may attempt to reshape his psychological patterns in obedience to the patterns of his machines" (Burke 1984, 63). Later he asks, "How many people today are rotting in either useless toil or in dismal worklessness because of certain technological successes?" (Burke 1984, 101).

The technological psychosis is evident in *Brave New World*; much like Burke's "Helhaven," the culture has succumbed to a mechanized view of the world, and that view has created, in parallel, categories and classes of humans; the preoccupation with technology has led that culture to re-see humans *as* technologies. Doing so, of course, resituates humans as objects, a transformation of terms that is perhaps the *opposite* of a purification that leads to cooperation. By representing what happens when our terms determine our response, *Brave New World* offers a warning. And certainly, Burke in the 1930s and 40s was paying attention to such warnings and term shifts, as he catalogued "examples that he been culling from the *New York Times* to show 'the ingredients of war lurking undetected in language that may seem on its surface to be the language of peace'" (Burke, A., Jensen, and Selzer 2018, "Introduction").

Just as *Brave New World* offers a set of terms that might lead to a reduction of conflict, it also reorients its audience out of the scientific and into the literary as the preferred perspective, another attempt at transcendence. It does so through a clever re-orientation of the literary (high culture) with the savage—John the Savage, the Shakespeare fanboy whose insights focalize Huxley's dystopian thesis. While the natural path for the novel's audience would be to align the literary with the cultured, Huxley asks us to reorient ourselves and see reading Shakespeare as a defiant, uncivil act. This allows the literarily-inclined readers to claim for themselves a new orientation to their own social position—to merge themselves with other rebels instead of standing outside the political realm, inactive.

Danger-Response

In general, dystopian arguments may be seen as a particular case of what Burke refers to as a danger-response, an interpretation of a stimulus (in this case, a situation) as dangerous which leads to action (Burke 1984, 150). However, unlike the heat of fire or the pain of disease, abstracted stimuli may not lead to an immediate or ameliorative response: "We do not persuade a man to avoid danger. We can only persuade him that a given situation is dangerous and that he is using the wrong means of avoiding it" (Burke 1984, 150). Dystopian scenarios name that danger, and are secular prophecies, new orientations toward the present and toward history (or historiography). Burke further suggests that even new discoveries can quickly become dystopic landscapes: "Such is the case with those elaborate regimens of social diet which we build up by a slowly selective process until certain ills gain prominence and authority enough to grow self-sustaining or creative. These ills become powers in themselves, leading us on to still further interests, all farther and farther afield from our original patterns of humane gratification" (Burke 1984, 182). Burke's instinct seems to be to warn, to extrapolate, and to predict an unwelcome social condition.

Wartime SF might be seen as entirely engaged in this danger response. Even the more optimistic works of the Golden Age depict conflicts and cultural tensions that their writers used as plot devices. What we might focus on, then, are the rhetorical features of the texts that act as "stimulus"— beyond the narratological aspects of the stories, how do they literally enact a bodily fear response by creating *identification* between readers and the characters in the stories? In *Brave New World*, Huxley presents us with two potential points of identification, John the Savage and Bernard. As the outsider character, the Savage is easy for us to identify with cognitively, if not emotionally. Bernard, on the other hand, is described, as most dystopian protagonists, as flawed enough to be relatable and not the strong-jawed hero common in most SF: "Too little bone and brawn had isolated Bernard from his fellow men, and the sense of this apartness, being, by all the current standards, a mental excess, became in turn a cause of wider separation" (Huxley 1998, 67). We can share substance with Bernard, become aligned to his interests and, as his terms shift, so ours will follow.

Entelechy

This essay intentionally ends with perhaps Burke's most important contribution to SF studies. Burke borrows "entelechy" from Aristotle, who used the term to mean "the inner potentiality that could make matter into form" (Blakesley 2002, 138). Blakesley clarifies Burke's use of the word:

"When he says that at the very start our terms jump to conclusions, this is what he has in mind" (Blakesley 2002, 139). The words we use to describe and interpret our situation end up determining our positions, our trajectories, and thus our ends (puns intended throughout). Our word choices become "shorthand for motives, which in turn are shorthand for situations"; by analyzing the patterns and clusters of words used in a given discourse, we can foresee our own ends. And this drive to find our ends is a major part of what makes us human—we will always, Burke argues, extend our terms (and thus actions) to their logical conclusions, even when doing so harms us.

This is what SF literature does best; Burke's "Helhaven" essay is an exercise in entelechial extensions, finding causes and effects in the way we figure language about our worlds. But the entelechial logic flourishes in the novel form, as it allows characters opportunities to compare and contrast their own time to the distant future time and place described. A novel like Edward Bellamy's *Looking Backward* (1888) can explore the problems of industrialism and unregulated markets by transporting a protagonist from the familiar world the original reading audience lives in to an ideal or horrific extension of those conditions. In *Looking Backward*, for example, Bellamy's argument is formed by the descriptions of the year 2000 provided by narrator and protagonist Julian West, who, after using hypnotherapy for insomnia, wakes up in a utopian Boston more than a century after he fell asleep. West tells his story directly to an audience, allowing him to contrast the norms of the fictional future Bostonians with the era of unregulated industrial growth he just left. The contrast of *Bellamy's* audience's norms in the *fin de siècle* fervor with the imagined norms of a utopian future provides both the plot and the logic. West can critique his own culture (including the use of footnotes to explain his audience's motives to themselves) by imagining a future in which humanity corrected its own course and did not allow their terms to jump to conclusions.

In utopian literature, the logic of extrapolation works in the negative: by showing contemporary readers what is needed for a society to progress to the ideal, utopian texts ask audiences to contrast their own conditions with that perfected other world. Bellamy's readers in the late 19th century are confronted with this in each chapter through a variety of rhetorical strategies. As West notes early on, "The reader who observes the dates alluded to will of course recognize in these disturbances of industry the first and incoherent phase of the great movement which ended in the establishment of the modern industrial system with all its social consequences. This is so plain in the retrospect that a child can understand it, but not being prophets, we of that day had no clear idea what was happening to us" (Bellamy 1888, 11). Bellamy-through-West hopes to make the trajectory of his present time much clearer. Throughout, West's interlocutors use leading questions to jump the audience to the correct attitude toward various social changes: "'Were sidewalk coverings not used at all?' she asked. They were used, I explained, but in a scattered and utterly unsystematic way, being private enterprises" (Bellamy 1888, 99). Lectures, histories, and even romantic liaisons help Bellamy show us how his current conditions might progress from 1887 to 2000, letting him argue that humanity must *necessarily* make adjustments to reach this utopian future. While the novel is often credited with "predicting" the emergence of a credit-based economy, novels using entelechial extension are not concerned so much with accuracy as they are serving as kind of early alert system for readers. SF novels using these extensions present their terms and they jump readers to conclusions as a way of creating reflective readers who might, possibly, head off their impulses to "perfect" their ideologies to their logical, terrible ends.

Conclusion: Purifying the War Through SF

What does it mean that Burke has (apparently) this occupational psychosis? Burke is preconditioned by the linguistic texture in which he finds himself, embedded in the set of terms and relationships that also gave rise to SF as a genre. It is for this reason that Burke's work should be taken more seriously as already SF—and that SF should be taken seriously as a kind of rhetorical theory. SF in the period between the wars certainly had much to be pessimistic about; and the stories told in dystopian literature seem wildly at odds with the wonder-filled mysteries and space operas of the Golden Age and pulps. But both sets of SF are strongly motivated by a desire to establish new terms and produce a better future. The War—both World Wars, in fact—mark the SF in the first half of the 20th century not by the content of the stories but by their rhetorical aims of identification, warning, and reorientation of the reader outside of him (or her)self. The stories themselves perform their rhetorical theories of purification: They show us how to identify the self with other, how to align our interests, and how to fall across the bias through making difference a principle of wonder, not fear. These wartime texts, though, also set the terms for the SF that came after—terms that also must, eventually, undergo their own reexamination. That task lies with the next generation of SF scholars, with hopes of warding off another war.

NOTES

1. While Freedman's thesis is specifically about "science fiction," this essay uses "SF" to describe the genre. That terminology shift, though, should not be a reason to discount Freedman's primary thesis; instead, as the second section reviews, the major shifts in the genre during the time period this essay addresses means that a single terminology ("scifi," "magazine era," "Golden Age," "dystopia") is probably inadequate anyway. Overall, the social–rhetorical function of science fiction played during the lead up to World War II led the many members of the genre to read quite differently from the space opera "hard" science fiction that was also prevalent in this time.

This essay emphasizes and builds its argument on the end of World War II era science fiction that engages a specifically dystopian rhetoric, but since, the war and social concerns inevitably marked all literature of this era, even the pulpiest of space opera stories can be seen as a literature working to encompass and reflect on its time, and while these subgenres of SF are both far afield of the more "literary" texts invoked in Freedman's project, this essay hopes to show how the wildly divergent kinds of SF texts in the 1930s, '40s, and even '50s share a similar rhetorical stance. To maintain the notion that all literature is rhetorical and all members of a genre are working to the same rhetorical ends, this essay avoids specifying "dystopian" literature or "hard" science fiction in favor of the term that, in Burke's terminology, "falls across the bias" and bridges the two ends of the genre. Therefore, while Freedman's premise is used here to introduce the idea of SF as always/already engaged in theoretical work prior to critics reading into that work, the essay respectfully seeks to broaden the scope of his claim. To that end, this essay uses SF as a primary identifier for broad statements of the historical genre's theoretical potential, but "science fiction," "scifi," "utopian," and "dystopian," are used when appropriate to discuss the various positions for those varieties of SF we have staked out as a field.

2. The New Rhetoric movement is closely tied to both Burke's work and Chaim Perelman's work, but Burke's repeated defense of the pragmatism-influenced theories means he is often considered the leader of the movement, if one could be identified.

3. Suvin's book chapter, "Estrangement and Cognition," may be seen as an attempt, through rhetorical theory, to unfreeze the text while maintaining Suvin's core thesis that SF works on and with its audience to construct a sense of reality. A rhetorical approach would put more emphasis on the text's ability to use the estrangement as a way of negotiating the conflicting sense of culture and history with which each text is preoccupied.

4. Jameson references the "Desire called Utopia" throughout his book. The initial construction referenced here emerges from his reading of Ernst Bloch, but the remainder of Jameson's book works to complicate Bloch's thesis.

5. For a discussion of the trajectory of Burke's work on his core concept of Dramatism across half a century, see William Reuckert's *Kenneth Burke and the Drama of Human Relations*.

6. Citations for all of Burke's monographs referenced in this essay refer to the University of California Press editions.

7. Emphasis original. While this first section of *The Philosophy of Literary Form* does not address war directly, both Reuckert and Weiser connect the book's thesis to Burke's core concept of dramatism, which is essential to his attempts to explain the purification of war.

8. Weiser's introductory chapter identifies four threads: "falling on the bias," "translation," "ambiguity and incongruity" and "the comic corrective," that led Burke to his master theory of war through dramatism; literature or literary language is implicated in all four.

9. The "traditional" view of rhetoric in the opening of *A Rhetoric of Motives* is almost entirely Aristotelian, ignoring, as many rhetoricians did in the mid–20th century, the Sophist tradition.

10. Burke's use of the pronoun "he" throughout can be problematic; Burke's erasure of race, gender, and other markers of privilege has often been a problem for Burkeian scholars applying his theories to contemporary concerns. For a thorough discussion of Burke's difficulties with race, see Brian Crable, *Ralph Ellison and Kenneth Burke: At the Roots of the Racial Divide* (Charlottesville, Virginia: University of Virginia Press, 2012).

11. For an extended discussion of the implications of embodiment for identification and conflict, see Debra Hawhee, *Moving Bodies: Kenneth Burke at the Edges of Language* (Columbia: University Press of South Carolina, 2009).

12. Blakesley is paraphrasing Burke in *Counter-Statement* in this quote.

13. Reuckert's *Preface* is his clearest statement of his belief in this book that Burke's theories are dependent on the literary. Reuckert's version of Burke's unfinished *A Symbolic of Motives* is also dependent on this premise.

14. I would like to thank Jack Selzer for providing me with an early draft of the editor's introduction to this much-anticipated publication of Burke's "lost" sequel to *A Rhetoric of Motives*.

15. Capitalization original.

Works Cited

Appel, Ed. 2004 (06:54), November 1. Comment on Clarke Rountree and Mark Huglen, "Editor's Essay: Toward the Next Phase," *KB Journal* 1.1. http://www.kbjournal.org/node/73.

Attebery, Brian. 2003. "The Magazine Era: 1926–1960." In *The Cambridge Companion to Science Fiction,* 32–47. Edited by Edward James and Farah Mendlesohn. Cambridge: Cambridge University Press.

Bellamy, Edward. 2000. *Looking Backward: 2000–1887.* Boston: Ticknor & Co., 1888. Reprint. New York: Signet Classic (Penguin).

Blakesley, David. 2002. *Elements of Dramatism.* New York: Longman.

Burke, Anthony, Kyle Jensen, and Jack Selzer. 2018. "Introduction" to *War of Words* by Kenneth Burke. Berkeley: University of California Press. Kindle edition.

Burke, Kenneth. 1951. "Rhetoric—Old and New." *The Journal of General Education 5, No. 3:* 202–9.

_____. 1968. *Counter-Statement.* 2nd ed. New York: Harcourt, Brace and Company, 1931. Reprint with additional preface and notes. Berkeley: University of California Press.

_____. 1969. *A Rhetoric of Motives.* 2nd ed. New York: Prentice-Hall, 1950. Reprint. Berkeley: University of California Press.

_____. 1974. *The Philosophy of Literary Form: Studies in Symbolic Action,* 3rd ed. Baton Rouge: Louisiana State University Press, 1941. Reprint. Berkeley: University of California Press.

_____. 1984. *Permanence and Change: An Anatomy of Purpose,* 3rd ed. New York: New Republic, 1935. Reprint as "revised 3rd edition" includes new and revised sections. Berkeley: University of California Press.

_____. 1988. Letter to Malcolm Cowley, 9 August 1945. In *The Selected Correspondence of Kenneth Burke and Malcolm Cowley, 1915–1981,* 267–8. Edited by Paul Jay. New York: Viking.

_____. 2003. "Toward Helhaven: Three Stages of a Vision." In *On Human Nature: A Gathering While Everything Flows, 1967–1984,* 54–65. Edited by William H. Rueckert and Angelo Bonadonn. Berkeley: University of California Press.

_____. 2010. "The Carrot and the Stick, Or." In *Equipment for Living: The Literary Reviews of Kenneth Burke,* 402–9. Edited by Nathaniel Rivers and Ryan Weber. West Lafayette, Indiana: Parlor Press.

Cheng, John. 2012. *Astounding Wonder: Imagining Science and Science Fiction in Interwar America.* Philadelphia: University of Philadelphia Press.

Clark, Gregory. 1997. "Kenneth Burke, Identification, and Rhetorical Criticism in the Writing Classroom," *Conference Paper Repository,* KB Society archive. http://www.kbjournal.org/clark-kbirc.

Crable, Brian. 2012. *Ralph Ellison and Kenneth Burke: At the Roots of the Racial Divide* Charlottesville, Virginia: University of Virginia Press.

Freedman, Carl. 2000. *Critical Theory and Science Fiction.* Middletown, CT: Wesleyan University Press.

Huxley, Aldous. 1998. *Brave New World.* London: Chatto and Windus, 1931. Reprint with Foreword. New York: HarperPerennial.

James, Edward, and Farah Mendlesohn, eds. 2003. *The Cambridge Companion to Science Fiction*. Cambridge: Cambridge University Press.

Jameson, Fredrick. 2005. *Archaeologies of the Future: The Desire Called Utopia and Other Science Fictions*. London: Verso.

Miller, Carolyn. 1984. "Genre as Social Action," *Quarterly Journal of Speech* 70 (May): 151–167.

Reuckert, William. 1982. *Kenneth Burke and the Drama of Human Relations*, 2nd ed. Berkeley: University of California Press.

Roberts, Adam. 2016. *The History of Science Fiction*, 2nd ed. London: Palgrave McMillan. doi:10.1057/978-1-137-56957-8.

Suvin, Darko. 2010. "Locus, Horizon, Orientation, and Possible Worlds." In *Defined by a Hollow: Essays on Utopia, Science Fiction and Political Epistemology*, 111–136. Oxford: Lang Press.

_____. 2014. "Estrangement and Cognition," *Strange Horizons*, November 24. http://strangehorizons.com/non-fiction/articles/estrangement-and-cognition/.

Weiser, M. Elizabeth. 2008. *Burke, War, Words: Rhetoricizing Dramatism*. Columbia: University Press of South Carolina.

Zappen, James. 2009. "Kenneth Burke on Dialectical-Rhetorical Transcendence," *Philosophy and Rhetoric* 42, no. 3: 279–301.

Speculations on the Interconnectedness of Edward Bellamy, His Utopian Writing and the Civil War

ANNETTE M. MAGID

Edward Bellamy's utopian works, *Looking Backward* and *Equality* had a profound effect on nearly one million readers. Even though some critics considered Bellamy's supporters naïve in their beliefs that *Looking Backward* literally foretold the coming age (Egbert 1979), half a million copies were sold by 1935, and it has never been out of print since it was first published. In fact, in 1935 *Publisher's Weekly* listed it as one of the four most influential works published since 1885.[1] It is also interesting to note that not only were readers inspired by Bellamy's approach to the economy, politics and society, but his utopian visionary projections also inspired writers, both positively and negatively, to respond with their own envisionment of America's future. Bellamy, who was a strong critic of capitalism, devised a utopian community which utilized an industrial army and promoted nationalism, an economic system embraced by leaders, worldwide. Bellamy's main goal for writing two volumes focused on the social order was, in fact, to help guide individuals to embrace a "common sense" approach toward the complete "organization of society" (Bellamy 1967, 3).

Since no one can confidently predict a perfect society, especially a perfect society in the next millennium, such literature is more properly classified as SF rather than as utopian. Whether viewed as utopia or SF, documents exist to prove that his ideas influenced a plethora of countries, including Russia, Great Britain, Japan, India and others.[2] As Egbert suggests, "A utopia is a reflection of one author's reaction to his contemporary historical situation and its problems, and represents his attempt either to offer another model than the present society as a basis for criticism of that society, or else to show a way out of the present society into a future one which resolves those historical problems" (Egbert 1979, 13). The aim of utopian literature is to embrace all fields of human endeavor in order for the writer to attempt to imaginatively portray his deepest beliefs about the proper arrangement of his society's institutions for the good of all. I suggest that Bellamy's political, sociological and literary focus was a possible reaction to the devastation he witnessed when soldiers returned home, physically and emotionally scarred following the Civil War. Authors such as Vinton, Geissler and Roberts, who wrote utopias immediately following Bellamy's highly successful novel, also reflect the effects of the Civil War in their work; however, the focus of this essay will remain with speculations on the interconnectedness between Bellamy's utopias and the Civil War.

Even though America had a Civil War and laborers were mistreated at the beginning of industrialization, nothing deterred the throngs of individuals who emigrated to America and pushed to the West. America continued to represent a chance for a better life, where one could have liberty and material prosperity. Following the Civil War, the transformation of the United States from an underdeveloped agrarian society into a great industrial power caused unprecedented expansion in material prosperity, mainly due to the considerably greater efficiency of machine versus hand labor. While the Civil War brought death and devastation, industrialism developed machine technology, which created a highly exploited labor force. The laboring class had to fight for its right to organize, to bargain collectively, and to strike. Bellamy included the conflict between labor and capital through his protagonist, Julian West, who represented public opinion, which was frequently against the laborers. West personally experiences the inconvenience brought on by the strikes, as it threatens to delay his marriage. It is interesting to note that later, after West has been in utopia and returns to Boston in a dream, he is able to see the reasons behind such strikes.

The rhetorical approach within Bellamy's utopic novel is reflected in Burke's theory regarding wartime SF texts which had a "necessary connection between boundaries and futures, positing boundaries—the terms and frames we use to select reality—as a way to act in the present with the goal of intervening in the future" (Mays, Rivers and Hoskins 2017, 11). As Burke suggests regarding differentiation of cultures as seen in wartime SF texts, Bellamy used *Looking Backward* as a "space for cultural exploration." Julian West, Bellamy's protagonist, clearly identifies with the division of society into the four classes, or nations, which he identifies as "the rich and the poor, the educated and the ignorant" (Bellamy 1967, 5). West identifies his set of divisions as "rich and educated." Furthermore, West distinguishes the dichotomy of existence regarding those who lived in the late 19th century, using the analogy of a coach proceeding across unpaved, treacherous roads, peopled by the rich in the select seats at the top of the vehicle that was propelled by the harnessed masses of humanity. Bellamy uses this analogy as a metaphorical template for the imbalance between the very rich, the capitalists—those at the top of the coach in the "very breezy and comfortable" seats—and those impoverished "brothers and sisters [who were strapped to] the harness," pulling the coach (Bellamy 1967, 6–7). In addition, Bellamy stipulated that "in truth [...] the main effect of the spectacle of the misery of the toilers at the rope was to enhance the passengers' sense of the value of their seats" (Bellamy 1967, 8–9). This image echoes Burke's approach to rhetoric, which in his terms, serve as both the disease and the cure—by which he means that violence arises from the same source as the cure (Mays, Rivers and Hoskins 2017, 11).

Bellamy observed that society in the late 19th century could not be helped, nor did it want to change. He identified the "hallucination" of the rich who thought that they were better than those who were burdened to pull at the rope. The rich thought that they were made of "finer clay" and belonged to a "higher order of beings" (Bellamy 1967, 8) and they deserved to be riding in comfort upon the upper deck of the coach. Of course, those in the seats on the coach were aware that they could fall off, just as some wealthy families who owned huge tracts of property in the South did during the Civil War, but those who remained on the coach (analogous to the Southern plantation owners) had to struggle to hold on to their positions, as well as their wealth, more desperately than before. Bellamy further speculated that if the passengers could only have felt assured that neither they nor their friends would ever fall from the top, he realized that it is probable that, beyond contributing to the funds for liniments and bandages to aid the injuries sustained by those who were metaphorically burdened with pulling the weight of the rich, those at the top were not willing to leave their high status nor would they change. In his scenario, he used the carriage as a vehicle physically supporting the comfort of the rich. As can be extrapolated from Burke's philosophy, given a situation which is associated with a specific term, such as "slavery" as a problem, the society of the South was trained to regard the term of slavery by looking "in one direction rather than another for possible solutions." The term "slave" in the South dehumanized workers who were necessary to harvest and perform everything needed to keep the wealth of the plantation owners flowing at a steady rate. It is interesting to note that in the present time, early 21st century, society is returning to the image of the poor performing menial tasks for the rich. In fact, just as Bellamy predicted, those who are labeled in the 21st century as the idle rich, would have done extremely little about those who dragged the coach. The rich, after all, considered themselves destined for greatness.

While "commiseration was frequently expressed by those who rode in the coach," Julian West mentioned that the wealthy coach riders would:

> exhort the harnessed people [the workers] to patience, holding out hopes of possible compensation in another world for the hardness of their lot, while others contributed to buy salves and liniments for the crippled and injured. [Bellamy 1967, 8–9].

Bellamy suggests that "there was always some dangers at […] bad places [perhaps during or following Civil War, which initiated a general overturn] in which all would lose their seats" (Bellamy 1967, 7). This image again reflects Bellamy's awareness that those wealthy individuals whose fortunes were overturned in the war, ended up in a low socio-economic place and were forced to suffer the indignities of poverty and a hand-to-mouth existence. As M. Elizabeth Weiser explains in *Burke, War, Words*, poetic naming was, for Burke, a means for "evincing change," or more specifically, a means for how "poets and activists could exhort and how sociologists and semanticists could more accurately measure the present to predict future actions" (Mays, Rivers and Hoskins 2017, 11). It is through Bellamy's use of rhetoric throughout his utopian novels that he employs an effective means for suggesting as well as eliciting change.

The initial scenes begin with West declaring his wealth, his fine education and himself as one who enjoyed "all the elements of happiness" available to "the most fortunate in that age," (Bellamy 1967, 5). West still suffers from insomnia, reflecting a lack of peace of mind rather than the absolute happiness he professes to possess. West's motivation for living, the antithesis of those unfortunate, maimed and impoverished soldiers Bellamy witnessed returning from the Civil War, was "'living in luxury,' with the pursuit of the pleasures and refinements of life" (Bellamy 1967, 5). All of West's means of support came "from the labor of others, rendering no sort of service in return. [His] parents and grand-parents had lived in the same way" [and West] "expected that [his] descendants, if [he] had any, would enjoy a like easy existence" (Bellamy 1967, 5). West also identified himself as entitled to have "the world [support him] in utter idleness [even though he, may have been] one […] who was able to render service" (Bellamy 1967, 5–6), but chose to continue to live off of his great-grandfather's "accumulated […] sum of money on which his descendants had ever since lived" (Bellamy 1967, 6). If one of Burke's suggestions in "The Rhetoric of Religion" is to be assessed for its merits of accuracy, he postulates that "[t]he future will inevitably be what the particular combination of all men's [*sic*] efforts and counter-efforts and virtues and vices, along with the nature of things in general, inevitably add up to" (Burke 1970, 272).

Julian West exhibits selfish and narcissistic behavior, which indeed becomes balanced out with Dr. Leete's logical, sharing lectures. For example, Dr. Leete told of clever methods to select more appropriate people for Congress. Having a variety of individuals from various guilds, as Bellamy (through Dr. Leete's discussions) suggests, offers a method to have a combination of men who could work together to decide the future of our country. In fact, Bellamy utilizes Dr. Leete's discussions to share his viewpoint that the president would be more adaptable in his position if he became familiar with the various types of individuals in Congress, thereby enabling him to experience the "efforts and counter-efforts" (Mays, Rivers and Hoskins 2017, 12) of those representatives in his government in order to be a more effective leader (Bellamy 1967, 116–17). The anger and warring tendencies exhibited in various groups of men would be resolved. However, Bellamy's approach to establishing a peaceful, non-combatant government had some flaws. His idea of separating the technical professions, such as engineers and architects, into the constructive guilds while members of the liberal professions, such as doctors, teachers, artists and men of letters, were allowed to seek "remissions of industrial service" because "they do not belong to the industrial army," creates a very divisive class system which could lead to rancor in the country. In short, what Burke identifies as "wartime SF texts" characterize the genre presented in Bellamy's utopias as a space for cultural exploration, fueled by the discussions that logically followed such changes.

The Premise of Looking Backward *and* Equality

Looking Backward begins with a preface dated December 26, 2000, and explains that it speaks of the future and the "progress that shall be made" (Bellamy 1967, 94). The first chapter opens in Boston in 1857 with the first-person narrator, Julian West, discussing his engagement to Edith Bartlett. The marital property, his house, which is part of the nuptial agreement and is to be completed before their marriage, has not been completely remodeled and is the only thing that stands the way of matrimony. Issues dealing with physical property cause West to suffer from insomnia, which adds an ironic emphasis to Bellamy's Nationalist message throughout his utopian novels. Bellamy observed the destruction of physical property and the devastation of the Civil War, which possibly led him to conclude that the only way property can be enjoyed is when all property is distributed equally among all inhabitants, so no frustration and jealousy result.

Bellamy uses his utopia *Looking Backward* to tell a story and create a world. Unlike some literary works which can be clearly analyzed internally without reference to the age during which it was written, it is critical when analyzing a utopia to understand the context of the work. The world serves as a clever medium to present his beliefs in a highly enjoyable, ostensibly romantic, novel. Bellamy's protagonist spent the night before his transmigration into the 21st century at the home of his fiancée denouncing the working class. When he returns home to sleep in his tomb-like sleeping chamber in his house's lower level, West is in fact spiritually dead. Like West, death-like existence is an integral part of Bellamy's psyche. West awakens in modern Boston in the 21st century with "new freedom mirrored in the splendor and expanse of the city spread out before him. The view of urban utopia and the sense of ventilation and spaciousness immediately affect his mood" (Bellamy 1967, 52).

In the 22 chapters of his novel, Bellamy discusses his theories of non-violent revolution and social change by introducing them in conversations between Dr. Leete and West. Dr. Leete prepares West with low-keyed lectures filled with parables and homilies. These lectures are the direct opposite of the diatribes Bellamy experienced from his father, Rufus. Bellamy uses the inventive idea of a multiple-station radio to add a message from a spokesperson, Dr. Barton, as a final means of justification for the utopia. *Looking Backward* can be assessed as a religious fable that has two parts: one is the resurrection of Julian West and the other is Dr. Leete's catechism concerning the creation and management of utopia. The transformation of West from an inhabitant of his current world to a time traveler in a New World provides a fanciful device designed to give color to an otherwise "non-fanciful issue" (Bellamy 1967, 51). The details, such as the model industrial army, which are explained in different parts of the book, are conflicting. The psychological drama of conversation, using carefully presented rhetoric, much like Burke espouses, serves as the means of expounding Bellamy's concepts of utopia.

The first draft of *Looking Backward* was written in third person omniscient but Bellamy changed it to identify West as the narrator and the subject of the miraculous relocation into utopia. The magic of conversation (Bellamy's favorite device) saved the "repentant sinner" (Bellamy 1967, 54). The first-person protagonist presents apt immediacy and creates an on-the-spot reporter's monologue as well as an easy method to move into dialogue whenever the writer deems conversation necessary. It is again due to Bellamy's need to thwart the heated arguments of his bickering parents that inspired civilized discussions between Bellamy's characters concerning revolutionary thinking and non-conventional behavior.

The use of a first-person narrator also has an effect on the love theme in *Looking Backward*. The entire premise of West's finding his way to the year 2000 was caused by his attempt to complete a house for his bride-to-be

Edith Bartlett. By merging his philosophy concerning labor and materialism into a romantic mixture, Bellamy was able to offer his ideas to the reader in a more palatable manner. In fact, the love relationship was resolved when West "folded the lovely girl [Edith Leete] in [his] arms, the two Ediths were blended in [my] thoughts" (Bellamy 1967, 55). West reawakens on May 31, 1887, but Bellamy's novel ends with a final dream that returns him to the home of Dr. Leete and the arms of his beloved Edith Leete (Jameson 2016, 64). Bellamy used his novella's Postscript as a platform to state his philosophy on the "principles of evolution, as well as the next stage in industrial and social development of humanity" (Bellamy 1967, 312–14). Just as utopia came to West in the late 20th century when his attitude changed about his material possessions, Bellamy felt that utopia would also come to mankind through a change of heart (Bellamy 1967, 55). Bellamy's own individual change of heart was demonstrated when he abandoned his father's theology and developed his own brand of personal guidance.

In one sense, *Looking Backward* and *Equality* echo utopian romantic tales, such as Washington Irving's *Rip Van Winkle* (1820) that is also set after an American war—in Irving's fantasy, after the American Revolutionary War—in which the protagonist awakens after a long sleep to discover his changed world. While Bellamy lived in his father's house for many years as a bachelor in seclusion, he was hardly asleep. The rhetoric of *Looking Backward* and *Equality* offers guidance to Americans moving through a technologically changing world. Instead of espousing Marxism in his changed world, *Looking Backward* and *Equality* suggest a manner of dealing with the Machine Age which promotes the positive aspects of industrialization (Isaac 2002, 353–405).

Bellamy's upbringing, his education and his individual philosophies shape his utopian novels. Through a thorough analysis, the focus of *Looking Backward* becomes evident. Since Bellamy viewed the 19th century as a time filled with contrasting messages, the need for the fantasy of a utopian world was essential in order to escape the oppression of reality brought about by the onslaught of the Civil War. By focusing on a love theme, Bellamy tried to include women in a positive role for the future, but he fell short of his goal because he could not envision the male/female relationship in any way other than one in which the male dominated. One must keep in mind that three years before he totally gave up the dominance of his father's religion and wrote his utopian male-dominated *Looking Backward*, Bellamy married his young stepsister whom his parents had adopted (Bellamy 1887, 3A). The influence of his father-dominated household remained an overbearing influence on Bellamy in his dream-filled utopia, and throughout his relatively brief 48 years.

Early Influences on Bellamy

Many specific occurrences in the life of Edward Bellamy shaped the characterizations and theories within Edward Bellamy's utopian novel, *Looking Backward* as well as its sequel, *Equality*. The mere place of one's birth can have a profound effect on the decisions a person makes later in life. Bellamy was born before the Civil War in Chicopee Falls, Massachusetts, a highly industrialized center for manufacturing swords, bayonets, and cannon produced by the Ames Manufacturing Company (Bowman 1986, 1). Some of the guns manufactured for the Civil War were made in the J. Stevens Arms and Tool Company, later called the Massachusetts Arms Company. Some of the firearms made in Chicopee Falls were contractually sold to the Confederate Army as well as the Union Army (Graf 2009, 187).

In his highly industrialized town, Bellamy witnessed the power of machine over man and the success of armament manufacturers who produced artillery that inevitably maimed soldiers during Civil War battles. Since he could not be part of the military complex, he took a different career path, studying law and practicing briefly in Massachusetts (Sreenivasan 2008, 33). Bellamy became an editor for the *Springfield Union* and then an editorial writer for the *New York Evening Post* (Sreenivasan 2008, 33). Edward's father, Rufus, a Baptist minister, may have had parishioners who participated in the Civil War and later returned home, no doubt maimed, either mentally or physically (Bellamy 1877, 4).

While living in this hub of entrepreneurial energy during a period of emerging dehumanization, Bellamy's poor health allowed him extended hours to imagine his own discussions with heroes and kings, no doubt wearing fanciful textile garments he may have seen produced from the cotton mills, and adorned with bronze from the bronze manufacturer in Chicopee Falls. Bellamy was able to devote considerable time to his studies because he spent much time alone in his room, away from his family. He not only enjoyed his private time, but he needed it to maintain his equilibrium. Part of his need for solitude and introspection can be attributed to the fact that his parents were opposite personalities. His mother Maria, who was greatly respected in the community, was described by one of her relatives as "extremely intelligent," "inclined to pessimism" and possessing "a dry humor" (Bellamy 188?, 24). While Maria was a precise, formal woman, her husband Rufus, a congenial overweight minister, was much less inclined toward precision and self-imposed rules (Bellamy 188?, 24–5).

An arena of perpetual skirmishes during his childhood emerged from the fact that Bellamy's father was a Baptist minister and his mother a highly devout Calvinist. Edward was subjected to heated turmoil and continual perplexity concerning each parent's religious principles. The influence of his religious parents is evident. Edward was so strongly enmeshed in Christianity in his younger years that he said, "He ceased to feel any interest in reading that did not relate to God's service" (Bellamy 1967, 146–47). It was not until Bellamy actually "came to feel a sense of intimacy and to enjoy an indescribably close and tender communion with what seemed to him a very real and sublime being" (Bellamy 188?, 1A) that he agreed to become part of his father's religion. It seems that he chose his father's religion so that he could gain acceptance from that highly critical parent and possibly form some lasting relationship with him. A young man needs his father, perhaps more than he needs his mother, to guide him through his adolescent years. The influence Bellamy's father had on his sons was profound. Upon his deathbed, Rufus wrote a lengthy list of books and tasks for his son Paul (then 13) to master "during the next four or five years" (Bellamy 1967, 146–47). Rufus taught his sons the importance of studying history as well as learning from the past. It is from this guidance that Bellamy adopted the philosophy that "history is the key to knowledge" and that "if you know how the human race behaved under certain stresses and strains in the past, you can pretty well plot its course in the future" (Bellamy 1967, 147). His encounter with the Civil War and the resulting approach he adopted in *Looking Backward* and *Equality* reflect this.

At the age of 14, Edward was converted and on April 3, 1864, shortly after his birthday, he was baptized and became a member of his father's church. Since Bellamy was a voracious reader, a writer such as Horatio Alger, who used his writing as a forum for his sermons, may have had an influence on him. Even though Bellamy attempted to avoid non-religious books after his conversion, the writings of Alger were sermon-like and may have appealed to him. In addition, Bellamy would have been exactly the age for which Alger had intended his books. The major difference between Bellamy and Alger was their political philosophy. Bellamy was a socialist while Alger was an apologist for capitalism. Ironically, Bellamy's message was almost identical to that of Alger: energy and industry are rewarded and indolence suffers. Another possible influence of Alger's sermon-like books may have been his self-made approach to formal education. Bellamy, too, felt that formal education was not as valuable as his self-disciplined education in Latin, French, German, Italian and Greek. As an integral part of the education he sought for himself, he "wrote a list of ten items necessary for self-education" (Bellamy 188?, 12). Just as with Alger, much of Bellamy's personality was shaped by his self-determination. Bellamy's interests also involved both his reading and his writing. Learning from his father's example, he used writing as a springboard for short sermons criticizing the behavior of the masses. His personal education also included honing his writing skills to the level of a professional writer. By the age of 20, the strong literary style he developed earned him a frequent spot in the *Springfield Union*, writing editorials and book reviews.

Although Bellamy was very religious, he resented the formal visits of parishioners who disturbed his studies and his reading time (Morgan 1944, 38). I also think he was jealous of the time that the parishioners took from his relationship with his father. When Bellamy took on the Baptist religion, he may have thought that he would have his father all to himself; however, he just became another individual who needed the minister's time. He did not seem to be treated with any special regard. Through their religious fervor, his father and mother harnessed Bellamy with a religious yoke of guilt. He thought that by joining the Baptists, he would be released from the heavy moral burden his parents used to inhibit his potentially boisterous behavior. Indeed, at times, "boys will be boys," but it was a harsh method to control a young child. Bellamy's plan succeeded for ten years until he left his father's church at 24 years old. It is interesting to note the following industrious activities in which Bellamy engaged during the ten years he was affiliated with his father's church: he studied at Union College and in Germany; he was admitted to the bar, but instead of pursuing a law career, he took an editorial post with the *Springfield Union*. After a brief time as a journalist at William Cullen Bryant's *New York Evening Post*, he wrote four romantic novels (Bellamy 188?, 10–11). This highly productive period of his life offered less notoriety than the popularity of his utopian novel, *Looking Backward*.

Even after his conversion, his parents constantly reprimanded him even though he was a rather well-behaved boy. His parents told him that "he was a grievous sinner, accursed from God with whom he must make peace or suffer the most terrible consequences" (Morgan 1944, 37). The heavy burden placed upon his young shoulders could have pushed Edward to become an introverted individual; but, in spite of his parents' castigations, he gained personal strength when he found his vocation as a writer. In an excerpt from one of Bellamy's notebooks, he stated that "the chiefest [*sic*] of all causes of sorrow and the most piteous [is] parental love" (Widdicombe and Preiser 2002, 231). A utopian world in Bellamy's adolescent years might have been one in which mothers, after nursing their children was concluded, shall:

> be relieved of nearly all other care of them, and fathers shall have no intimate relations with them. At an early age they shall be educated in kindergartens, their education and corrections shall not be determined by their parents, but by the State, consulting with the youth [Bellamy 188?, No.6: 7–9].

In one of his notebooks, Bellamy also mentioned that since society was "arranged to provide … for children's welfare … better than the parents possibly could" (Bellamy 188?, No.6: 7–9), parental love is "no longer useful" (Bellamy 188?, No.6: 7–9). To further emphasize Bellamy's attitude toward his contentious household, he stated in the notebook that "the fraternal and sisterly tie and all family ties [will be] loosened as a consequence of discontinuance of family life" (Bellamy 188?, No.6: 7–9). Each individual had the ability to excel to his or her highest personal level of competence, without assaults from anyone else, especially parents and siblings. Even though little is known about Bellamy during his one-year attendance at Union College, he "prevailed upon one of the professors to give him a special course in literature" (Bowman 1986, 5) and in his journal wrote that he was more a "reader rather than a student, devoting much more attention to the college library than to the college textbooks" (Bellamy 188?. *Notebook XI*, 12). Being such a voracious reader helped him become a singular thinker and copious writer.

Bellamy's insatiable appetite for high adventure and military exploits fueled his fascination with war heroes such as young Napoleon. It should be noted that "[b]efore young Edward completed his secondary education, he wrote essays indicating his interest in war heroes: 'Philip and Alexander,' 'The Marshalls of Napoleon,' and 'Notes on Military Tactics'" (Bowman 1986, 4). It is seemingly incongruous that although Bellamy hated war, he was interested in a military career. It is ironic that he yearned for the glory of Napoleon while being rejected at West Point because he suffered from tuberculosis. He was constantly being compared to his brothers, and was left at a disadvantage due to his early childhood illnesses and his failure to attain a post at West Point.

It was recorded that Bellamy's rejection was "because of physical inadequacy" (Morgan 1944, 41). Perhaps, because he could not pass his physical examination in 1867 for entrance, his dream of a military career was subtly transferred into his quest to prove his prowess and worth to his family in a different way. Even though he had to change the focus of his career from the military to a career of law and soon after to a more permanent career in writing and journalism, he never lost interest in military tactics (Egbert 1979, 32).

Besides his parents, his teachers and other writers, there were other people who influenced Bellamy's adulthood. One such influential person might have been considered the black sheep of the family. This relative gave shape to Bellamy's philosophy of life and was his boyhood hero. Captain Samuel Bellamy, a pirate, socialist, philosopher and orator gave Bellamy the inner strength to reject what was socially accepted and espouse ideas that were not the norm. Bellamy later adopted each aspect of Samuel's life, other than his piracy. The socialist in Samuel is strongly exemplified in Bellamy's *Looking Backward* and *Equality*. The philosopher in Samuel is exhibited early in Bellamy when he writes his first articles at age ten. Finally, the orator in Samuel carried on as an inheritance for him, since Bellamy enjoyed lecturing all his life (Bellamy 1967, 20–25).

The philosophy Samuel shared with Bellamy moved his thoughts away from his immediate problems with his parents. It was through Samuel that Bellamy learned how to cope with his overbearing parents. Samuel explained to Bellamy that a person was "the offspring of mankind and his mother is humanity" (Bellamy 1967, 11); therefore, his parentage was not as important as his entire heritage and what that person finally did with his life. Bellamy hoped that his life would be happier but since his present life was unalterable, he had a need to create an imaginary perfect society in which all within its bounds could live in harmony. This was the beginning of Bellamy's search for utopia. It was also the beginning of the development of Bellamy's inner resolve to eventually leave the church of his father and find his own way.

In addition to his insatiable reading interests, no doubt inspired by his mother who, during his childhood, provided him with a copious book list and told him to "read a book" when he seemed bored, Bellamy also had an opportunity travel during his reading period at Union College. At his mother's insistence, he went with his cousin, William Packer, and his cousin's mother to visit Dresden, Germany, where they stayed in a German home. Bellamy learned German and wrote letters home about German socialism which he had studied prior to his trip (Morgan 1944, 369).

> Bellamy became aware of the suffering of the urban poor while studying in Germany. He was also influenced by Laurence Gronlund, author of *Co-operative Commonwealth* and the first writer to try to explain socialism to Americans [Sreenivasan 2008, 33].

Laurence Gronlund and Bellamy both introduced socialist ideas to late 19th century America. Bellamy wrote a review of a late edition of Gronlund's *Co-operative Commonwealth* that appeared in Bellamy's newspaper *The New Nation*. It indicates great differences in how they each envisioned socialist relations of production and the transition to socialism (Bellamy 1891, 224–5).

Prior to the Civil War

Utopian communities were quite popular in the United States prior to the Civil War (1861–65). Dreamers such as Ann Lee helped form the efficient, productive Shaker communities along the East Coast. Even though the Shakers left England in the early 18th century to seek a more peaceful existence in America—their beliefs included, among other things, the divinity of all humans—and to share their view of the uselessness of human warfare (Reece 2016, 28), they met with fierce opposition and outright hatred. "Several Shakers were jailed within the first two years of their arrival in the American colonies, because they were preaching pacifism at the time of the American Revolution" (Sreenivasan 2008, 307). One of the Shaker community leaders, Joseph Meacham wrote in his journal, "we cannot, consistent with our faith and conscience, bear the arms of war, for the purpose of shedding the blood of any, or do anything to justify or encourage it in others" (Reece 2016, 29). In order to avoid imprisonment during the war of 1812, the Shakers paid a "muster fee" which allowed the dissenter to pay money toward hiring a substitute soldier; however, by the time of the Civil War, the elders said that paying for substitute soldiers violated their pacifist principles (Reece 2016, 29). The elder from the New Lebanon Shaker community, Frederick Evans, went to President Lincoln and explained that many Shakers, before joining the order, had fought in the Revolutionary War and the War of 1812, but "because of Shaker doctrine, they had refused to draw their military pensions, which Evans figured to be exactly $439,733" (Reece 2016, 37). Even though it was against Lincoln's better judgment, he allowed the Shakers to be exempt from serving in the Civil War.

Ann Lee and the Shaker community were well known for their craftsmanship, making items they shipped to buyers across America, such as barrel hoops, furniture, and brooms. They were also known across America for their innovations—the circular saw, invented by a Shaker woman; the cooling fan; the stickpin; the common clothespin; the silk reeling machine; the apple corer; and seed packets—all of which were shipped throughout America by the hard-working utopian community (Reece 2016, 36). Since some of the Shaker communities were located in New England, not far from Bellamy's Chicopee Falls home, it is not difficult to conjecture that some of the notions embraced by the Shakers such as "communal ownership in a property-less agrarian community" (Reece 2016, 37) may have been ideas written, filed and later seen in the news office of the *Springfield Union* at which Bellamy was employed during his journalism career. Some of the Shaker community thoughts may have been threaded through Bellamy's utopian vision. Some ideas that seem to echo Shaker thinking include Bellamy's belief:

> …with all his heart, mind and soul that capitalism, because of its productive ingenuity, would evolve slowly and logically and peacefully to a higher plane where material abundance would be shared by society as a whole rather than hoarded for the benefit of the few at the expense of the many [Widdicombe and Preiser 2002, ix].

Like the Shakers, for Bellamy the idea of "using force in a free society to achieve political and economic ends was abhorrent to him"; however, he was nearly intolerant in *Looking Backward* toward those unwilling to contribute their share of work to help the social order he envisioned. In the novel, those resisters were sentenced to solitary confinement with a diet of bread and water until they were ready to accept their duty to society (Widdicombe and Preiser 2002, ix). Further inferences to the Shakers through a reference to their unique seed growing enterprise seems to be reflected in Bellamy's less coercive solution included in *Equality* where he proposed that those who were unwilling to work cooperatively within the freely established framework of a democratic society would be given "tools and seeds" and be permitted to withdraw to lands specifically set aside for them where they could experiment with their own individual life style (Widdicombe and Preiser 2002, ix). With Bellamy's revised theoretical solution fleshed out in *Equality*, he offered a potential resolution to the consideration of the desirability of attaining the goals of a utopian community.

> A utopia tries to force on readers the problem of how to respond (acceptance, self-change, reform or transformation of society) on each particular dimension considered by the utopia; the new light cast by the utopian text encourages readers to ask the practical question of how to reflect on and act in their own world [Davis 2001, 56].

Some utopian communities, identified as community experiments, include those established by Fourier's followers, can be categorized as "intentional,"[3] as compared to Bellamy's theoretical *Looking Backward*; however, in both the Fourier communities and Bellamy's utopian novels, neither require violence against those unwilling to live within the confines of the community.[4] Laurence Davis clarifies the role of utopias which he describes as equally intentional and theoretical; as not based on "fanaticism of any kind"; nor are they focused on "the quest for ethical perfection; but [they function as] a vivid exercise of ethical imagination" (Davis 2001, 57). In the 19th century, utopian socialists criticized the institution of private property and the growing gap between rich and poor, as well as restrictive conceptions of sexual morality and family relationships (Davis 2001, 79). Fourier's followers established utopian communities in the Ohio River Valley, while Owens tried to establish a utopian community in Indiana, and others attempted to establish communities along the West Coast of the United States. Such communities set the stage for the people's desire for experimental, more sexually free communities. Due to a variety of issues, most of the communities did not thrive. The failure of the earlier utopias established in America is reflective of the truism that they focused on issues that did not offer suggestions of transformation, or betterment for the readers' present conditions, neither for the individual nor for society in general. This set the stage for Bellamy to create a fictional community that promoted the strength of the nation and the cooperation of individuals within his fictitious utopia. *Looking Backward* promoted logical conversations; popularized intertextual questions and answers; included inventions not yet invented; and avoided including lascivious behavior as well as terrorizing, deadly conflict as a means to achieve his utopian goal.

Consequences of the Civil War

The Civil War left lasting consequences, not only for those who participated in the horrendous conflict, but also those who became observers of the aftermath. Prior to the onset of the war, thousands of 19th-century Americans envisioned a swift, romantic conflict which would be quickly resolved and life would get back to its former existence. Such postulations were either an attempt to calm frantically worried mothers and wives or to comfort themselves; however, thousands of other Americans dreaded a long, bloody war that would spin out of control (Cook, Glickman and O'Malley 2008, 37). Prophetic thought was an underlying condition of American life that shaped how people perceived and acted during the crisis. Perhaps Edward Bellamy, a voracious reader, may have been initially inspired by the prophecies which continually appeared in 1861 publications. For example, as appearing in the *Congressional Record*, regarding both Northerners and Southerners who may have been potential soldiers, was the account of John Pentland, who expected "fun and frolic" when he joined the 29th North Carolina Infantry on his 19th birthday. He prophesied a romantic war of "about six months." As Pentland recalled, the war promised "a chance to wear a uniform and to see the world, to shoot some Yankees and to run 'em north, and then to come back home and lord it over those who hadn't been [Civil War soldiers] and be a hero and court the gals" (*Congressional Record* 1898, 2607–2608). Perhaps Bellamy's plot line in *Looking Backward*, especially the romanticized relationship of Edith Leete and Julian West, may have been vicariously inspired by a reading of pre-war hopes for a speedy and bloodless resolution.[5] Once Bellamy formed his premise, he devised a utopian novel that embraced change, innovation and societal transformation.

> In *Looking Backward*, Bellamy presented the organization of the ideal state; he made very little change in it in *Equality*; instead, he devoted more space to the political and economic chicanery that had turned a democracy into a plutocracy [Bowman 1986, 64].

By the beginning of World War I, three main categories of SF existed: the Extraordinary Voyage, typified by writers such as Jules Verne from France, who adopted a cautious approach to exploring the science side of his fiction, choosing to use only proposed or possible current inventions in stories such as *Five Weeks in a Balloon* (1863). In a similar approach, Bellamy, like Verne, wanted to explore the beneficial aspects that scientific discoveries could have on humankind. Bellamy's *Looking Backward* fit into the second category, Tale of the Future. The third category is the Tale of Science or Marvelous Invention, which is exemplified by another SF writer, British H.G. Wells whose *The Time Machine* (1895) fits perfectly into this category. Wells thought that "humans could evolve into a better species, but they needed to be aware of what mistakes they had already made and what was likely to occur if they did not learn from their previous errors" (Minyard 1998, 8). Many American writers created SF stories, possibly alluding to war. The stories ranged from ghost tales such as Edgar Allan Poe's *Edward Arthur Pym* (1838), which combined Poe's scientific articles exploring the origin and makeup of the universe with a macabre psychological horror story of a destroyed pirate ship which still sailed with only the dead aboard, to Ambrose Bierce's story, "An Occurrence at Owl Creek Bridge" (1890), which alluded to the death and devastation of the Civil War. It should be noted that Bierce, the youngest son of poor farmers, attended a military academy for one year and enlisted in the 9th Indiana Volunteers. He participated in some of the bloodiest battles of the Civil War, including Chickamauga, where 34,000 men died. His stories reflected his experiences in the war (Bierce 1994, iii).

Early Economic Issues

Seeing the maimed men return home, Bellamy was made aware that no matter the amount of wealth one possessed, war decimates all material possessions and renders those affected penniless, both emotionally and financially. He rallied against the devastation of the Civil War in his utopian works. Not only did he seek a method to do only positive, non-harmful, actions to achieve his ideal society, he also created a place that was helpful economically for the inhabitants so that all individuals who adhered to the guidelines he set forth could thrive and experience financially comforting success. For Bellamy, "capitalism had failures in distribution, distortion of wealth, and restrictions on individual freedom" (Widdicombe and Preiser 2002, i). In *Revisiting the Legacy of Edward Bellamy (1850–1898) American Author and Social Reformer*, one of the editors, Herman S. Preiser, states that Bellamy's utopian works are excellent examples of what Bellamy labeled as "democratic socialism," "in part because of the foreign overtones" (Widdicombe and Preiser 2002, ii). Preiser's articles printed in 1995 editions of *The Capital* also identified *Looking Backward* and *Equality* as studies of "democratic socialism." Preiser argues that Bellamy actually solicited correspondence from socialists in France, Germany, Australia, and New Zealand, which Preiser suggests, "at the very least," indicates an attraction to the ideology of democratic socialism, whether or not Bellamy accepted the label of that ideology (Widdicombe and Preiser 2002, ii). I assert that the term "socialist" was not a comfortable term for Bellamy since he was raised in a home by a Calvinist mother, who was herself the daughter of the Rev. Benjamin Putnam of Springfield, Massachusetts, and a Baptist minister father. Both parents were staunch capitalists, adhering to the most accepted economic plan within the United States.

Socialism implies a breech from serving as an honorable United States citizen. In fact, several scholars, including John W. Baer in "Defends Bellamy" in *The Capital* (1995), which discusses Bellamy's assessment on the distribution of wealth. Robin Hahnal, a highly regarded professor of economics, also analyses Bellamy's critique of capitalism in his comprehensive *Panic Rules: Everything You Need to Know About the Global Economy* (1999). In addition, Preiser provides a study of "unfair competition and repressive labor practices" (Widdicombe and Preiser 2002, ii), all of which indicate Bellamy's focus on the basic tenets of democratic socialism. Furthermore, during my trip to Harvard Library to access Bellamy's notebooks and other writings, I found references to his comments on the "debauching effects of wealth" (Bellamy 1870, 12). The effect of seeing the devastation of war and the huge expense which only resulted in tremendous loss is reflected in articles he wrote in the *Springfield Daily Union*, which critique the market economy and its "industrial feudalism," "commercial princes," and the piling up of money (Bellamy 1873, 4). It is difficult not to envision Bellamy's awareness of the wealth of the plantation owners in the South and the belittling of the work force in the factories of the North as the Industrial Revolution evolved. Bellamy suggested that he had a "cure all for our labor and capital frictions and smash-ups" (Widdicombe and Preiser 2002, ii).

Beginning a Theory of Nationalism

Since Bellamy's upbringing was in a highly industrialized center for textiles and bronze manufacturing, his focus on industrialization seems in line with his promoting of a utopia focused on nationalism. He foresaw that through his nationalism, he embraced a peaceful transition evolving from the free choice of each individual. This attitude is derived from his understanding of United States history and the effects of the Civil War on society. Bellamy was disenchanted with the descendants of the pioneers, who did not live up to his perception of achievement through personal struggle.

Instead, these descendants became scheming exploiters who took farms from soldiers who were away fighting for American freedom. Bellamy saw this as an insidious pattern throughout American history (Bellamy 1967, 146–47).

In addition, Marxian socialism was viewed as a method of evolutionary progress, and in Bellamy's utopia, his version of Marxianism was peaceful, incorporating a series of nonviolent movements that were designed to benefit each person. It is interesting to note that Burke reflects a similar thought in his *Rhetoric of Motives,* which states that even though there appears to be inconsistencies in Marx's thought, "rhetors seem to compromise their own ethics for the 'greater-good' of motivating the ethical actions desired in others" (Mays, Rivers and Hoskins 2017, 56). While some of Bellamy's observations regarding the notion that "greed and self-seeking were all that held mankind together" (Bellamy 1967, 146–47), he did not take into account human nature and how individuals might react if the government equalized everyone's financial worth, and doled out credit cards (actually more closely aligned to present-day debit cards) for them to make purchases and withdraw funds from a predetermined amount of allotted bank-held money. "The maxim he wished to emphasize was 'we do not live to work but work to live' (Bowman 1986, 51–52)—true living meant 'to live the fullest, freest, most developed life we can'" (Bellamy 1967, 146–47). In his 1874 essay, "The Policy of Public Works in Dull Times," which appeared in the *Springfield Union*, Bellamy supported the concept of government employment of the unemployed by pointing out that the government always had money, that the work that could be provided was not makeshift but necessary, and that, therefore, the work accomplished was not wholly for the benefit of the unemployed citizens (Bellamy 1874, 4). According to noted Bellamy biographer Sylvia Bowman, Bellamy had multiple examples that fit the template for his theory that the government should provide employment for the unemployed. Bellamy not only read Comte and Louis Blanc,[6] he also "knew that the mayor of Boston had asked in 1873 that the municipality provide a public building for the employment of the unemployed, and in 1883, the mayor of Springfield … introduced a bill in the state legislature which would have permitted the establishment of municipal industries which would have provided employment for the temporary or permanently unemployed" (Bellamy 1893, 39).

In order to test the waters of public reaction to his nationalistic theories, he wrote short stories based on notes from his journals and notebooks. He also wrote editorials based on ideas that motivated people in respect to the work they selected. It should be noted that Bellamy believed that all men should work and that physical labor was important for all. He also considered as an ethical sense of duty the public spirit created by the brotherhood of man and an enthusiasm for humanity which was parallel to patriotism in time of war (Bellamy 1967, 147). Once again, the underlying issue of the Civil War may have been partially instrumental for his approach to organized labor. He formulated thoughts based on his reading, his writing and his experience, which added to the worldwide appeal of nationalism that he incorporated in *Looking Backward* and *Equality*.

Bellamy also had many futuristic visions which provided more opportunities for the inhabitants of his utopia. Doctor Leete serves as a guide in the futuristic world for Julian West, showing West around and teaching him about all the advances of the new age that occurred during the 113 years West was asleep, entombed in the basement of his renovated home. West wakes up in the basement of Dr. Leete's home and learns that working hours have been reduced; retirement age with full government-provided benefits is age 45, and public kitchens provide meals, thus taking one of the burdens of housewives out of their personal responsibility. Items could be selected and are then delivered, similar to the way the present-day Internet functions. Most important for the concept of nationalism is that the productive capacity of the United States is nationally owned, and all items are distributed equally to its citizens. Bellamy uses a clever question and answer (Q & A) technique to provide the reader with his theory while presenting it as an extremely palatable context of knowledge acquisition of a young man who finds a love interest in a household over a century after he awoke.

The reader learns about Bellamy's notion of consumer cooperatives, which Bellamy may have learned from the 1844 treatise the *Rochdale Principles,* based on serving the community which also entails responsibility and democratic control. Dr. Leete, ostensibly Bellamy's voice within *Looking Backward*, explains the notion of financial equality through the use of a bank card connected to the only bank, a national bank, which services all in the community. Bellamy also includes a prototype radio on which a person could choose to hear a sermon or music. Many of these visions involved timesaving devices for women's chores such as dishwashers and table setters.

Concluding Considerations

Even though *Looking Backward* and *Equality* are American utopian novels, there is a British flavor to the mannerisms and tone utilized in the utopias. Bellamy's early encounter with "stark and revolting" poverty that he observed all over London and elsewhere in Europe during a trip as an adolescent[7] had a profound effect on his dream of a perfect society (Bellamy

1967, 47). The distinctly American influences on Bellamy, related to the effects of his encounters with remnants of the Civil War, are more negative as is evidenced in the short sermons throughout his work criticizing the behavior of the masses. Perhaps the influence of the devastation and uselessness of the prolonged Civil War jaded his opinion of humankind. Part of the negativity comes from the preaching of imminent world catastrophe predicted for materialistic, loose-tongued, non-conformers outside of Rufus' Baptist Church. Bellamy observed:

> What an unutterably funny spectacle we mortal men present. We stroll along side by side gaily disporting, gravely plodding in fine apparel and fine spun refinement of companionship. Yet we cannot see where we put down our feet. We know there will come a step—it may well be the very next—beyond which we shall take no other but of a sudden drop eternal fathoms deep [Bellamy 1967, 48].

It is no wonder that Bellamy was impressed by martial order and includes special insignia and music for his fictionalized utopian characters in *Looking Backward* so that they could function at a more advantageous level with the proper leaders without dropping into "eternal fathoms."

Another characteristic that helped to influence the tone and content of *Looking Backward* is illustrated through Bellamy's ability to utilize his energy and industry throughout his life. He became a member of discussion clubs such as the Cabot Institute, where he had a forum to discuss his views on Marxian socialism. Later, the Nationalist political party in which Bellamy was active and which eventually was absorbed into the Populist movement, promoted state capitalism as a way to achieve state socialism and was based on the Nationalist party. It was through Bellamy's unflagging energy and industriousness that the political party to which he devoted much of his time became so powerful (Morgan 1944, 79).

In 1891 at the height of his success, Bellamy established the *New Nation* Magazine as "a vehicle for dissemination of Nationalism" (Bellamy *Autobiographical* 188?, 2A). Bellamy had begun to take his vision of utopia very seriously and devoted himself entirely to traveling and lecturing. But his health began to fail. His final years were spent writing *Equality*—the dry, overstated sequel to *Looking Backward*. It is ironic that four years prior to his writing *Looking Backward*, Bellamy thought that he was going to die. Perhaps this gave him a stronger inspiration to write his dream before he succumbed to "the most common tragedy that is the fight of a man against disease" (Bellamy "Notebook" 188?, 13).

According to Bellamy, the American people had to first be converted through circumstance and revelation to the idea of solidarity in a National Party (Bellamy 1967, 55). So long as "most Americans," like fictionalized West, remained class-bound and blind to the truth of brotherhood, all the inventions and increased efficiency only made their problems of strikes, lockouts, unemployment, slums and starvation more difficult to solve. Bellamy combined an economic determinism similar to Marxism and a traditional American doctrine of progress as the basis for the National Party in *Looking Backward* and *Equality*. For West's friends to insist on "perverse individualism" was to forestall the great transformation illuminated by the process of history that Bellamy espoused (Bellamy 1967, 56). If America was scarred by the Civil War, Bellamy had hope that the future would proceed devoid of warring conflicts.

Notes

1. The other three were *Das Kapital*, *The Golden Bough* and *The Decline of the West* (Widdicombe and Preiser 2002, 3).

2. Other countries that were influenced by Bellamy's utopian visionary works include: Australia, Canada, Germany, the Netherlands, Indonesia, South Africa, New Zealand, Scandinavia, France, Belgium, Italy, Poland, Czechoslovakia, Yugoslavia, Hungary, Bulgaria, Romania, Spain, Portugal and Switzerland (Widdicombe and Preiser 2002, 231).

3. A term used by Lyman Taylor Sargent in *Utopianism: A Very Short Introduction*.

4. Laurence Davis wrote an analysis of Isaiah Berlin in which he asserts that the inhabitants of utopia would lack freedom as well as require violence (Davis 2001, 56).

5. Jeremy Black notes the strong connections between cultural approaches to warfare and the "War and Society" approach, "not least the tendency of traditional military historians to ignore both in their work" (Black 2003, 8).

6. Blanc believed that workers could control their own livelihoods, but knew that unless they were given help to get started the cooperative workshops would never work. To assist this process along Blanc lobbied for national funding of these workshops until the workers could assume control (Kaufman 1879, 143–45).

7. Bellamy's Aunt Harriet Parker financed his first trip to Europe to attend his British cousin's funeral (Bellamy 1967, 47).

Works Cited

Bellamy, Edward. 1870. "Notebook II." *Unpublished Papers of Edward Bellamy* (unpublished documents). Cambridge, MA: Houghton Library, Harvard University. Viewed, 9 March 2010.

_____. 1874. "The Policy of Public Work in Dull Times," *Springfield Union*, 21 November.

_____. 1877. "Wastes and Burdens of Society" *Springfield Union*. 15 November: 4.

_____. 188?. "Notebooks" and *Autobiographical Fragment, Unpublished Papers of Edward Bellamy* (unpublished documents). Cambridge, MA: Houghton Library, Harvard University. Viewed, 9 March 2010.

_____. 1891. "'The Co-Operative Commonwealth': Mr. Gronlund's New Edition of This Important Work Reviewed." *The New Nation*, vol. I. 2 May: 224–5.

_____. 1893. "City Industries," *The New Nation,* vol. I. 14 February: 39.

_____. 1967. *Looking Backward 2000–1887*. Cambridge, MA: The Belknap Press of Harvard University Press.

Bierce, Ambrose.1994. *Civil War Stories*. New York: Dover Publications, Inc.

Black, Jeremy, 2003. *Rethinking Military History*. London: Routledge, 8.

Bowman, Sylvia E. 1986. *Edward Bellamy*. Boston: Twayne Publishers.

Cook, James W., Lawrence B. Glickman, and Michael O'Malley. 2008. *The Cultural Turn in US History: Past, Present, and Future*. Chicago: University of Chicago Press.

Congressional Record, March 8, 1898: 2607–2608.

Davis, Laurence. 2001. "Isaiah Berlin, William Morris and the Politics of Utopia," *The Philosophy of Utopia*, Barbara Goodwin, ed. London: Frank Cass.

Egbert, Nelson Norris. 1979. *Problems of the Form and Content in Six Utopian Responses to Edward Bellamy's Looking Backward: 2000–1887.*" Albany: State University of New York at Albany.

Graf, John F. 2009. *Standard Catalog of Civil War Firearms.* Iola: Krause Publications, 11 March: 187.

Irving, Washington. 1820. "Rip Van Winkle" in The Sketch Book of Geoffrey Crayon, Gent. New York: C.S. Van Winkle.

Isaac, Larry. 2002. "To Counter 'The Very Devil' and More: The Making of Independent Capitalist Militia in the Gilded Age," *in The American Journal of Sociology.* Sep., vol. 108, n. 2: 353–405.

Jameson, Fredric. 2016. *An American Utopia: Dual Power and the Universal Army*, Slavoj Žižek, ed. London: Verso, 64.

Kaufman, Rev. E. 1879. *Utopias: Or Schemes of Social Improvement from St. Thomas More to Karl Marx.* London: Kegan Paul & Co.

Mays, Chris, Nathaniel A. Rivers and Kellie Sharp Hoskins, Editors. 2017. *Kenneth Burke + the Posthuman*. University Park: The Pennsylvania State University Press.

Minyard, Applewhite. 1998. *Decades of Science Fiction*. Lincolnwood, IL: NTC Publishing Group.

Morgan, Arthur E. 1944. *Edward Bellamy*. New York: Columbia University Press.

Reece, Erik. 2016. *Utopia Drive: A Road Trip Through America's Most Radical Idea.* New York: Farrar, Straus and Giroux.

Sargent, Lyman Taylor. 2010. *Utopianism: A Very Short Introduction*. Oxford: Oxford University Press U.S.A.

Sreenivasan, Jyotsna. 2008. *Utopias in American History*. Santa Barbara, CA: ABC-CLIO.

Widdicombe, Toby, and Herman S. Preiser. 2002. *Revisiting the Legacy of Edward Bellamy (1850–1898) American Author and Social Reformer: Uncollected and Unpublished Writings Scholarly Perspectives for a New Millennium*. Lewiston: The Edwin Mellen Press.

Clouds Over the Valley

Images of War and Peace
in the Films of Hayao Miyazaki

Erin M. Roll

"What is a king when his country lies ruined,"[1] Sheeta, the young heroine of *Laputa: Castle in the Sky*,[2] chastises the evil government agent Muska
as they confront each other in the ruined catacombs of the titular castle.
"No matter how powerful your weapons, or numerous your poor robots,
you can't survive apart from the earth." War is not too far away from the
forefront in many of the films of Hayao Miyazaki, and it is not a glorious
business. In many of the films that Miyazaki created and directed, including with Studio Ghibli, war appears in some form, whether it is as dark
clouds on the horizon, threatening to bring a violent storm, or whether it is
front and center, with warplanes and war machines.

Miyazaki is regarded as one of the most revered and influential ani-
mators, both of his generation and of the animation field in general; Susan
Napier has noted that his films have become an essential part of the larger
cultural discourse in Japan and beyond: "Miyazaki's works were part of the
national debate in Japan during the 1970s through the 1990s (and, indeed,
arguably, from the Meiji period opening to the West) about what it means
to be Japanese in an increasingly global world" (Napier 2002, 474). In this
essay, I intend to discuss the depiction of war in some of Miyazaki's films,
and analyze that imagery alongside Miyazaki's own words on the subject of
war, his own upbringing in post–World War II Japan, and the critical readings of different scholars on the subject. It would be possible to dedicate a
longer paper, or even a book, to the socioeconomic and political messages
that may be interpreted in most, if not all, of Miyazaki's films. However, for
the purposes of brevity and clarity, I have chosen to concentrate on three
particular films: *Nausicaä and the Valley of the Wind* (1984); *Laputa: Castle
in the Sky* (1986); and *Howl's Moving Castle* (2004).

I suggest that Miyazaki's approach to war in these three films, in the main, is not a simplistic black-and-white approach, but a more nuanced approach that serves as a warning to the people on both sides of the battle lines. Rather than a black-and-white treatment of war as "good guys" versus "bad guys," Miyazaki presents a series of shades of gray: good people who have evil sides, antagonists who are a lot like the protagonists, and a questioning of whether something done for "the greater good" is truly for the greater good. Rather, in Miyazaki's films that address the subject of war and armed conflict, war is depicted as part of a larger viewpoint on humanity and the universe: good and evil; kindness and rage existing in the same person or the same object; a questioning of nationalism and blind patriotism; the effect that war and conflict have on ordinary people who do not hold any power; and in some cases, a reminder that the good and the bad in life must be taken together. Of these concepts, it appears that at the root of them is the idea of rage: what anger and rage will cause otherwise good people to do, or what happens when an object that one person uses for good falls into the hands of someone who will use it for evil. At the end of some of Miyazaki's films, we often see rage being brought to its head in a violent, apocalyptic cataclysm: a time when it seems that the world as the characters know it is coming to an end. These cataclysms—the battle of the ohmu at the Sea of Decay, the fall of Laputa, the bombing of the two opposing kingdoms in *Howl's Moving Castle*—must take place before the scales are righted—indeed, if the scales are even righted.

Miyazaki's Background

Miyazaki was born in 1941, early on in World War II. His father and uncle were part of the family business, Miyazaki Airplane, which manufactured planes and aircraft parts for the Japanese imperial air forces during the war. Helen McCarthy notes in her biography of Miyazaki that in his early childhood, the war had life-changing effects, from his family's being forced to evacuate to starting school in the early post-war years (McCarthy 1999, 26). And these years would impact his work as an artist, she writes: "Like many children in postwar Japan, the youngster decided he wanted to become a comic artist while in high school. His abilities at the time were limited—he couldn't draw people, having (like war babies all over Europe) only drawn planes, tanks, and battleships for years" (McCarthy 1999, 27).

Dani Cavallaro, meanwhile, notes that Miyazaki's family background, having relatives who were involved in producing warplanes, and living just outside Tokyo at the time of the air raids and the bombings of Hiroshima and Nagasaki, played a significant role in the development of his worldview on war. It is this upbringing and family history, she states, that has led to Miyazaki taking a pacifist worldview, as a way of coming to terms with his family's own role in World War II. Cavallaro also states that Miyazaki has had to deal with feelings of guilt stemming from how his own family, moving as they did to a town well outside of Tokyo during the war, were spared much of the brunt of war's destruction (Cavallaro 2006, 7).

For Miyazaki, growing up in post–World War II Japan led to some conflicting feelings about what it truly meant to love country and culture. He would describe these conflicting feelings, on what it meant to be Japanese while being repulsed by his country's warlike heritage, in a series of essays in *Starting Point*. In one essay, he describes his feelings as he joined a children's literature study group while attending university: "My father would say things, like, 'Even Stalin said the people have no sin.' But these older men who were part of 'the people' occasionally talked about having killed people in China. Weren't Japanese perpetrators in the war? Weren't my father and others mistaken? Having been raised by such parents, wasn't I a product of their mistakes?" (Miyazaki 1996, 200). Furthermore, Eric Reinders makes the argument that Miyazaki's feelings on Japan's history, nationalism and pacifism in this era are especially evident in his 1997 film *Princess Mononoke*: "[Miyazaki's] politics belong to the post–War despair of a nation that had invaded other nations on the basis of ideological garbage, and was crushed in return. The post–War period has been called the 'age without kami' (*kaminaki jidai*)" (Reinders 2016, 8–9).

In 1991, with the outbreak of the Gulf War, Miyazaki wrote a column which appeared in Japan's *Shukan Asahi* (Asahi Weekly). In it, Miyazaki described his suspicion with "national claims of 'righteousness'" and "just causes," cautioning against the concept of Japan becoming involved in the Gulf War. And this in turn informs his vision as a filmmaker and a father: "When I look into the faces of my sons, I think that no matter how poor Japan might become, I wouldn't want to send them off to war. And I feel the same for other people's sons. As a filmmaker, I have continued to think that the main challenge we face in Japan today is to survive without being crushed to death by our oppressive society" (Miyazaki 1996, 147).

The postwar era in Japan, and the years hence, have been a complicated era to address for science fiction and fantasy authors and filmmakers, besides Miyazaki and Studio Ghibli. Motoko Tanaka—the author of *Apocalypse in Contemporary Japanese Science Fiction*, an analysis of apocalyptic imagery in Japanese films, anime and manga from World War II to the present day—notes that apocalyptic imagery has appeared at various points in Japanese history and culture, just as such images may be seen in other global traditions and cultures: "Apocalyptic themes in Japanese culture can be observed not only in the Buddhist notion of cyclical life but also in premodern legends which describe natural disasters such as major earthquakes and the subsequent recreation of communities" (Tanaka 1994, 2). But Tanaka notes that it is the twin bombings of Hiroshima and Nagasaki in 1945, along with Japan's examination of itself as a country and a culture in the years since, that has had an especially strong grip on the nation's collective consciousness in the 20th century onward: "The traumatic experience of defeat in World War II has shaped Japanese contemporary culture by destroying the traditional identity of Japan and the Japanese people" (Tanaka 1994, 2). Certainly we may see echoes of the twin bombings and their aftermath in Miyazaki's fantasy films. *Nausicaä and the Valley of the Wind* takes place following the violent cataclysm of the Seven Days of Fire; flashbacks to that moment show cities being leveled by flames, ohmu and Giant Warriors. When Muska activates the destroying ray in Laputa's core in *Laputa: Castle in the Sky*, it is difficult not to notice that the cloud billowing up from where the ray has struck the earth resembles a mushroom cloud or a nuclear blast. It is also possible to see in the film the concern for the misuse of technology that Tanaka has noted. Even *Howl's Moving Castle*, a film that begins on a relatively cheerful and whimsical note, reaches its climax as bombs and war machines start to rain fiery destruction upon the town.

Are the films meant to be message films? The general critical consensus appears to be no. Miyazaki has been quoted in numerous interviews as saying that the films are meant to be an entertaining story for the viewer, first and foremost. As Helen McCarthy writes, "It has been said that [*Nausicaä*] is an antiwar movie, a pro-ecology movie, a feminist movie, even a political movie. Miyazaki says otherwise. While acknowledging that a director can do nothing to influence how an audience perceives his film, he says that all he wants to do is entertain" (McCarthy 1999, 89). She adds, "There are messages galore for those who want to look for them and a solid story for those who don't" (McCarthy 1999, 89). I would suggest, however, that some of the messages regarding war in the films are so plain that they are there even for someone who might not be looking for them.

However, around the time of the making of *Howl's Moving Castle* in 2004, Miyazaki was upset and angered about the U.S.–led war in Iraq, which began in 2003. Miyazaki described this in a 2005 interview with *Newsweek*, when asked about the 2001 film *Spirited Away* receiving an Academy Award: "Actually your country had just started the war with Iraq, and I felt a great deal of rage about that. So I felt some hesitation about the award. In fact, I had just started to make *Howl's Moving Castle*, so the film is profoundly affected by the war in Iraq" (Gordon 2005, 62).

Recurring Themes

On the subject of war, there are a number of recurring themes and images that appear in *Nausicaä and the Valley of the Wind*, *Laputa: Castle in the Sky*, and *Howl's Moving Castle*. Based on my viewing of the films, I believe that these images and themes can be broken down into several major categories: the depiction of institutions; the actions of individual characters; the ruins left behind by a disaster that occurred many years ago; the symbolism of landscapes and natural phenomena; and the significance of a final, highly destructive battle or cataclysm.

I will begin with how the three films tend to portray institutions, especially governments and armies. What I notice, quite frequently, is the imagery of a person, or a country, trapped between two larger countries or groups of people. The Valley of the Wind is in the midst of the warring Tolmekians and Pejites, Sheeta is being sought by the Dola Clan on one side and Muska, his agents, and the army on the other. *Howl's Moving Castle* opens with the prospect of several different kingdoms and principalities teetering on the brink of war, and each one of these countries is trying to seek out Howl, in his different wizardly personas, to aid their respective causes. Taken in the main, these films generally do not portray nationalistic ideals, nor full-fledged military forces, in a sympathetic light. Though Miyazaki makes a point of having many of his characters be neither completely good nor completely evil, military figures in his films are more likely to be "bad guys" rather than "good guys." The brutish, often dense army general in *Laputa: Castle in the Sky* curses Sheeta's unwillingness to reveal what she knows about Laputa, and threatens to use force to get information out of her. Still later, the army soldiers are seen gleefully looting Laputa's catacombs, helping themselves to the treasures and artifacts stored there. The Tolmekian and Pejite leadership in *Nausicaä and the Valley of the Wind* comes across as bullying, short-sighted and narrow-minded; the Tolmekian forces, especially, stage an armed coup of the Valley of the Wind, in the guise of benevolence and protection against the forces of the Sea of Decay. In *Howl's Moving Castle*, the military pomp and pageantry come across as increasingly absurd and futile as the film progresses; the heroine, Sophie, does not share the town's excitement in the military parades, and the senselessness of the war is thrown into sharp relief when the reason for the battles is finally revealed at the film's end.

Besides militaries, it is possible to suggest that the films, particularly *Laputa: Castle in the Sky*, might be a commentary of sorts on the subject of empires and powers in general. The Laputan empire, if it can be called it such, has fallen, with its descendants having returned to earth. Sheeta may have a royal title and be descended from kings and queens, but she makes no indication that she cares for royal status. Instead, she speaks fondly of the sowing and reaping songs from her mountain home, where it may presume that Sheeta's ancestors settled after leaving Laputa. The castle itself literally falls at the end of the film, when Sheeta is forced to trigger the destructive spell, leaving the tree at the castle's core to float away.

With the possible exception of Muska, the government agent who is the primary antagonist in *Laputa: Castle in the Sky*, it appears that there are no genuine, full-fledged villains in these three films. The Tolmekians try to bully the Valley of the Wind into submission with promises that the Tolmekians will reverse the Sea of Decay, but Nausicaä shows some degree of mercy toward Kushana, the Tolmekians' empress and commander. The bumbling sky pirates in *Laputa: Castle in the Sky,* initially enemies to Sheeta and Pazu, eventually become friends and allies. One would expect that Sophie would have every reason to hate the Witch of the Waste, but Sophie shows pity toward the Witch after she is stripped of her powers. In *Nausicaä and the Valley of the Wind* and *Howl's Moving Castle*, there is no clear-cut boundary between hero and villain. Indeed, there are moments where a hero may display almost villainous qualities. A recurring image in the film, as I shall discuss, is the fear of what someone may do in a state of rage. This extends from Nausicaä herself to the swarms of ohmu and the Tolmekian and Pejite armies, and to Howl's night flights against the different armies' aerial squadrons, as he takes on the form of a raven-like phantom: the physical manifestation of Howl's darker nature, as I shall discuss later on.

Besides the actions of the individual characters, and the storyline itself, the physical landscape in Miyazaki's films plays a role in showing the effects of war. Even in peaceful places, there are hints of the turmoil on the outside threatening to creep their way in, and all three films have an example of a peaceful place with war and violence threatening to overtake it. In the peaceful little green valley in *Nausicaä and the Valley of the Wind*, windmills turn day and night to keep the toxic winds and clouds of the Sea of Decay at bay, and the people themselves try to resist the onslaught of the Tolmekians. In *Laputa: Castle in the Sky*, the giant tree at the top of the titular castle is surrounded by storm clouds, symbols of a violent hurricane as well as of the man-made storm of war and military buildup that is taking place far below on earth. And in *Howl's Moving Castle*, as Howl and Sophie enjoy an all-too-brief respite in a field of wildflowers overlooking Howl's childhood home, a warship from one of the warring nations appears on the horizon. "What difference does it make," Howl replies bluntly when Sophie wonders if the approaching airship is one of their country's, or one of their enemy's.

In all three of the films, there is a fiery, almost apocalyptic climax. *Nausicaä and the Valley of the Wind* ends with the clash between the ohmu, the Giant Warrior, the Tolmekians and the people of the Valley of the Wind. Muska unleashes Laputa's destructive power on the army's warship, which is only halted when Sheeta and Pazu trigger a destroying spell that breaks the castle apart. The city in *Howl's Moving Castle* erupts in flames as bombs fall upon the city, as the war moves from distant seas back onto land, and the titular castle itself falls to bits as Sophie, Howl and their compatriots try to make things right. And as I have noted, when looking at the imagery in several of Miyazaki's fantasy-oriented films, it is not difficult to see visual hints of Hiroshima and Nagasaki: ominous clouds on the horizon, fiery death being rained from some hostile deity or a sinister machine in the sky.

But despite the presence of war and destruction, there is always hope, especially represented by children and young people. Miyazaki's heroes and heroines, with one or two exceptions, are children, or at least no older than teenagers. Sophie, Howl and Nausicaä appear to be in their late teens, while Pazu and Sheeta appear to be not much older than 11 or 12. As is customary in many of Miyazaki's films, it is noticeable that the children or the younger generation usually sets things right, often in an effort to fix the mistakes or right the wrongs that adults have done. And yet there is hope as well; even if the ending is not entirely a happy one, Miyazaki seems to be casting his young heroes and heroines as the carriers of hope for the world and for the next generation.

Nausicaä and the Valley of the Wind

Nausicaä and the Valley of the Wind began life as a series of manga, first published in 1982.[3] The manga was turned into a full-length animated feature in 1984.

The film is, at its core, the story of people trying to survive in a world badly wounded by a long-distant apocalypse. Nausicaä, the titular princess, makes her home in the Valley of the Wind, a peaceful green valley hemmed in on all sides by war and destruction: the warring Tolmekian and Pejite peoples, and the Sea of Decay: a massive toxic forest. Susan Napier, in her essay on disaster imagery in Japanese science fiction films, argues that the world of the film is very much a dystopian one, albeit one with a kernel of hope at its core: "*Nausicaä* does contain, however, a protagonist in the traditional mode, a young girl, interestingly. There is also at least a suggestion of a pastoral utopia in the peaceful kingdom she inhabits" (Napier 1993, 347). Napier also makes the argument that *Nausicaä and the Valley of the Wind* is meant to be read as a cautionary tale, a reminder of what will happen if humanity makes the wrong choices, or at least fails to make the right choices. In this sense, she says, *Nausicaä and the Valley of the Wind* bears something in common with literary dystopias such as George Orwell's *Nineteen Eighty-Four* and Aldous Huxley's *Brave New World*, two other works that can be interpreted as warning the present with a dire vision of the future (Napier 1993, 348).

As the film progresses, more is learned about the catastrophe that led to the formation of the Sea of Decay. A thousand years before, the land was afflicted by the Seven Days of Fire, a cataclysm in which seven demons inflicted massive destruction upon the earth, killing thousands and laying waste to the land. Very early on in the film, a patrol team is seen passing through a deserted village, including a house that still has skeletons inside. As Nausicaä's gruff old mentor Yupa grimly surveys the ruined house, he picks up a discarded doll that is lying on the floor, and it crumbles to bits between his fingers. There is very little dialogue in this scene, but the meaning is painfully clear: what has happened is a catastrophe of monumental proportions. A viewer is left to wonder if the doll's owner survived or perished.

The exact nature of the Sea of Decay, what exactly makes it so deadly, is a mystery. Nausicaä routinely makes trips to the Sea of Decay to collect specimens of the plant life that is starting to take root there, and to observe the ohmu: giant creatures that may best be described as a cross between rhinoceroses, armadillos and giant beetles, among other animals. It is clear that most of the humans in the film fear the ohmu, but Nausicaä respects them and cares for them, at one point trying to reason with a young ohmu that has gone rogue from the rest of its herd. This is one of our first hints at Nausicaä's role as a diplomat of sorts, a peacemaker. It is through her studies, and her return to the Sea of Decay while she is a prisoner of the Tolmekians, that Nausicaä realizes that the plants below the Sea of Decay's surface are gradually filtering out the toxins from the soil and the water: a hint that the land's blight—the root of much of the humans' conflict—is starting to heal itself.

It is possible for the reader to see, in this depiction of the Sea of Decay, anxieties about a world in which warfare increasingly depends on nuclear weapons or biological warfare. As we have noted, for Miyazaki's generation, the aftermath of Hiroshima and Nagasaki, and the thousands of people who were afflicted with radiation sickness in the decades that followed, looms especially large; it is not difficult to see in the Sea of Decay lingering anxieties about a once-populous place now decimated and ruined by poisons. The forest's toxic nature appears to be biological in nature, stemming from rotting ohmu corpses, but it is also possible to view the forest as being radioactive: a fallout zone of sorts. Whatever the nature of the poison, it is clear that even a thousand years after the Seven Days of Fire, a person cannot enter the Sea of Decay without protective breathing gear. The Sea of Decay is, in this sense, very similar to a real-life radioactive fallout zone or an area sealed off due to a biological outbreak. Indeed, when seeing the Valley of the Wind inhabitants fretting over a swath of orchards that is under threat because of spores, it is not difficult to find parallels between the plight of the orchards and a biological attack.

Beyond the Valley of the Wind there are two larger kingdoms: the kingdom of the Tolmekians and the kingdom of the Pejites. It is learned over the course of the film that these two kingdoms have been in conflict with one another for quite some time; the Valley of the Wind is caught between these two countries, both geographically and politically. Nausicaä, like the Valley, ends up physically caught between these two nations as well; the Tolmekians capture her so that they may exploit her knowledge of the Sea of Decay, while the Pejite leaders distrust her because she attempts to stop their planned attack on the Tolmekians. The Tolmekians are described as "a brutal military state" when the people of the Valley of the Wind speak of them. When the Tolmekians arrive, under the direction of the empress Kushana, they direct the Valley's people to surrender all of their weapons that the Tolmekians might protect them from the Sea of Decay. This is a rather brutal might-makes-right form of benevolence. We will protect you if you do exactly as we say, these actions seem to be saying. However, any illusion of benevolence on the Tolmekians' part soon vanishes when the Tolmekians kill Nausicaä's father, Jihl.

The Pejites are encountered, as people, later on in the film. The Pejites' kingdom, recently bombed out by the Tolmekians, is for all intents and purposes a ghost town; nothing is left but miles of bombed-out, ruined and abandoned houses and shops, littered with infected ohmu corpses and dead insects. The surviving citizenry has fled via a supply ship; we might say that the Pejites are for all intents and purposes refugees as a result of the Sea of Decay. The Pejites' leadership initially do not trust Nausicaä and insist on having her thrown into the ship's brig, especially after she protests their plan to launch a counter-attack on the Tolmekians and the Valley. But some of the women and children among the Pejites insist on helping Nausicaä escape, supplying her with clothing and having a serving maid take her place in the cell. This, I contend, is another indicator that Miyazaki did not intend to have one side purely good and another side purely evil; to put it another way, there are good people and bad people on both sides of the lines.

This duality is seen within the individual people as well. Nausicaä, for example, is not a perfect angel. I assert that she is indeed capable of killing, and she proceeds to strike down an entire room of Tolmekian soldiers, in a frenzied rage, after they have slain her father. Still later, we meet Asbel, a Pejite prince (whose sister has been abducted by the Tolmekians) who becomes Nausicaä's friend and ally. Despite his boyish nature,

Asbel shows that when we first meet him, he has no qualms about blasting the Tolmekian ships and their crews out of the sky in his one-person fighter aircraft. Jihl is ready to die a hero's death; he sits up in bed as well as he can, his sword in his hand, as the Tolmekian soldiers break down the door. As Kushana's personal guard comes in following Nausicaä's slaying of the soldiers, Nausicaä prepares to strike at them as well, but Yupa quickly comes to stand between her and the guards, with the result that the sword strikes him and draws blood. Yupa is revealed to be a master swordsman, as Kushana notes with grudging respect, but Yupa chastises the Tolmekians for their heavy-handed intrusion into the Valley. He is a warrior, but it is in this situation that he becomes the gruff peacemaker. "If you must make war, you must have reasons," he says. In this same scene, it can be seen that Nausicaä is clearly horrified at what her rage at the Tolmekians has made her do, as she watches blood trickle down the blade of her sword. At dawn the next morning, she is sobbing in Yupa's arms as she confesses her fear that she will kill again.

The presence of weapons at various locations around the castle, in Jihl's chambers and the basement, shows that the people of the Valley of the Wind are not a completely pacifist people, but the weapons in the castle are either for display or kept away and disused. The people of the Valley are also made to surrender their own personal weapons when Kushana and the Tolmekians announce their intentions. Still later, the Valley people commandeer a tank and regain their weapons to mount an assault on the Tolmekian-held castle. The Tolmekians and the Pejites, particularly the Tolmekians, are over-confident to the point of arrogance in their belief that they alone will be able to subdue the Sea of Decay. It is plain to see, in their words and behavior, their unwavering faith in the effectiveness of military might and firepower, no matter how often Nausicaä tries to convince them that the repeated use of weaponry is only making the problem of the Sea of Decay worse. It is telling that at one point, Nausicaä is given the opportunity to kill or torture Kushana when the latter becomes her prisoner. But Nausicaä treats her kindly, even though she has every reason to hate or fear her.

The Tolmekians and Pejites are locked in a battle for a supreme weapon: the Giant Warrior, a creature similar to those that brought about the Seven Days of Fire. The Tolmekians stole the nascent Giant Warrior from beneath the Pejite kingdom, while the Pejites are responsible for unleashing a swarm of insects against the Tolmekians in an attempt to get the Giant Warrior back: a sort of postapocalyptic fantasy arms race. The Giant Warrior is one of the most dangerous objects in the film; the sphere containing the nascent creature arrives in the Valley when the Tolmekian ship carrying it (and Lastel, the captured princess of the Pejites) crash-lands. As the Valley people are made to haul it up the slope from the wreckage, they look at it with a sense of foreboding, if not a growing sense of terror. There is an awareness that whatever is in that sphere could cause untold death and destruction if unleashed. The absurdity of the ongoing power struggle and the pending conflict is highlighted with the realization, through Nausicaa's own research and discoveries, that the Sea of Decay is gradually filtering out the toxins on its own, and that the repeated battles of the Tolmekians, Pejites and other nations over the centuries has only enraged the ohmu and made the Sea of Decay even worse.

The film comes to its completion in the final, apocalyptic battle on the plains outside of the Valley of the Wind; the Tolmekians and the Valley people prepare for a standoff, but a swarm of enraged ohmu (which the Pejites have provoked into swarming onto the Valley by using a baby ohmu as bait) appears on the horizon. The Tolmekians soon unleash the Giant Warrior, which unleashes a series of atomic bomb-like blasts upon the ohmu before it decays. In one final sacrifice, Nausicaä throws herself into the melee in an attempt to forestall the ohmu, and is presumed to have been killed. But she is brought back to life—or awakened, depending on the viewer's preferred interpretation—by the touch of the ohmus' tentacles, and her once-pink robes have become stained blue with ohmu blood. Depending on the viewer's own philosophical viewpoint, it is difficult not to see these last moments as a sacrifice that has to be made for the greater good, that Nausicaä died (or nearly died) for the sake of all concerned, not just the people of the Valley of the Wind.

The film ends just as the battle is over and Nausicaä is reunited with her people and Asbel. There is no guarantee that the land and the Sea of Decay will recover completely, but there is a promise that a better future may come. "Children, watch well and tell me what I cannot see," the aged Obaba says. She literally speaks of her inability to see what is happening as the ohmu help revive Nausicaä, but considering what has been seen in these three films, it could be interpreted as a hint that the younger generation may help the previous generations work toward the goals of peace and a better world.

Laputa: Castle in the Sky

Laputa: Castle in the Sky is the next film in the Miyazaki canon, released two years following *Nausicaä and the Valley of the Wind*. It is also one of the first films to be released under the banner of the newly-founded Studio Ghibli (Odell and Le Blanc 2009, 62–63). As with *Nausicaä and the Valley of the Wind*, Laputa continues the themes of conflict, destruction, and of good and bad existing within the same person or people. In this film, we see other varieties of warlike imagery, but of a different form, of manmade war machines parading across the landscape and through the sky. It is notable that in this film, objects and places can be seen that have dual purposes: one peaceful and one warlike, depending on who is trying to use them.

Laputa,[4] the titular castle of the film, is believed to have been a fictional place, the stuff of legends and fairy tales, but there are a few people who believe that the castle well and truly exists. It is the search for this castle and its secrets, in the tradition of classic adventure stories, that is at the center of the film. Sheeta, one of the film's two young protagonists, is introduced as a farm girl, an orphan living in the mountains. Before the start of the film, she is abducted by Muska, a sinister government agent whose motives are not yet clear to the viewer. Sheeta escapes from the airship that is presumably carrying her to the country's seat of power. She actually falls from the ship, but the blue, teardrop-shaped crystal pendant around her neck allows her to float safely to earth. It is upon landing that she meets Pazu, the film's other young protagonist, who has seen her falling. As the film progresses, one learns that Muska and the government are targeting Sheeta because of her perceived connection to, and knowledge of, the floating sky kingdom of Laputa. On the other side, Dola and her band of buffoonish sky pirates are also after Sheeta and her crystal pendant, but for a much more obvious reason: Laputa is rumored to be a veritable trove of lost treasure. Pazu also wants to journey to Laputa, but for a nobler purpose. One learns that Pazu's father, an aviator like his son hopes to be, has died some years earlier; he had spied Laputa through the clouds while flying through a storm, but his story was mocked and ridiculed. It appears that Sheeta is unaware of most of her heritage's secrets, aside from a few stories and spells passed down from generation to generation in her family. Her most prized possession is the blue crystal pendant, also a family heirloom, with what turns out to be a Laputan emblem engraved on it. Both the government and the Dola pirate clan are eager to get their hands on the crystal, since it is proven to hold the key to finding Laputa and revealing its secret capabilities.

Sheeta, like Nausicaä, is capable of great strength when needed; early on in the film, we see that she is not averse to knocking Muska out with a wine bottle so she can escape from the airship, and she bites the arm of one of the government agents attempting to recapture her midway through the film. Pazu reveals himself to be quite skilled with weapons, when Dola slips him a handheld cannon and some rounds of ammunition. But it should be noted that Pazu uses the cannon either for self-defense or for blasting holes through walls.

Muska's exact role with the government is a mystery. It is clear that he occupies a senior position, in that the army apparently answers to him. He claims, outwardly, that Laputa is a dangerous object that must be found and destroyed in the interests of world peace, and it is possible that the story that he has told to Sheeta, he has already told the army generals to justify the search for Laputa. Near the end of the film, however, when Muska gains access to the giant crystal in Laputa's core, he gleefully turns its destructive power onto the army airship and all aboard it; his speech about needing to protect the world from Laputa was, quite simply (though not surprisingly), a front for his own quest for world domination. It is rather troubling to consider how Muska may have easily swayed others to work with him with his outwardly stated motive of preserving world peace. One has to consider how many other historical figures, including tyrants, have used these same motives to persuade others to follow them, with disastrous results. The fact that Sheeta yells for the soldiers to run for their lives is also a telling indicator; these soldiers were part of the forces that pursued her and took her into captivity, and yet she does not want to see them get hurt. Whether it is simply concern for a fellow human being's lives, or whether she is realizing that they too have been duped by Muska, or some mixture of the two, is subject to debate.

There are at least three varieties of object in the film that are peaceful in one person's hands, destructive in another person's hands. The first is Sheeta's pendant. The second variety is the Laputan flying robot, a variety of automaton that can be either a protector or a killer, depending on who is commanding it. The third object is Laputa itself. By themselves, the objects themselves are benign; whether they are for good purposes or for evil depends on whose hands they are in. Sheeta's pendant gives her the ability to float, which saves her life when she falls from the airship at the beginning of the film. But when her pendant ends up in the hands of Muska, he uses it to activate the destroying mechanism in Laputa's inner core. This is a continuation of the theme that we have already seen in Nausicaä, of objects being used for good or ill, or of humanity having both good and evil qualities. "A stone so powerful brings happiness, but it can also bring misery," the old miner Uncle Pom advises Sheeta.

Sheeta reveals to Pazu that along with the crystal, she was given a ceremonial name in a strange ancient language. Muska eventually reveals to Sheeta that her ceremonial name translates to "Lucita, True Ruler of Laputa," therefore identifying her as a descendant of the Laputan royal family. In addition, Sheeta later confides to Pazu that her grandmother taught her a number of useful spells, presumably of Laputan origin, when she was a little girl. But Sheeta says that along with the useful and safe spells, there were a number of spells that were potentially dangerous, including a destructive spell that Sheeta dares not speak of. Sheeta's fear of what the spell will do if she has to use it—and she does, in order to stop Muska at the end of the film—is similar to Nausicaä's confiding to Yupa her fear of what her rage may make her do. It is also similar to Howl's own dual nature in *Howl's Moving Castle*, his darker, more destructive side that threatens to consume him, even though it is with good intentions that he reverts to that darker side. In this, I suggest that one may also see a parallel of a country having a powerful weapon, but also the terrible knowledge of what that weapon may inflict.

The Laputan flying robots are one of the most recognizable objects associated with *Laputa: Castle in the Sky*. The first robot seen in the film, the one that falls from the sky, is clearly capable of destructive force, as is seen in its ability to blast the army's castle headquarters to pieces. But it will not harm Sheeta; it recognizes her crystal pendant, and it makes every effort to protect her. And yet, Sheeta is terrified of the robot's destructive force even when it is trying to fend off the soldiers. Still later, on Laputa itself, to similar robot is seen quietly roaming the gardens in the castle's upper canopy. This robot is shown to be nothing but gentle; birds and squirrels perch on its head and arms, it picks up the glider and moves it because it has come to rest on top of a bird's nest, and it leads Sheeta and Pazu to the grave of past Laputans (presumably Sheeta's ancestors) at the base of the giant tree. Seeing that the two robots are benign, it is somewhat jarring, later on, to see Muska unleash a squadron of similar-looking robots to attack the army's airship. For the viewer, this may be interpreted as a reminder that that which can be used to destroy can also be used to help—and vice versa: "Sometimes we love our fake people, sometimes we fear them. But the Laputan robots remain firmly amoral. They are tools whose moral status is determined by our use of them. We can use them to help a tree grow, or to kill people. We can use wind power to conquer the skies, or to quench a yak's thirst" (Reinders 2016, 41).

Several elements of the film, such as clothing and machinery, suggest that the film takes place in the late 19th century.[5] However, some of the other technology, especially the military's weaponry, bear a resemblance to the World War I era; the troop train and the airships are reminiscent of battlefield vehicles of the time, while the soldiers' helmets and trench coats appear to be a combination of British and German infantry uniforms. It is never told, exactly, whether the country in the film is headed to war. But the sheer scale of troop buildup, and the presence of the massive troop trains and warships, does strongly suggest that the country is preparing for large-scale conflict.

Are the soldiers, in themselves, evil? Since they are on the same side as Muska, or at least appear to be so, there would be a temptation to say yes. But it becomes clearer and clearer that Muska and his inner coterie of agents are operating at cross-purposes to the army generals and soldiers. Yet even if the soldiers aren't entirely evil, they certainly aren't entirely good either.

"Squeeze the brat! She'll talk!" the general roars in his frustration at Sheeta's silence.
"Spoken like a man in uniform," Muska says dryly.

When the warship arrives at Laputa, the soldiers immediately start looting and plundering the castle of its treasures as Pazu and Sheeta look on in disgust. And one of the senior officers taunts Dola and the captured pirates with a handful of treasure, along with a none-too-subtle reminder that the pirates will all be hanged when the army returns to earth. Miyazaki described his approach to depicting the military forces in *Laputa: Castle in the Sky* thusly: "I wanted to show the military as large-as-life as possible, because no matter what Pazu tried, there was no way he could ever have won against them." Miyazaki also notes that the film made an effort to show how strong and mighty the military forces are compared to the ragtag band of pirates, and also to highlight the military's less-than-savory aspects (Miyazaki 1996, 346).

Landscape and geography, once again, play a role in hinting at the effects of war. Like the ruined villages left behind in the advancing Sea of Decay, Laputa is a ruined, abandoned, place, but it is a nicely ruined place, with the classical architecture on the castle's upper level slowly being enveloped by trees, flowers, and mosses. The castle appears to be divided into two distinct regions. The upper levels of the castle are composed largely of the branches and foliage of an enormous tree, and it is here that Sheeta and Pazu come to land after being swept away from the Tiger Moth, the Dola clan's ship, in a storm. The tree canopy has every appearance of being a place of peace and refuge, with birds and small animals, as well as the lone robot, making their home there. The lower portion of the castle is a multi-tiered, layer cake-like edifice of stone labyrinths. As the film takes the viewer into the castle, we discern that the core of the castle contains a giant levitating crystal, identical in composition to Sheeta's pendant. It is the weight of the castle that keeps the castle suspended where it is in the sky, instead of floating off into the stratosphere. It is clear that the castle has not been inhabited, at least not by humans, in a very long time; the castle has decayed and crumbled in spots, but while the upper half has the appearance of returning to a bucolic idyll, the lower half has the appearance of a ruined place. We may say that the upper half is peaceful, the lower half warlike. One half is natural, the other half is the work of man. The entire island is hidden from view in the sky by a massive wall of storm clouds, and these clouds themselves could have multiple meanings. On one hand, they are a source of protection for the island, initially keeping soldiers and treasure-seekers away. On the other hand, the image of a giant mass of clouds floating in the sky hints at Laputa's darker, hidden purpose, capable of raining death down on the ground below.

McCarthy suggests that there may be some class symbolism at work in the film, regarding the dichotomy of the castle's two levels: "Nature has gentled the city's cold crystal heart not through man's agency but by simply taking over once he had gone, cloaking the symbols of oppression in greenery and flowers and tangling the machinery of domination in the roots of a mighty tree" (McCarthy 1999, 229). Admittedly, one does not know the exact details of the social hierarchy on Laputa, whether the castle was home to royalty only or to aristocrats and peasants both. Furthermore, the castle's lower levels were where the throne room, the crystal, and the stone tablet controlling the destroying rays were located, and Muska notes that only royalty was allowed to enter that part of Laputa. Yet McCarthy's interpretation does provide some food for thought; it would certainly fit in with a skeptical view of empires and kingdoms in general in Miyazaki's films. Indeed, in *Howl's Moving Castle*, one does see a more obvious depiction of a palace shielded from war while the ordinary populace is vulnerable to falling bombs.

As with the battle of the ohmu and the Giant Warrior in *Nausicaä and the Valley of the Wind*, there is the final, violent confrontation. When Muska activates the destroying rays in the castle's core, and blasts some unknown target on earth with them—sending up the atomic-like blast—he says that the rays are the fire that destroyed Sodom and Gomorrah in biblical times, and the Arrow of Indra in the *Ramayana*. This moment, one that ties legendary horrors of the past in with the horrors of the present, fits in well with Motoko Tanaka's description of apocalyptic imagery in folklore over the centuries. One gets a foretaste of this scene earlier in the film when the robot is destroying the government's castle headquarters on earth, after Sheeta's pendant has awakened it out of its centuries-long period of dormancy. Eric Reinders sums up this scene, in comparison with other catastrophic imagery from Miyazaki's works: "But we see another of Miyazaki's visions of hell—the wreckage of buildings consumed by fire, like the ancient cities from *Nausicaä* burnt and trampled in the Seven Days of Fire; or the cities bombed in *Howl*, or like the firestorm after the Kanto Earthquake in *[The] Wind Rises*" (Reinders 2016, 39).

It is during the battle that Muska reveals to Sheeta that the two of them are in fact related; both are descended from separate lines of Laputa's royal family. Muska indicates that the family split into two lines when the family left the castle, for whatever reason, and returned to earth. The film never makes clear exactly why the castle was abandoned, whether because of war, catastrophe or simply a desire to abandon the sky for the earth.

In the end, the only way for good to prevail is for the castle (in its present state) to be destroyed. Sheeta and Pazu, holding hands, recite the destroying spell that has terrified Sheeta for so many years. And one sees the stone half of the castle crumble to earth (taking Muska with it), allowing the crystal, the giant tree and its inhabitants to ascend slowly to the heavens. During the closing credits, one sees the tree floating in low-earth orbit, its limbs and its roots now broadly spread out. One may infer that the weight and the confines of the castle kept the tree from flourishing as it should have; by extension, one might argue that the warlike half of Laputa was weighing down and stunting its peaceful side. From a purely artistic or narrative standpoint, a massive battle scene does make for a good climax. A number of critics and experts have read the symbolism of this last battle, and its aftermath, as indicative of something deeper. For example, Pamela Gossin states that the endings of Miyazaki's films tend not to adhere to the conventional example of the happy ending. Rather, she says, there is a sense of life continuing on in its own way. In the case of *Laputa: Castle in the Sky*, she notes, the castle floats away after the violent cataclysm, with the natural reclaiming itself from that which is manmade: "It is Easter Island all over again, or Pandora" (Gossin 2015, 229). Gossin's discussion of the natural reestablishing itself harkens back to the Sea of Decay, when Nausicaä reveals that the Sea of Decay is slowly healing itself without the interventions of humanity. It is subject to debate, however, to say whether destruction must always take place in order for good to prevail. The Sea of Decay and Laputa appear to begin recovering after their respective cataclysms, but the films certainly show the Seven Days of Fire and the battles leading up to Laputa as terrible events, due often to man's arrogance.

A number of critics tend to view *Laputa: Castle in the Sky* as an allegory about the misuse of technology, especially when that technology falls into the wrong hands. The misuse of technology largely manifests itself in the use of machines of war and destruction. McCarthy, for example, has this to say regarding the subject of technology in the film: "[Miyazaki's] skepticism about science and technology as tools of progress is often inferred from the way in which increasing levels of technological control equate with increasing levels of violence, greed and injustice in his work; yet this is not a comment on technology but on man's inability to use it wisely" (McCarthy 1999, 95).

There is a great deal that the viewer is not told in the film: why are the troops mobilizing, why was Laputa abandoned centuries ago, how did Muska convince the government that it was necessary to search for Laputa, and so forth. So it appears that as a viewer, one is left to read between the lines on some of the film's subject matter. What one also has, perhaps even to a greater extent than what was seen in *Nausicaä and the Valley of the*

Wind, is a sense that something must be destroyed in order for the world to begin again. In this case, it appears that it is Laputa's warlike nature that must be shed in order for the castle to begin a new life.

Howl's Moving Castle

"The country is ablaze," the enigmatic wizard Howl laments quietly as he slumps before the fireplace in *Howl's Moving Castle*, "from the northern border to the southern coast."

Released in 2004, *Howl's Moving Castle* is based on the novel of the same name by British author Diana Wynne Jones. Dani Cavallaro argues that *Howl's Moving Castle* is an example of how war has moved from the background in Miyazaki's films to the forefront. She also argues that in Miyazaki's previous films, including *Nausicaä and the Valley of the Wind*, *Laputa: Castle in the Sky*, and *Princess Mononoke*, the tendency was to assign the blame of war or conflict to one person, group of people or object. But with *Howl's Moving Castle*, Cavallaro asserts that war is presented in a much broader view than it had been in Miyazaki's previous films. Rather than being a background presence, she states that war is now seen as much more of a widespread evil, creeping into every aspect of society (Cavallaro 2015, 44).

In the case of films such as *Nausicaä and the Valley of the Wind* and *Laputa: Castle in the Sky*, I would question whether the war is truly in the background; certainly the conflicts between the Tolmekians, the Pejites and the Valley people are quite prominent in *Nausicaä and the Valley of the Wind*. For *Laputa: Castle in the Sky*, one doesn't know the exact nature of the war for which the army is preparing, but the military presence and the buildup are quite clear. Reinders describes *Howl's Moving Castle* thusly: "It's not a war story, it's a love story set in a time of war" (Reinders 2016, 141). He also notes a continuation in different war-related themes carried over from other films in the canon: "We find a continuation of certain themes from earlier films, such as the refusal to join a war effort, and the struggle not to take sides in a conflict, though we are little concerned with environmental issues, adolescence or love of one's culture" (Reinders 2016, 153).

Howl's Moving Castle is set in the fictional country of Ingary, which appears to be modeled heavily on western and central Europe. The time period, like that of *Laputa: Castle in the Sky*, appears highly suggestive of the late 19th century or early 20th century. The protagonist of the film is Sophie, the eldest daughter of the Hatter family. Fate and family wishes have consigned her to working as an apprentice milliner.

As the film opens, we are greeted by the sight of flags hanging from every single house and shop in town, of warships sailing through the skies, and of a grand military parade marching through the town as the populace cheers. Still later, soldiers are seen offering rides on the miniature flying vessels, as civilians dressed in their best finery eagerly take part. By the middle of the film, however, another parade of sorts will be seen: a dispirited populace heading out of town, with all of their worldly goods packed with them. Sophie, watching from the steps of her shop, remarks that eventually the town will be completely empty. The subtext of this moment seems fairly apparent: the excitement and novelty of the coming war has given way to grim reality, and it is the ordinary people, rather than the rulers and aristocrats, who are suffering the most. In this, one may see a similarity to the plight of the Pejites in *Nausicaä and the Valley of the Wind*: the Pejites' city is abandoned due to strife and conflict, leaving its surviving citizenry to roam on an airship for a safe place to settle. When war comes, it is the ordinary people who will suffer the most.

Sophie shows no interest in any of the military pomp and pageantry that has all of the town in thrall. At one point, as she is on her way to the pastry shop and café where her sister works, she is propositioned by two soldiers, who only leave her alone when Howl unexpectedly arrives and asks her to accompany him. An unfortunate encounter with the Witch of the Waste—whom the viewer is led to think will be the main antagonist—turns Sophie from a young woman into an old one, and she goes off to find Howl in order to figure out how to break the spell. Along the way, she encounters Turnip Head, a scarecrow with useful magical powers (and a secret that is revealed at the film's end); Markl, the world-weary, often cynical young boy who acts as Howl's second-in-command; and Calcifer, the fire demon who keeps the titular moving castle running. Our first glimpse of Howl's castle—a rambling, clanking monstrosity on mechanical fowl's legs—is in the film's opening, lumbering in and out of the mists on the mountains overlooking Ingary. Once again, one has the imagery of clouds, like those that hover over the Sea of Decay, or those that guard Laputa, albeit briefly, from the turmoil outside.

Howl's Moving Castle goes to great details to point to the absurdity and futility of war, and the questionable motives that drive nationalism and patriotism. The two kingdoms at war are virtually alike in every way, with the only difference being the insignia of their flags. Besides physical bombing, the film is highly critical of propaganda. At one point, the film shows another variety of bombing: after two physical bombs fall on the harbor— as a badly bruised warship, once the pride of the fleet, limps into port— an airship drops flyers and pamphlets on the crowd, as the policemen urge the crowd to avert their eyes. The viewer will also notice numerous posters on the walls of the city, depicting soldiers raising their weapons in battle, doubtlessly rallying the citizenry to the cause of the war and the state. Still later, one learns a little bit of how the war is being presented in the local press:

> "But the paper says we won," Markl says in one scene, looking up from a newspaper. "Don't believe such lies," the (now harmless) Witch of the Waste says from her armchair.

One soon learns that Howl, being a wizard, is being sought after by two different opposing countries, except that one country knows him as Jenkins and another knows him as Pendragon. Two envoys, each from a different country, come to the castle door (disguised as an ordinary shop front) and present Markl with an almost identical message urging Howl to do his patriotic duty. It is amusing to the point of absurdity to know that two opposing nations are seeking out Howl, each one being unaware that "Jenkins" and "Pendragon" are one and the same, and that Howl will have nothing to do with either nation's plans.

The bright, cheerful colors and sights that characterize much of the film are the polar opposite of Howl's night flights. These are nightmarish sequences in which Howl, in his other form as a raven-like figure, flies over landscapes being consumed by battle and fire as warships rage overhead. Howl flies into the midst of the ships, sabotaging their cannons and bombs. But it becomes clear that Howl's night flights into the battle are taking a physical and psychological toll on him. With each flight, he becomes more and more consumed by his raven form, which gradually becomes more monstrous in appearance. "Keep on changing and you won't be able to change back," Calcifer the fire demon chides Howl on his return from one particular flight. It is easy to read this as a warning that Howl may one day be consumed completely by his darker side, the side of his rage. Howl's dual nature—of cheerful eccentric wizard and of raven-like specter—is a continuation of Miyazaki's depiction of light and dark in the same body. It is like Nausicaä and her fear of what her rage against the Tolmekians will make her do, and like Sheeta and her fear of the destroying spells that her grandmother taught her. It is the fear that one has of the darker side of their nature. "Howl's world is one in which people, as a result of traps or curses, are turned into something they are not, often for political purposes. Even someone as powerful as Howl finds it difficult to stand up to the establishment in his struggle to aid a people subjugated by terror" (Odell and Le Blanc 2009, 128). Taken in this context, one does see some connections to the other two films. And there is also the dichotomy of something (or someone) that can be used both for good and for evil.

Madame Suliman, the official court witch of one of the two kingdoms, appears to be the power behind the throne. She initially comes across as coolly gracious when Sophie is brought before her, but Suliman soon shows that she has a rather cruel side. Some would perhaps argue that Suliman is meant to be the real antagonist of the film, rather than the Witch of the Waste. And yet, the situation is much more complex and complicated than that. The scenes in which one meets Suliman are a continuation of what one has seen in the other two films; a suspicion of the motives of kings and empires, and a concern over whether they truly have the country's best interests at heart. Howl appears before Suliman, disguised as the country's king, and remarks that the palace is shielded from falling bombs by a magic spell, but those same bombs will only end up falling on neighboring houses and buildings: a predicament that does not seem to be of great concern to Suliman. It is then that the real king comes running in, gleefully rubbing his hands at the prospect of beating the other kingdom's army to a pulp, much like a little boy looking forward to a schoolyard brawl.

Suliman comes across as a Kushana-like figure, vowing that she can release Howl from whatever curse that binds him if he will help her and the kingdom. It is with almost clinical cruelty that she triggers a magic spell that sends Howl and Sophie into an illusory nightmare world once their ruse is found out. But even at the end, Suliman sits in her wheelchair and asks her "Let's end this foolish war." Even Suliman has come to recognize the futility of the armed conflict, suggesting that she is not meant to be a purely black-and-white antagonist, though certainly this could be subject to debate. It is not until the end of the film that the reason for the war is revealed. In almost *deus ex machina* like fashion, Turnip Head the scarecrow turns into a debonair young prince from one of the warring kingdoms (exactly which one is not specified). It is revealed that he has gone missing, and that was the reason for the different countries going to war in the first place. It is possible to feel a sense of "what was it all for?" when the prince reveals himself: a sense that all the war and buildup could have easily been avoided.

Conclusion

Miyazaki demonstrates in these three films that war is a complicated and brutal business, and that it is dangerous to draw the lines of "us vs. them," especially when weapons are involved. The films call into question blind loyalty to nationalistic ideals and the words of government leaders; certainly, the reasons for going to war that are presented in the films come across as futile, absurd, and pointless. Even more unsettling is the knowledge that good and evil, and serenity and rage, exist within the same person or the same nation, and that the line between those two polar opposites may be easily crossed. The nightmares of real-life wars, past and present, do manifest themselves in the film, like dark clouds on the horizon, but at the end of the films, there is the presence of hope, that things may one day be settled in one form or other. As Miyazaki writes in *Starting Point*, "In the end, that's where we must start from each time. Even in a chaotic, ruined world, there will always be good things and exciting things. As in *Nausicaä*, "We are like birds, forever going beyond that morning, spitting out blood as we fly" (Miyazaki 1996, 434).

NOTES

1. For quotes from the films, I am referring to the English-language subtitles that appear with the Japanese-language tracks. I acknowledge that the English translations may have grammar and syntax that may result in a different meaning from the original Japanese.

2. The film's complete title is *Laputa: Castle in the Sky*. The English-language translation produced by Buena Vista Home Entertainment, which I am using for this essay, omits the word "Laputa."

3. There are significant plot differences between the anime version of *Nausicaä and the Valley of the Wind* and the manga version. For purposes of brevity and clarity, I am referring to the anime version in this essay.

4. The Laputa in the film appears to be a nod to the island of the same name in Jonathan Swift's *Gulliver's Travels*; at one point in the original Japanese-language track of the film, Pazu makes a reference to Gulliver.

5. The photograph that Pazu's father took of Laputa is dated 1867/8, which would put the film sometime in the 1870s or later.

WORKS CITED

Castle in the Sky. 1986. Dir. Hayao Miyazaki. Buena Vista Home Entertainment, 2004. DVD.

Cavallaro, Dani. 2006. *The Anime Art of Hayao Miyazaki*. Jefferson, NC: McFarland.

_____. 2015. *The Late Works of Hayao Miyazaki: 1996–2009*. Jefferson, NC: McFarland. Overdrive e-book.

Gordon, Devin. 2005. "A Positive Pessimist." *Newsweek*. June 19. http://www.newsweek.com/positive-pessimist-119801.

Gossin, Pamela. 2015. "Animated Nature: Aesthetics, Ethics and Empathy in Miyazaki Hayao's Ecophilosophy." *Mechademia* 10: 209–234. DOI 10.5749/ mech.10.2015.0209.

Howl's Moving Castle. 2004. Dir. Hayao Miyazaki. Buena Vista Home Entertainment, 2006. DVD.

McCarthy, Helen. 1999. *Hayao Miyazaki: Master of Japanese Animation: Films, Themes, Artistry*. Berkeley, CA: Stone Bridge Press.

Miyazaki, Hayao. 1996. *Starting Point: 1979–1996*, trans. Beth Cary and Frederik L. Schodt. San Francisco: VIZ Media.

Napier, Susan. 1993. Panic Sites. "The Japanese Imagination of Disaster from Godzilla to Akira." *The Journal of Japanese Studies* 19, no. 2: 327–351. 10.2307/132643.

_____.2002. "Confronting Master Narratives: History as Vision in Miyazaki Hayao's Cinema of De-assurance." *Positions* 9, no. 2 (Fall): 467–489.

Nausicaä and the Valley of the Wind. 1984. Dir. Hayao Miyazaki. Buena Vista Home Entertainment, 2005. DVD.

Odell, Colin, and Michelle Le Blanc. 2009. *Studio Ghibli: The Films of Hayao Miyazaki and Isao Takahata*. Harpenden, UK: Kamera Books.

Reinders, Eric. 2016. *The Moral Narratives of Hayao Miyazaki*. Jefferson, NC: McFarland.

Tanaka, Motoko. *Apocalypse in Contemporary Japanese Science Fiction*. New York: Palgrave Macmillan, 1994.

PART II

World Conflicts

Epistemological Warfare(s) in Dystopian Narrative

Zülfü Livaneli's Son Ada
and Anthony Burgess' The Wanting Seed

EMRAH ATASOY

Epistemological warfare plays a crucial role in utopian thought since it is a matter of power practice to establish a utopian social order, which tends to be utopian or dystopian depending on the way it is regulated. Whoever holds the mainstream episteme at hand determines the means of social engineering and of regulation. Although the literary dystopia presents a dark, pessimistic vision, the utopian impulse does not vanish completely. The utopian hope is maintained at the end of dystopian narrative despite the dystopian impositions as the reader is guided through the lens/perspective of the protagonist. In the aftermath of such epistemological warfare, the social order might be severely damaged or completely destroyed; however, the survival, literal or metaphorical, of the protagonist attests to the ultimate maintenance of hope. In this light, this epistemological war throughout the narrative reveals the problematic nature of identity politics in dystopian narratives. Warfare becomes a tool through which the unique individual identity of the protagonist is reinforced.

Identity politics illustrates the utopian or nightmarish dystopian tendency in literary utopias and dystopias contingent upon the means of social engineering, normative ethics, and power politics. Frustration and rebellion might ensue due to certain practices of the governing structure such as standardization, collectivism, and sameness. The world may become a mishmash of utopian hope and nightmarish dystopian reality in these speculative visions. The individual may accordingly find himself/herself engaged in epistemological warfare with the system due to an identity crisis in dystopia, which Lyman Tower Sargent describes as: "a non-existent society described in considerable detail and normally located in time and space that the author intended a contemporaneous reader to view as considerably worse than the society in which the reader lived" (Sargent 1994, 9). It is this crisis of identity that prompts the individual/the protagonist to begin a quest for his/her own individual identity amidst epistemological warfare. Therefore, the discussion of identity politics in line with epistemological warfare through an analysis of Zülfü Livaneli's novel, *Son Ada* (*The Last Island*, 2008) and Anthony Burgess' novel, *The Wanting Seed* (1962) forms the core of this study as it is often at the heart of dystopian visions.

Part I: Quest for an Individual Identity and Epistemological Warfare in Utopian Thought and Dystopia

To begin, the concept of *utopia*, meaning, "no place" presents "a non-existent society described in considerable detail and normally located in time and space" (Sargent 1994, 9). It has been popularized and widely dealt with by scholars and critics, inspired by Thomas More's significant text, *Utopia* (1516). Since More introduced the word *utopia* I agree to and promote Sargent's functional categorization between a good place, e-utopian or a bad place, anti-utopian or dystopian. He describes eutopia or positive utopia as "a non-existent society described in considerable detail and normally located in time and space that the author intended a contemporaneous reader to view as considerably better than the society in which the reader lived" (Sargent 1994, 9). A utopian text in this sense projects an alternative social order in an envisioned society, which tends to be e-utopian or dystopian. Various means of social engineering are utilized to realize and regulate this vision. Creators of such literary e-utopias and dystopias have voiced their concerns, worries, desires, or retained their utopian hope through these positive or negative portrayals. They deal with politics of identity, either in generic terms or in an individual sense thereby spotlighting the public appearance or individual integrity. Hence, identity emerges as a highly significant aspect, which welcomes ideological contestations over multiplicity, multi-dimensionality and diversity to discuss the probability and feasibility of an *ideal* state (if such a state exists).

Identity formation plays a significant role in establishing a utopian or dystopian code of norms and ethics. Different types of identities are presented and molded to maintain a social order. How these identities are shaped and indoctrinated is contingent upon the practices of the power-holders, which relates to the maintenance of the political administration. How the order is regulated and maintained therefore determines the *utopian* or *dystopian* tendency to accomplish an ideal state. Formation of a collective social identity might be a blueprint for a transformational change and the key to a utopian reality for some utopists. Since we are "defined in part by our membership in a range of social groups into which we are born such as gender, social class, religion and race," these "appropriated social identities" (Hall 2013, 31–2) become functional in the writers' quest for a utopian realization. Therefore, the ruling body in such a representation strives to implant its ideological doctrine into the minds of its citizens by forming such a collective social identity, which mostly does not leave a room for the cultivation of an independent self. Through this identity, citizens are expected to conform to a normative code of ethics, which leads to their generic behaviors.

This seemingly *fixed* identity might also lead to the formation of yet another identity in an attempt to separate from the dogmatic structure of the imposed identity as a result of frustration and failure to sustain the functionality of the *utopian* political systems. This eventually opens up the possibility of an individual identity, especially in literary dystopias due to their complex and controversial narrative structures. A clash thus ensues between the omnipotent power-holder and a potentially misfit citizen/s who defies/defy the predestined nature the indoctrinated social identity. A struggle for individuality accordingly becomes the focal point for some characters, especially the protagonist who wages epistemic warfare against the system.

It should be clearly expressed that the protagonist cannot be completely free from the binding boundaries of the order as an individual identity is formed and maintained through socialization and interactive communication. What the protagonist attempts to reach is a state of the self which is not dictated by the political structure in the process of his/her intellectual cultivation and sophistication. Subsequently, the social sphere is a mutual interaction zone for both parties, though in different lights since social action becomes "a site of dialogue, in some cases of consensus, in others of struggle" (Hall 2013, 45). This strife against the system indicates the extent to which the protagonist desires to be self-dependent and to self-mold his own disposition. As the collective identity does not endow the character with unique properties, his/her sense of self-esteem diminishes, blocking the path to self-actualization in Maslow's hierarchy of needs.

The protagonist who yearns to raise his/her individual awareness endeavors to transcend the oppressive strictures of such an ideological identity, which involves "a process of stereotyping or 'cognitive simplification'" (Buckingham 2008, 6). The character's metaphorical and epistemological warfare aims to vitiate the efficiency of the collective identity that categorizes and labels citizens. The literary dystopia rather than the literary e-utopia (depending on how one defines an e-utopia or a dystopia) therefore attaches more importance and priority to the search for individual identity since it offers a fruitful site of controversy, dispute and plurality. In many e-utopian projections, we do see that essentialist categorizations of citizens are recounted as the ideal societal picture; however, these essentialist assumptions about identity engender problematic ramifications in nightmarish representations.

Thus, dystopias that retain the utopian hope, mostly through their open-ended structure increase the prospect of self-individualization and self-identity through epistemological warfare as opposed to literary utopias, which ideally avoid tension, constriction and predicament. The intricate internal dynamics of dystopias expedite the emergence of a self-sufficient individuality in a strident confrontation with the domineering ideological power. The complex structure of dystopian narrative in this sense accentuates the "potential for diversity and resistance to dominant identities" (Buckingham 2008, 8). As a dystopian text illustrates worse societies of repression, technocracy, and restraint, the protagonist launches his/her transformational individual resistance in this surrounding, in which individuals are "now encouraged to regulate themselves and to ensure that their own behavior falls within acceptable norms" (Buckingham 2008, 10).

The notion of acceptability and of normality is accordingly challenged by the assertive protagonist who flouts the doctrinal authority and its means of manipulation and construction of knowledge through a distortion of factual truth. The protagonist goes through an experiential journey "to confront novel hazards as a necessary part of breaking away from established patterns of behavior" (Giddens 1991, 78). In this regard, certain questions arise as a result of this confrontation: What triggers the protagonist's resistance? How does the imposition of a collective social identity generate the feelings of exasperation and dissatisfaction? How can such a frustration spark the protagonist's rebellion? To what extent is it functionally influential in an individual trajectory?

These analytical questions can be answered via the dynamics of the dystopian genre. The ruling power draws on manipulative strategies by distorting history and collective memory in order to establish a society of overall conformity. In its aftermath, a seemingly ideal order might be created, but this aspect is a far cry from the reality as this new society is probably subject to systematic dehumanization and callousness. The relativity of the ideal society does not satisfy all the citizens; on the contrary, this apathetic stereotyping induces a critical stance. To exemplify the means of manipulation to reinforce the position of the imposed social identity, the state in such dystopian illustrations can create a cult around the leader, and sublimation of that leader without questioning can result in a police state that employs physical and psychological violence to discourage dissent.

Moreover, the dystopian state can practice a strict separation of sexes, of parents from their children or of couples from each other to weaken and to destroy the familial bonds; and can manipulate history by misconstruing and twisting historical facts. This misrepresentation of history impinges upon the formation of a collective memory to the interests of the state instead of that of the individual. History is not represented objectively in a specific context due to the practical reasons of a certain country. On the contrary, history or historical awareness is either blocked or presented in a different light. The subjectification of history therefore limits citizens to a certain mind-set, placing an obstacle to individual thinking. Memory, collective or individual, is accordingly shaped under the strong influence of the state-sponsored historical perspective.

The normative values of the dominating power are therefore instilled through political and social indoctrination, which fosters passivity, resignation and acquiescence. These characteristics might be fixed and stable when recounted in a literary utopia, whereas they are in a state of flux and challenge in a dystopia, especially in critical dystopias, which facilitates the growth of individual identity. In this regard, these critical texts can be "emancipatory, militant, open" and are especially crucial in giving "voice and space to … dispossessed and denied subjects" (Moylan 2000, 188–89).

The characters who are given an opportunity to speak their minds are incited to take an initiative to purge their identities of lethargy, manipulation and their interpellation. Thus, their transition from "an initial consciousness to an action that leads to a climatic event that attempts to change the society" (Baccolini and Moylan 2003, 6) resists the notion of total conformity and bolsters individuality in the face of dystopian impositions. This struggle for an individual identity in dystopian narratives accordingly turns into an efficient means of retaining the utopian impulse and maintaining the utopian hope, especially in 20th century speculative texts. The following parts of this chapter deal with the quest for an individual identity in the face of an epistemological warfare in the representative literary dystopias. Prior to the analyses of two literary texts, Zülfü Livaneli's *Son Ada* (*The Last Island*) and Anthony Burgess' *The Wanting Seed*, I consider it useful to give a brief insight into utopianism in Turkish literature since the major part of the chapter is dedicated to the analysis of a literary Turkish anti-utopia or dystopia.

Part II: A Brief Insight into Utopian Thought and Exemplary Representative Literary Texts in Turkish Literature

The utopian thought continues to attract both intellectuals and ordinary citizens in Turkey, probably under the influence of the socio-political aura and conjuncture in the country, not only at the moment but also throughout the centuries. It is worth mentioning that utopian/dystopian novels such as Jack London's *The Iron Heel* (1908), Yevgeny Zamyatin's *We* (1924), Franz Kafka's *The Trial* (1925), Aldous Huxley's *Brave New World* (1932), George Orwell's *Animal Farm* (1945) and *Nineteen Eighty-Four* (1949), Ray Bradbury's *Fahrenheit 451* (1953), Anthony Burgess' *A Clockwork Orange* (1962), and William Golding's *The Lord of the Flies* (1954) are among the most-read and the best-selling books in Turkey. In addition, the numerous translations of Thomas More's *Utopia* (1516) also demonstrate the increasing interest in utopianism. It was re-translated by a Turkish scholar, Sadık Usta in 2016 from German into Turkish. This enormous interest in utopian thought gives way to such questions as: Do Turkish people envision utopias and dystopias? How is the utopian impulse reflected in Turkish literature? What are some concerns in these speculative texts? What does the epistemological warfare in these texts consist of? Why are these books so popular among Turkish readers? Why do people keep reading More's *Utopia*? Why is there a section of utopian literature in an inter/national book fair in Ankara?

To find probable answers to these questions, I start with the translations of More's text, and certain representative exemplary literary works. More's *Utopia* has been translated a number of times into Turkish, and continues to be translated. Disciplines such as political science, philosophy, history, sociology, and literature teach *Utopia* as part of their curriculum for both the undergraduate and graduate university levels. In addition to academic demand, the general reader is also interested in this text. Most of the translations are based on the English versions of the text, such as Ralph Robinson's translation (1551, 1556), Gilbert Burnet's translation (1684), Paul Turner's translation (1965), and Everyman's Library version (1992). Different translators such as Sebahattin Eyüboğlu, Mina Urgan and Vedat Günyol's collaborative translation from English into Turkish (1964, 1968), Zeynep Türker's translation (1970), Necmiye Uçansoy's translation (2004), İlhan Erşanlı's translation from French into Turkish (2009), Çiğdem Dürüşken's translation from Latin into Turkish (2009), Mahmut Özdil's translation (2011), and Sadık Usta's translation (2005, 2016) from German translated *Utopia* into Turkish. I had the chance to chat with the translator, Sadık Usta, and asked him why he wanted to re-translate a text that was already translated so many times. He answered by saying: "I decided to translate it again because a part from the original text was lacking in Sebahattin Eyüboğlu, Mina Urgan and Vedat Günyol's collaborative translation." Although Usta's translation is highly regarded, his text is still a translation of yet another translation, that is from German into Turkish. The collaborative translation is still regarded as the most popular one in Turkey.

In addition to the abundance of *Utopia*'s translations, a plethora of Turkish literary utopias and dystopias represent the growing interest in utopianism. These texts are significant in illustrating the social texture in Turkey, but due to the insufficiency of translated texts, international scholars do not have the opportunity to read these speculative novels. The utopian tradition did not start with modern Turkey but in fact dates back to the Ottoman Empire. Turkish literary utopias were especially popular in the 19th century under the strong influence of western culture, socialist and revolutionary opinions as well as the historical, social and political conjuncture of the period; consider *Tanzimat Fermanı* (1839, The Imperial Edict of Reorganization), *Islahat Fermanı* (1856, The Imperial Reform Edict), and *I. Meşrutiyet* (1876–1878, the first constitutional era).

Some of these texts such as the writer and translator, Ziya Paşa's *Rüya* (it is accepted as the first utopia of the Ottoman Empire by Sadık Usta, and touches on the socio-political aura of its time, 1868, *Dream*), the intellectual, writer, and political activist in the Young Turks movement, Namık Kemal's *Rüya* (1874 or 1875, *Dream*), the Crimean Tatar intellectual, publisher, and politician, İsmail Gaspıralı's *Darürrahat Müslümanları* (1906, *Muslims of Peaceful Land*), the novelist, and pioneer of women's rights, Halide Edib Adıvar's *Yeni Turan* (1912, *The New Turan*), and Molla Davud-zade Mustafa Nazım Erzurumi's *Ru'yada Terakki ve Medeniyet'i İslamiyeyi Rü'yet* (1913, *Envisioning Progress and Islamic Civilization in Dream*) have been translated into contemporary Turkish, simplified, and researched so that these texts can be more widely read. These novels include themes and issues related to dreaming, alternative imagined political and social systems, and religious concerns, just to name a few.

Turkish utopian tradition developed more under the influence of the foundation of the Republic of Turkey (October 29, 1923), and the ensuing Mustafa Kemal Atatürk's reforms such as the abolition of the caliphate (March 3, 1924), adoption of the new Turkish alphabet (November 1, 1928), and political rights to women to elect and to be elected (December 5, 1934). The decade of the 1930s witnessed the emergence of many literary utopias in this regard in the light of an epistemological warfare against the ingrained established norms in order to keep up with contemporary developments. Ahmet Ağaoğlu's *Serbest İnsanlar Ülkesinde* (1930, *In the Land of the Free Men*), Yakup Kadri Karaosmanoğlu's *Ankara* (1934, *Ankara*), Memduh Şevket Esendal's *Yurda Dönüş* (1940, *Return to Homeland*), Şevket Süreyya Aydemir's *Toprak Uyanırsa* (1963, *If the Land Wakes Up*), İlhan Mimaroğlu's *Yokistan Tasarısı* (1997, *Non-existent Land Design*), and Latife Tekin's *Unutma Bahçesi* (2004, *The Garden of Forgetting*) are significant texts from the early years of the republic and onwards.

Anti-utopian, dystopian trends are, on the other hand, influenced by historical events such as the military coups, especially the 12 September 1980 coup d'état, economic crises, technological developments, and other social problems. Among these cautionary novels are Adam Şenel's *Tele-andregenos Ütopyasında Evlilik Hayatı* (1967, 1984, 2003, *Marriage Life in Teleandregenos's Utopia*), Çetin Altan's *2027 Yılının Anıları* (1985, *Memoirs of Year 2027*), Cüneyt Arcayürek's *Ku-De-Ta* (1987, *Coup D'édat*), Zühdü Bayar's *Sahte Uygarlık* (1999, *Fake Civilization*), Alev Alatlı's *Rüya* (2001, *Dream*), Burak Özdemir's *Yıl 2 Bin Yüz 2* (2002, *Year 2102*), Ayşe Şaşa's *Şebek Romanı* (2004, *Gibbon Novel*), Tahsin Yücel's *Gökdelen* (2006, *Skyscraper*), Zülfü Livaneli's *Son Ada* (2009, *The Last Island*), Oya Baydar's *Çöplüğün Generali* (2009, *The General of the Garbage Dump*), and Ayşe Kulin's *Tutsak Güneş* (2015, *The Captured Sun* or *the Captive Sun*) as exemplary dystopian novels in Turkish literature.

Part II.I: Social Upheaval (and Epistemological Warfare) in Zülfü Livaneli's *Son Ada* (The Last Island)

"Forget that this is a Turkish book—there is no identity.
It's archetypal. And above all, not sentimental!"—Livaneli

Ömer Zülfü Livaneli[1] was born in 1946. Due to his political ideology, he was taken into custody for about three months during the coup of March 12, 1971, and was subsequently forced to leave Turkey and live in exile for nearly 11 years. He moved to Stockholm, Sweden, in 1972, and lived in Paris and Athens for a period of time, upon which he came back to Turkey. Livaneli gave conferences and taught at Harvard and Princeton universities. He was given numerous awards such as Cannes Film Festival Golden Palm Award in 1982, the Balkan Literary Award in 1997, Theodorakis Music Award in 2006, and Barnes & Noble Discover Great New Authors Award, USA in 2006.

Some of his books are *Diktatör ve Palyaço* (1992, *The Dictator and The Clown*), *Engereğin Gözündeki Kamaşma* (1996, *The Eunuch of Constantinople*), *Mutluluk* (2002, *Bliss*), *Serenad* (2011, *Serenade*), *Edebiyat Mutluluktur* (2012, *Literature is Bliss*), *Son Ada'nın Çocukları* (2014, *Last Island's Kids*),

Konstantiniyye Oteli (2015, *Constantinople Hotel*), *Huzursuzluk* (2017, *Disquiet*), *Elia ile Yolculuk* (2017, *Journey with Elia*) and *Gölgeler* (2018, *Shadows*). Livaneli has achieved enormous success as a writer, musician and film director as well as his political career. In 1996, he was appointed as a Goodwill Ambassador of UNESCO due to his contributions to world culture and peace.

His novel, *Son Ada* (*The Last Island*) presents an e-utopian social order on a desolate island with forty houses, in which the rules and expectations of the mainstream ruling body do not apply. The island is referred to by the narrator as the last oasis of happiness, joy, and tranquility in a world corrupted by capitalism, totalitarianism, greed, and the system of hierarchy. The experimental, mature, introverted narrator (number 36) explains the main features of this *last haven* as: there are only forty houses on the island; the owner of the island does not allow more immigration so as not to disrupt the beauty and balance of nature on the island. People address to each other by the number of their house, and they live in peace leading an idyllic life. They have no television reception; a weekly ferry brings the needs of the inhabitants; and the grocer (*bakkal*) meets their needs next to the pier. They have been living in peace with the *actual owners* of the island—the seagulls for a long time. There are no children on the island, and the dead bodies are either buried on the hill or sent back to the homeland on the ferry. Finally, there are no traffic jams, bureaucracy, taxes.

This paradise is disrupted by the migration of the President (*Başkan*), who decides to move to the island upon "having fallen from favor after his five-year iron-fisted rule and given his walking papers by the Revolutionary Council" (Livaneli 2008, 14). Although he states that he has immigrated to the island to maintain a peaceful life, he begins a gradual, substantial transformation of this arcadian order into a totalitarian order. He changes the nature of the island, namely the e-utopian dream into a dystopian nightmare through the allegedly democratic means; pruning the trees, which are the source of shade, changing the dress code, organizing an administrative committee, and killing the seagulls. The ecological balance is substantially shattered; and ultimately, the houses are burned to ashes by his tyrannical practices. Moreover, any criticism or divergence is denied and not welcome since he regards his endeavor as civilizing and sacred. He accordingly perceives any divergent inhabitant as a possible terrorist.

The writer, the narrator and the narrator's wife, Lara are presented as possible threats to the President's *democratic, civilizing* regime. Thus, divergence is strictly punished; the writer goes through temporary punishment in the course of the story, and is sent out of the island in the end. The island is ultimately reduced to ash, and the President is killed by the hunchbacked son of the grocer. In this regard, the novel demonstrates the sort of consequences that divergence could lead to, and how democracy is exploited.

In this novel, the migration of a character gives rise to the change of the whole structure of the island. In this regard, the flow of people is projected in two different lights. Initially, when the father of inhabitant Number 1 bought the island, invited residents, and commissioned forty houses to be built on the island, his unexpected migration stood for happiness, hope, promising future, peace with nature, and joyous life. This initial migration, initiated by the father and maintained by his son, allowed the inhabitants of the island to live in peace away from the rat-race, violence, and materialistic obsessions of the mainland.

This flow paved the way for the formation of a unique culture and ideology on the island. The idyllic life style of the island's inhabitants does not have land ownership, competition, materialistic ambitions, or the turmoil of the materialistic world. The inhabitants manage to establish a peaceful, harmonious relationship with nature on the island, which differs to a great extent from the *civilized*, *modern*, contemporary world. They have learned to appreciate the beauty of nature and live with seagulls as stated by the narrator: "A state of harmony was established at last between the humans and the seagulls, between these wild birds and these hermitic people who were seeking refuge from a previous life, agreeing to mutual non-interference by means of a silent pact" (Livaneli 2008, 7).

Hence, nature is presented as a source of tranquility, shade, and joy. This inspiring source does not pose a threat for the islanders. The narrator touches on the beauty of nature as: "It was as if some sacred secret were hidden in the tranquil nature of the island. How could one begin to describe … the whispering of the wind amid the cries of the seagulls, the scent of lavender?" (Livaneli 2008, 7). This dream starts turning into a gradual nightmare following the migration of another citizen, which indicates how the initial migration with positive connotations is substituted by another migration with enormous negative connotations and results.

The fate of the island goes through a drastic change when the President decides to buy the house of Number 24, and to migrate to the island. His decision leads to many other significant decisions regarding the island and life on the island in a destructive manner. Therefore, he turns out to be the destroyer of this last remaining paradise, the last peaceful island on earth, and effectively destroys the island by drawing on his so-called democratic discourse. The *taming* process of nature, the island, and the islanders is practiced at the cost of the e-utopian order on the island as his aim is to *civilize* nature and the islanders that have been allegedly devoid of civilization due to their *primitive* lifestyle.

The President's arrival is a turning point in the history of the island since a hierarchical order is strongly felt for the first time on the island. His existence is recounted by the narrator as the harbinger of doom, and the writer, Number 7 plays a pivotal role in reflecting the President's suppressive side; in this sense, the writer becomes a token of divergence, defiance, and rebellion, revealing the President's destructive nature through epistemological warfare.

The inhabitants feel the need to respect the President due to his socio-political status even though he is not in power anymore. Thus, a hierarchical level is established between him and the islanders. How the President dresses demonstrates that he pictures himself in a very different light than the *primitive, uncivilized* islanders: "The President was clad in a white suit, gleaming and immaculate, with a gray tie around his neck" (Livaneli 2008, 15). His first impression, as he greets the islanders, foreshadows the dystopian future of the island.

The narrator expresses that the President used "a tone of voice that was all too familiar to us, echoing back from days of yore, and in particular from our days of military service ... we were involuntarily and unthinkingly prompted to retort: 'Thank you, sir!'" (Livaneli 2008, 16–17). This scene indicates that a new power structure is to be built on the island. The new power exercise turns out to be what regulates social life on the island. Hence, the allegedly democratic social engineering is initiated by the experienced President who claims to bring welfare, materialistic richness, civilization, and wealth to the island. Intervention in social and cultural life on the island immediately starts. Due to his staunch belief in his own divine right to rule, he begins engineering the island by ordering his men to prune the trees, which results in the destruction of the canopy. This act is enough to shock the islanders, some of whom still believe that the President does not pose a threat to their island and life; however, a partial destruction or taming of nature is intensified.

When the islanders attempt to complain to him about depriving them of shade and the beauty of their trees, they are reminded of what civilization stands for by the President, and are made to feel as though they should apologize to him for not taming nature previously:

> It's possible that after living here all these years, you've grown used to certain irregularities—to some of the turmoil and disorderliness in your midst.... But human societies can't live this way. Civilization requires people to bring order to their lives and where they live.... You ought to be grateful to my men for taking care of the matter before they leave. Each time you pass along that road from now on, you'll see those tamed and orderly trees at your sides—pruned, cleared out and fixed up in keeping with park and garden traditions—and remember what it is to take pride in your island [Livaneli 2008, 35].

His impressive voice and eloquence reveal him as the sole figure of power and authority on the island, while lending a sense of inferiority to the islanders. When he finds out that some islanders do not agree with him, he reveals his hypocritical satisfaction regarding the difference of opinion, to which he responds by establishing an administrative committee consisting of five members. He creates a system in which every difference of opinion is accordingly labeled as anarchy.

Democracy, democratic discourse, and civilization become key terms in persuading the islanders and transforming the island into a place that can no longer be recognized or even inhabited. His discourse enables him to exercise as much power as possible through the administrative committee (consisting of the President, his wife, Number 1, the writer and another islander) established to regulate social life. As he continues to talk about civilization and arranging life on the island, he accentuates that democracy is "the presiding principle." (Livaneli 2008, 43). His acts are controversial and paradoxical in that he does not welcome any divergence or dissidence. Thus, he wears the mask of a democratic leader, yet in reality this is quite hypocritical.

Democracy is, in theory, supposed to stand for tolerance, plurality of opinions and ideas, and freedom of expression, but the President only makes use of democracy and democratic discourse in order to realize his personal wishes, which eventually ends in a nightmare for the islanders and the island. His eloquent speech is persuasive enough to convince the majority, which brings to mind the question of the rationality of the decisions made by the manipulated majority.

The islanders are made to feel nationalistic and pride in their island in the process of choosing the members of the administrative committee: "We had grown so excited, as a matter of fact, that we were all on the verge of crying out something like 'May our lives be sacrificed in the name of the island!'" (Livaneli 2008, 45). This gradual transformation changes the fate of the island and leads the islanders to a state of ignorance as they start believing in whatever the President utters and begin to regard the divergent figures as possible threats to the welfare of their island. They are made to believe that they will rise to wealth through hotels, casinos, and tourism that the President's offers as promising words about the significance of the island. Hence, this tragic transformation is initiated and maintained by the President out of a materialistic desire or wealth.

The administrative committee starts setting up rules, which are actually the rules that the President desires. After the hunchbacked son leaves milk, bread, and cheese on the terrace of the President, he is beaten by the President's henchmen for violating his privacy. This act leads to the formation of certain rules by the administrative committee:

1. No one is to approach a house beyond the designated security border and private property threshold of 6 meters without advance notice.

2. Service personnel in charge of distributing supplies are to fulfill this task between the hours of 9 and 11 every morning and in accordance with the property border rules stipulated above.

3. Any and all persons violating these rules established by the island committee will be severely penalized by the island's homeowners. [Livaneli 2008, 50].

These rules imply that those who do not abide by them are to be strictly punished by the committee out of a desire to maintain public order. In this sense, such an order denotes the suppressing of divergent figures, and reinforcing the sense of land ownership, hierarchy, and power relation.

The formation of the administrative committee leads to many restrictive decisions and movements. These decisions are democratic in disguise, yet, they are actually the decisions of one person: the President. As time goes by, the President's hatred of seagulls starts growing as the seagulls attack his grand-daughter and invade on his terrace. Even though he does not see the real figure walking on the terrace, he immediately labels the figure as a terrorist, which reflects his paranoid psychological state. This act causes every house and the whole island to be searched, intensifying the epistemological war, but the writer reveals the secret that it was only a seagull making that voice. The seagulls and the divergent writer turn out to be the President's two enemies as a result of this incident.

Accordingly, the President finds himself in war against nature, and proposes the annihilation of the seagulls, which pose a great threat from his point of view. Although many islanders are initially opposed to this insane proposal, they finally end up exercising the annihilation of the seagulls with guns provided by the President. The majority is persuaded to start the fight against the seagulls, which have been living in peace with the islanders for a long time. The memory of the beautiful, charming moments with the seagulls is erased by means of the alluring discourse of the President. This changing tension reveals one fact for the writer, the narrator and his wife: "But there's one thing I've learned from life: Evil is everywhere, and its power is difficult to defeat. Goodness is weak in comparison" (Livaneli 2008, 67).

The President's hypocritical side is gradually revealed. His personality and remarks indicate that he actually does not believe in democracy and equality. His conversation with Number 1 is quite pivotal in that it highlights his tyranny and his obsession with power:

> But don't forget, people aren't equal. There are the powerful and there are the weak, and life is a fight between the two.... You're a wealthy owner and you ought to act accordingly. Equality, friendship, democracy: this is all a bunch of bullshit made up by the weak. They make it up because they need these kinds of notions in order to live. But the powerful have one desire and one desire alone: More power! [Livaneli 2008, 69].

His remarks point out that every decision taken by the committee is to transform the peaceful island into an unpleasant place, which is justified by the following actions.

The island goes through some further experiences that accelerate the destruction of the islanders and the last paradise. The seagulls are exterminated to some extent; their eggs are broken; the seagulls attack the islanders in return, which makes it almost impossible to walk outside; and the foxes are brought to the island to annihilate the seagulls as the foxes would steal and eat the seagulls' eggs. Due to a decrease in the number of the seagulls on the island, an extremely poisonous type of snake emerges on the island. After one islander dies due to seagull attack, another islander dies in the aftermath of a snake attack. The President decides to bring snake poison to fight against the snakes; however, the islanders cannot bear the smell of the snake poison.

In order to do away with the snake problem, a famous expert is called to the island to solve the problem. The famous expert orders the islanders to set up poles so that the storks can build nests on the poles and hunt the snakes as the storks migrate to the south at that time of the year; however, the expert's plan fails. When it becomes clear that the seagulls are vital to the balance of nature, the President plans to reduce the number of foxes and to raise the number of seagulls, which becomes a kind of vicious cycle. Cyanide is brought to the island, and injected into meat left in the forest. This poison kills many other species as well, and has turned the island into "a death camp" (Livaneli 2008, 200).

As a last resort, the President suggests setting a controlled fire to make the foxes run out of the forest. The controlled fire gets out of control, and causes the houses, and the forest to be burnt away. The seagulls fly above the destroyed islanders after the fire in a triumphant mood, and the islanders find themselves in a wretched situation. Ultimately, the President decides to leave the island, and does not feel guilty for his tyrannical practices. On the contrary, he blames the islanders for their failure: "Everything that's happened to you has been the result of your ineptitude and siding with anarchists like that embarrassment of a writer. I'm leaving, to hell with all of you. This island doesn't concern me anymore" (Livaneli 2008, 207).

He points out that all the decisions have been democratic: "Besides, all the decisions made on this island were carried out democratically. We carried out whatever the majority vote resulted in. As a result, all the decisions bore everyone's signatures beneath" (Livaneli 2008, 208). Democracy becomes a useful tool through which he manipulated the islanders and destroyed the e-utopian dream. However, his despotism comes to a halt with the unexpected move of a seemingly-minor character: the grocer's hunchbacked son.

The hunchbacked son hits the President, and they fall off of a cliff together, which ends in their death. This dramatic moment inspires carnivalesque laughter of the sort that "defends freedom of thought" (Shanti 1999, 131). The hunchbacked son laughs at the absurdity of the whole world with his un-anticipated move, and brings the President's dream to an end. Consequently, all the islanders are chained up and put into prison. The President's heroism is praised in the end; he is buried in the cemetery of heroes; and the terrorists are condemned. What happens to the writer in the end? How can his epistemological war engender an ultimate utopian hope?

The writer is depicted as the main figure of dissidence with his eloquence, rebellious remarks, and his concern about environment. In order to alienate the writer from other islanders, the President makes it public that the writer is a political convict that has escaped from prison, therefore an enemy of the regime. Subsequently, he is sent out of the island by his men, and becomes the scapegoat for the President's failure.

All throughout the novel, the writer does not agree with the President's and the majority's decisions. He reveals the *terrorist* walking on the terrace of the President (the seagull); opposes to the annihilation of the seagulls; refers to killing seagulls as massacre, barbarous, not civilized; warns the islanders about the new despotic regulations; and expresses the reason for the rise of the number of the snakes. Consequently, he becomes a dangerous target, and is ultimately disliked by almost all the islanders (except the narrator, his wife Lara, and a few others). The President punishes this dissident character by sending him out of the island. He ends up exercising his despotic power over the writer, which pinpoints his undemocratic exploitation of democratic discourse. Even so, the high probability that the writer is not dead in the end should be interpreted in a positive light. Although the last island is ultimately destroyed, the real writer through divine justice (if there is any) seems to sympathize with the fictional writer as the symbol of hope. The writer's possible survival is to communicate hope and blooming of a new order:

> I only know that there's a strange rumor going around. In the cafeteria, in the laundry room, or on the way to being interrogated, there are whispers to the effect that the Writer is still on the loose. Apparently, some have seen him, as he was on his way back to the island. They say he's going to start living there again these days. That he's going to plant new trees. Build new homes. And that some of his old friends are going to go help him. The island's going to come back to life, they say. We're going to live on the island again. We're going to re-establish our paradise on earth [Livaneli 2008, 182].

In conclusion, Livaneli's novel recounts how the migration of one character to the last haven leads to the total destruction of the utopian life on the island, and how the regime does not show any tolerance towards diversity of opinions, ideologies. The totalitarian rule on the island does not respect nature, and eventually disrupts the ecological balance. Democratic discourse becomes a manipulative tool in substantial social upheaval towards the dystopian end on the island, and democracy is presented as an excuse for the destruction of the island by the President: "Everything has been done in a way consistent with the principles of democracy" (Livaneli 2008, 167). Livaneli's illustration of this dark deteriorating social order might have a negative impact on the psychology of some readers, who are confronted with despotism, tyranny, discrimination, and intolerance of the President. Yet, it is not wrong to argue that Livaneli accentuates the significance and maintenance of hope and the utopian impulse in the face of a nightmarish reality through the writer's epistemological war and his struggle for his individual identity. The next part of the chapter engages itself with the analysis of Anthony Burgess' *The Wanting Seed*, which in a similar vein deals with the theme of epistemological warfare, identity politics, and the probability of utopian impulse.

Part III: Anthony Burgess' Inspirational Sources as a Novelist of Speculative Fiction

Burgess as a prolific writer develops a unique style although he starts his career late as a writer. His travels, his experiences, and his familial relations as well as the social, historical, and political events have a huge impact on his fiction and on his narration. He writes in the tradition of the spy thriller, the epic narrative, the exotic novel, the science fiction fantasy, the bourgeois novel, the mechanical stage farce, the fictional biography and the structuralist novel reflecting subordination, satire, intrigue, control mechanism, grotesque distortions of temporal and spatial settings, of minor characters, and of plot incidents, artificiality, intellectuality, duality, free will, defective will, linguistic inventiveness, illusion-vision relationship, opposition, fragmentation of values, split characters, juxtaposition of different journeys, and thematic concerns (Moran 1974, 208–11).

Burgess associates himself with modernism, and depicts modernist themes such as alienation, decay, futility, frustration, and fragmentation. In addition, loss of man's belief in progress, reason, order, war, and civilization is mirrored in his fiction. He points out that modernism "expressed itself as a rejection of the doctrine of Liberal Man—progressing, mastering his environment, finding salvation in science and the rational organization of society" (Burgess 1978, 56–57). Apart from drawing on modernist themes, he uses history and myth (from a broad perspective) in such a way that he draws an analogy between the problematic present and the peaceful past.

Language becomes a crucial tool in illustrating these themes in his narration. He attaches great importance to the use of language in that he attributes a writer's achievement to "the fundamental skill of putting words together in new and surprising patterns, which miraculously reflect some previously unguessed truth about life" (Coale 1981, 135). He believes that language, subject matter, and content co-exist, and are influenced from each other accordingly. In his view, language can be used to reflect Manichaean dualistic doctrine, and consciousness or the perspective of a fictional character. In addition, it can be an indicator of social class in England, which he dislikes, and fights against (Coale 1981, 137–8).

Similar to the role of language, Pelagianism and Augustinianism play an important role from a philosophical standpoint as he explains:

> What I really wanted to do was to present the English mind as tending to waver between Pelagianism and Augustinianism. The British mind being primarily Pelagian, accepting the notion that people are all right, really, you know, you needn't worry too much about things like grace, divine grace. Things all work out pretty well. This gives you socialism, then you get some disappointments [Churchill 2008, 13].

Similarly, Manichaeism or Manichaeanism has a profound effect on his fiction. It refers to the religion which was founded by the Persian Mani or Manichaeus (c. 216–276 AD) and mainly questions the existence of evil in the world. His doctrine interprets the world from a dualistic perspective meaning that the universe consists of opposing forces such as Light/Darkness, and Good/Evil. These forces are in a constant struggle with each other. It regards materiality and the body as the power of darkness, therefore the source of evil in the world, whereas the spirit coming from divine power, God is regarded as the source of good and light.

Part III.I: Epistemological Warfare and Individuality and Self-Sufficiency in *The Wanting Seed* by Anthony Burgess

This part focuses upon the critical analysis of Burgess' futuristic dystopia or serious entertainment, *The Wanting Seed*[2] (1962), which has not received the critical evaluation or appreciation that it deserves, probably due to the success of his most famous novel, *A Clockwork Orange* (1962). Although both novels were published roughly around the same time, *A Clockwork Orange* has gained more inter/national prominence as compared to *The Wanting Seed*. Both novels are influenced by his trip to Leningrad, and by Russian life. *A Clockwork Orange* is widely appreciated with its unique use of language, transformation of the protagonist, Alex, and representation of subculture and the dark social order. The novel is set in a future city governed by a totalitarian state, which is indifferent to the problems of the young. It is narrated in a slang called *nadsat*, a mixture of

Russian and English expressions by the protagonist, Alex, a 15-year-old boy, who is involved in violence, rape, and robbery with his small gang. Burgess recounts the protagonist, Alex as "hero or anti-hero … an exemplar of humanity: he is aggressive, he loves beauty, he is a language-user … he is to the state, a mere object, something 'out there' like the Moon, though not so passive" (Burgess 2011, 141).

Upon his imprisonment, Alex experiences Ludovico's Technique, a form of technique aiming to rehabilitate criminals, which leads him to associate violence with nausea. He is released from prison after two years as he is *healed* now. Through this novel, Burgess depicts and criticizes various issues such as power of choice, dualistic forces in the universe, repressive nature of government, and conformism. Moreover, he harshly criticizes behavioral interference emphasizing the importance of free will. He argues that human being becomes a clockwork orange, which means that "(s)he has the appearance of … an organism lovely with colour and juice but is in fact only a clockwork toy to be wound up by God or the Devil or (since this is increasingly replacing both) the Almighty State" (Newman 1991, 63).

Similar to *A Clockwork Orange, The Wanting Seed*, a Malthusian comedy, presents comic elements, alternate chapters, cyclical structure, imagination, and dystopian themes with its unusual use of language and engagement with the problem of overpopulation. The envisioned world is set in the future and divided into three parts, Enspun (English-Speaking Union), Ruspun (Russian-Speaking Union), and Chinspun (Chinese-Speaking Union). The action takes place mostly in Enspun. It depicts the lands of English-speaking people suffering from the problem of population excess. The novel does not limit itself to depiction of a certain group, but is enriched in its portrayal of characters from many different strata of society.

The novel is influenced by the historical background with its emphasis upon sexuality, population, and episteme on both governmental and individual levels. The early periods of the 1960s heralded a radical and gradual social transformation in society in Europe and Britain. In relation to this gradual change, Burgess explains his concerns: "Also I was interested in what was already apparently happening in England. Homosexuals were rising to the top. Indeed, we had a homosexual prime minister, Edward Heath … there is a homosexual mafia, not only in England, but also in California" (Coale 2008, 131–32).

Apart from the historical events, the novel pictures the significance of free will, and the struggle between dualism, Pelagianism and Augustinianism from a philosophical standpoint. Conflict is placed as a focal point due to Burgess' belief in significance of conflicts in novels: "Novels are about conflicts. The novelist's world is one of essential oppositions of character, aspiration, and so on. I'm entitled to an eclectic theology as a novelist, if not as a human being" (Cullinan 2008, 64). Moreover, Catholicism and Malthusian outlook on population are also influential in comprehending the text as Burgess states: "it's a very Catholic book. It's a total vindication of the encyclical. You know, of course, what the encyclical leaves out of account is the acceptance of natural checks, you know, is in fact Malthusianism" (Churchill 2008, 13). Additionally, it has other elements such as "elemental poetry, broad jokes, science fiction and political philosophy consort[ing] together, couched throughout in a highly pedantic and jawbreaking vocabulary" (Prichard 1987, 22).

The title depicts the dystopian setting and themes as it reflects the controversial, ambiguous mutual co-existence of the good and the evil in the nature of man. It is inspired by an old English folk song, "The Wanton Seed," which is collected in James Reeves's *The Everlasting Circle* (1960):

> As I walked out one morning fair
> To view the fields and take the air
> There I heard a pretty maid making her complain
> And all she wanted was the chiefest grain
> Chiefest grain,
> And all she wanted was the chiefest grain.
>
> I said, My pretty maid, what do you stand in need.
> Oh yes, kind sir, you're the man who can do my deed,
> For to sow my meadow with the wanting seed
> Wanting seed,
> For to sow my meadow with the wanting seed.
>
> Then I sowed high and I sowed low
> And under her apron the seed did grow,
> Sprung up so accidentally without e'er a weed,
> And she always remembered the wanting seed
> Wanting seed
> And she always remembered the wanting seed [Reeves 1960, 276].

Ambiguity between *wanton* and *wanting* is functional in the thematic discussion of the speculative text as it is based on a duality, conundrum, and a dichotomy. Torn between Pelagianism and Augustinianism, the novel seeks to find an answer as to the nature of the seed. This is the seed of knowledge, of the good, of war, of duality, and of the evil.

Various seeds are sown within the normative and constitutive structure of the society but these seeds are open to question. What does the seed stand for? What is the source of the seed? What is it that makes the seed wanton or wanting? How are eschatological[3] times represented in relation to the protagonist's gradual, challenging journey? Possible answers to these questions exemplify how the actual facet of truth is distorted by the regime, which desires to form an absolute conformity culture so that possible resistance can be circumvented. Burgess accordingly draws specific attention to significance of having knowledge/episteme in order to thwart possible manipulation: "They must have knowledge. And they haven't got enough knowledge. They disdain knowledge. All knowledge comes from a segment of society that they now reject" (Riemer 2008, 31). Thus, the feasibility of such a *utopian/dystopian* scheme or blueprint in open to question through Burgess' skeptical stance.

The critical interpretation of the text accordingly discloses the functional texture of the system in an attempt to observe how social engineering is applied and how such socio-political application engenders resentment and frustration in the personal vision of the protagonist through his epistemological warfare. It also pictures how such engineering leads to encroachment on individuality, freedom, and an epistemological systematization as a result of coercive practices, which, to a great extent, produce a culture of ignorance within the society in order to circumvent uprising and insurgency. Unveiling the operation of the system initiates and expedites the process of a possible radical transformation in society through the ensuing uprising of the protagonist whose viewpoints on government are shattered upon first-hand observation and experience. One may question the reliability of the protagonist's narrative and his critical judgment of the system as the reader is guided through his perspective although a certain degree of the other stance is presented. His narration generates a kind of sympathy due to the state practices that constrain individual progress and self-improvement.

The political body purports to employ these sanctions for the benefit of the society and its citizens; however, such a priori assumption results in the desire for herd mentality, and unquestioned, absolute conformity. Some characters, especially the protagonist experience ensuing frustration and realization in the wake of the repressive regime, which exploits knowledge and truth by diffusing its power, socially and politically. This situation creates deceit, disinformation, and misrepresentation. This residual awareness gives rise to a clash or an epistemological warfare between the protagonist and the ontological regime, which enables the possibility of a change.

Gradual transition from ignorance to experiential knowledge brings the nature of the mainstream truth into question and facilitates probable development of individuality, social transformation, and the maintenance of a utopian impulse. Thus, the protagonist's struggle (through his transformational journeys) against the dystopian regime leads to the exposition of the fabricated nature of truth as a discursive practice in the face of the arbitrary rule and cultural production of ignorance. *Anagnorisis* in an Aristotelian sense, that is recognition (although it has a negative connotation in tragedy) can be considered to be constructive and generative in the hopes of re-shaping the society transcending these oppressive boundaries. This exposition reinforces a new epistemological idea of transformation and renewal of collective values as opposed to the normative dystopian political system, which indoctrinates its citizens with its manipulative ideology. A major tenet of a revisionary knowledge is that it can give the prospect of a utopian hope and of a sanguine view about the future.

The suppressive means of manipulative social engineering reveals how the state shapes such a manipulated mind-set to maintain its order. Social life, organized accordingly, therefore exemplifies the absolute, omnipotent power of the state and its despotic nature. The protagonist's experiential journeys and his transition to self-awareness, introspection, and maturity expose how this engineering becomes efficacious and prevalent on a large scale within the society. A taxonomy of social engineering from the general to the specific thus illustrates its crucial role in manipulation and gubernation.

The State in the novel goes through a cycle, Pelphase, Interphase, and Gusphase. The governing Pelagian regime promotes homosexuality and several other measures to cope with overpopulation and famine such as paying citizens for infanticide and abortion (though later on cannibalism, eating clubs). Individual choices and decisions are not respected. The State sees itself as protective of the whole society and collective life and identity. However, when the regime is disappointed at man's inability to live up to the expectations, the Interphase replaces the Pelagian regime, which brings repressive strictures. The Interphase is then followed by Augustinian regime. It eases the despotic practices and ends in more chaos. When such a regime fails, a Pelagian regime is to be reinstated. Such a tyrannical rule is met with strong rejection on the part of the protagonist, Tristram. Burgess' novel, in this sense portrays Tristram Foxe's struggle against such an anti-utopian system, and projects how he is taken from one place to another eliciting the operation of the regime through epistemological warfare in order to realize his individual identity.

Tristram's awareness is raised on both political and individual levels. His keen eye for observation enables him to evaluate the socio-political aura more critically as compared to his wife, Beatrice, and other characters. His critical remark as to the nature of the state demonstrates his individual awakened status since he refers to espionage and the power of the Population Police: "Things have changed…. The State doesn't ask any more. The State orders, the State compels…. It's going to be the same everywhere … we're living in dangerous times" (Burgess 1962, 72–3). As opposed to the former Tristram, he transforms into a cautious citizen in his path to individuality and self-sufficiency.

Tristram experiences the despotic socio-political strictures and manipulation of ideological discursive episteme on order, war, education, family, and sexuality. Therefore, his new sense of critical self-awareness is reflected in his prospective instructional approach to war and social order. Such a new state of analytical experience increases the possibility of de-subjugated, un-suppressed episteme in a Foucauldian sense. This also raises the probability of re-organizing an alternative social order and identity politics in a more ideal way as opposed to the authoritarian regime. Burgess himself insinuates the aura of possible drastic change: "At the end they're looking forward to a new Pelagianism. One doesn't know what it would be like. It may last a long time, there's no need to repress anymore" (Churchill 2008, 14).

The final romantic reunion of the couple, Tristram and Beatrice who are both transformed mentally and psychologically as a result of experiential journeys, opens up the possibility of a more harmonious social order and a new form of identity politics with a focus on individuality. It is not enslaved by the manipulative discourse of ideological regime and its encroachment on individual, social and cultural freedom.

Part IV: Conclusion

Power in an epistemological sense plays a significant role in dystopian fiction. Its maintenance becomes the site of warfare, controversy, strife, resistance, and hope, especially for a revisionary epistemology. The ruling power and the discontented, defiant protagonist/character(s) are involved in this epistemological warfare through numerous literary and metaphorical experiential journeys, which open up the probability of a radical transformation towards prospective constructive changes. Dystopian narrative correspondingly facilitates the probability of a new individuality through its intricate internal dynamics, which engenders the protagonist's active participation and intervention in an epistemological warfare. Both Livaneli's and Burgess' novels project a discursive manipulation of episteme on multiple constituents of a cultural and social order in a fictional sense. However, what these alternative projections illustrate is unfortunately not limited only to an imaginary, make-believe realm. Although the reader is presented with a dark social picture, the protagonists' substantial transformation becomes ultimately the seed of the utopian hope towards a potential progressive society. The open-ended narrative hints at the hope of a revisionary epistemology and a new form of e-utopian identity politics in the aftermath of the protagonists' experiential journeys to a utopian awakening and an e-utopian prospective future in stark contrast to the dystopian present.

NOTES

1. I would like to express my gratitude to the writer, Zülfü Livaneli for his help and interest in this chapter since he contributed immensely to my comprehension of his text through e-mails.

2. *The Wanting Seed* is regarded as dystopia, anti-utopia, futuristic dystopia, serious entertainment, a Malthusian comedy, a novel of eschatological mode by John H. Dorenkamp, speculative novel, critical utopia.

3. John H. Dorenkamp calls *The Wanting Seed* the novel of eschatological mode, inspired by Walker Percy's term (107). Eschatology is a branch of theology which engages itself with the final events, man's final end, and the future of man. Percy points out that an eschatological writer is "a writer who has explicit and ultimate concern with the nature of man and the nature of reality where man finds himself" (qtd. in Dorenkamp 107) (Dorenkamp, John H. 1981. "Anthony Burgess and the Future of Man: The Wanting Seed." University of Dayton Review 15.1, 107).

WORKS CITED

Baccolini, Raffaella, and Tom Moylan. Introduction. 2003. "Dystopia and Histories." *Dark Horizons: Science Fiction and the Dystopian Imagination.* Eds. Raffaella Baccolini and Tom Moylan. New York: Routledge, 1–12.

Buckingham, David. 2008. "Introducing Identity." *Youth, Identity and Digital Media.* Ed by David Buckingham. The John D. and Catherine T. MacArthur Foundation Series on Digital Media and Learning. Cambridge, MA: MIT Press.

Burgess, Anthony. 1962. *The Wanting Seed.* New York: W.W. Norton & Company.

_____. 1978. *Ernest Hemingway and His World.* New York: Charles Scribner's Sons.

_____. 2011. "Anthony Burgess on *A Clockwork Orange.*" *A Clockwork Orange: Authoritative Text, Backgrounds and Contexts Criticism.* 1st ed. New York: W.W. Norton & Co.

Coale, Samuel. 1981. *Anthony Burgess.* New York: F. Ungar Pub. Co.

_____. 2008. "Guilt's a Good Thing." In *Conversations with Anthony Burgess,* edited by Earl G. Ingersoll and Mary C. Ingersoll. 115–134. Jackson: University Press of Mississippi.

Churchill, Thomas. 2008. "Going on Writing Till Ninety or One Hundred." In *Conversations with Anthony Burgess,* edited by Earl G. Ingersoll and Mary C. Ingersoll, 3–23. Jackson: University Press of Mississippi.

Cullinan, John. 2008. "Dealing with the Hinterland of the Consciousness." In *Conversations with Anthony Burgess.* edited by Earl G. Ingersoll and Mary C. Ingersoll. 46–73. Jackson: University Press of Mississippi.

Dorenkamp, John H. 1981. "Anthony Burgess and the Future of Man: The Wanting Seed." University of Dayton Review 15.1, 107–111.

Elliot, Shanti. 1999. "Carnival and Dialogue in Bakhtin's Poetics of Folklore." *Folklore Forum* 30 (1/2): 129–139.

Giddens, Anthony. 1991. *Modernity and Self-Identity: Self and Society in the Late Modern Age.* Stanford, CA: Stanford University Press.

Hall, Joan Kelly. 2013. *Teaching and Researching Language and Culture.* 2nd ed. New York: Routledge.

Livaneli, Zülfü. 2008. *Son Ada (The Last Island).* Translated by Ayşe Şahin. English editor, Alexandra Ivanoff. Istanbul: Doğan Kitap.

Moran, Kathryn L. 1974. "Utopias, Subtopias and Dystopias in the Novels of Anthony Burgess." Diss., University of Notre Dame.

Moylan, Tom. Preface. 2000. *Scraps of the Untainted Sky: Science Fiction, Utopia, Dystopia.* Boulder, CO: Westview Press.

Newman, Bobby. 1991. "*A Clockwork Orange*: Burgess and Behavioral Intervention." *Behavior and Social Issues* 1.2, 61–70.

Pritchard, William H. 1987. "The Novels of Anthony Burgess." *Anthony Burgess: Modern Critical Views.* Ed. Harold Bloom. New York: Chelsea House Publishers, 13–28.

Reeves, James. 1960. *The Everlasting Circle: English Traditional Verse*. London: Heinemann.
Riemer, G. 2008. "Cynical About the Great Words." *Conversations with Anthony Burgess*. Eds. Earl G. Ingersoll and Mary C. Ingersoll. Jackson: University Press of Mississippi, 24–45.
Sargent, Lyman Tower. 1994. "The Three Faces of Utopianism Revisited." *Utopian Studies* 5.1, 1–37.

Three Options and Three Science Fiction Novels Concerning the Algerian War of Independence

RUY BURGOS-LOVECE

A variety of definitions of science fiction have been proposed since its recognized inception with Mary Shelley's *Frankenstein*.[1] Among them, it could be argued that Darko Suvin's is the most solid and enlightening: "SF is … a literary genre whose necessary and sufficient conditions are the presence and interaction of estrangement and cognition, and whose main formal device is an imaginative framework alternative to the author's empirical environment" (Suvin 1979, 7). Estrangement is the attitude resulting from "confronting a set normative system—a Ptolemaic-type closed world picture—with a point of view or look implying a new set of norms" (Suvin 1979, 6). Cognition is an approach that "first posits [the essence of phenomena] as problems and then explores where they lead" (Suvin 1979, 7). The "imaginative framework alternative to the author's empirical environment" is based on what Suvin defines as a novum: "a totalizing phenomenon or relationship deviating from the author's and implied reader's norm of reality" (Suvin 1979, 64).

To Suvin's definition, we can add Delany's concept of a genre as "a way of reading (what we may henceforth call a protocol of reading), a structuration of response potential" (Delany 1980, 176). Just as we can't read a poem the way we read a novel, we can't read SF the way we read mundane fiction. As its name indicates, mundane fiction deals with *the world as we know it*; what could be called factual reality.

The equivalence between *the world as we know it* and factual reality involves some caveats: first, the word *factual* must be based on Gould's definition of facts as aspects of reality that have been "confirmed to such a degree that it would be perverse to withhold provisional assent" (Gould

1983, 255); second, it must be accepted that, since this assent is provisional, facts are not forever; third, it must be accepted that *the world as we know it* today is neither as we knew it yesterday nor as we will know it tomorrow and; fourth, it must be accepted that, in its anthropocentricity, *the world as we know it* is not equivalent to the absolutely unknowable world as it is. In summary, factual reality is the ever-changing status of our current anthropocentric knowledge of the world. Therefore, it should be called *present* factual reality. This, in turn, implies that there are *past* factual realities and yet unknown *future* factual realities.

For its part, SF deals with *the world as it **could** be*. Delany explains: "in the discourse of mundane fiction the world is given…. In SF, the world of the story is not given, but rather a construct that changes from story to story" (Delany 1980, 178). Asimov concurs: "What, then, is it that is required in a *good* science fiction story, that is *not* required in anything else? It is a *society*, based and organized on reasonable technological and scientific change so that it is quite different from the one we live in." And then he adds his personal experience: "I can write a mystery novel (and have) in seven weeks, because I am using our contemporary society and do not have to make it up. It takes me a minimum of seven to nine months to write a science fiction novel" (Asimov 1986, 8). Lest it be thought that SF's license to build new societies leads to fantasy,[2] Asimov clarifies that the changes needed to establish new societies should be "rational ones in keeping with what [is] known about science, technology and people" (Asimov 1991, 11).

In particular, Malmgren specifies that SF texts can be classified as extrapolative novels, where the author "accepts the current state of scientific knowledge, projects from it either in time or in space, and tries to imagine and articulate the resultant situation or conditions" (Malmgren 1991, 12), and speculative novels, where the author "is cut loose from the current state of affairs (but not from the convention which dictates that any novum must be grounded in scientific research)" (Malmgren 1991, 13). Notice that, in both cases, limits are imposed to keep the text from wandering into the *anything goes* of fantasy.

In summary, while mundane fiction must stay within the confines of past and present factual realities—thus denying the reader the benefit of perspective and a better gestalt—SF's license to create new worlds allows it to explore human nature in possible but carefully structured factual realities. From Jules Verne's prediction of the electric bulb[3] to Iain M. Banks brilliantly conceived Culture[4] society, SF uses the power of art and literature to illuminate possible future realities that may allow us to see, influence and, hopefully, improve our present.

Robert A. Heinlein, one of the *big three* in what could be called classical anglophone SF—the other two are Isaac Asimov and Arthur C. Clarke—wrote that SF is "the only fictional medium capable of interpreting the changing headlong rush of modern life" (Heinlein 1977, 23). Then he added, probably exaggerating, "[f]or the survival and health of the human race, one crudely written science fiction story containing a single worthwhile new idea is more valuable than a bookcase full of beautifully written non-science fiction" (Heinlein 1977, 27).

The three novels involved in this essay depict two possible futures and an allegory for France concerning the Algerian conflict. As true works of SF, these novels comply with the requirements in Suvin's definition: a work of SF must provide *estrangement*, "that feeling of alienation one is lead to experience when something familiar is taken out of context and repositioned so that it is perceived in an entirely new light" (MacLean 1994, 9); and a *novum*, "an innovation of some sort, something different in comparison with the 'normal' or empirical reality which surrounds the author" (MacLean 1994, 5); and be written according to *cognition*, "a way of thinking that has been influenced by modern Western science and philosophy, a pattern of thinking which is bound by cause and effect reasoning" (MacLean 1994, 6).

Charles de Gaulle gave a radio and TV speech in Paris on September 16, 1959. In this speech—a key turning point in the Algerian War—he offered three options to Algerians: "francisation" [francization] (total assimilation into France), "*gouvernement des algériens par les algériens*" [government of Algerians by Algerians] (a close union with France), or "*sécession*" [secession] (total independence from France) (DeGaulle 1959). The first two options had been explored, respectively, in two SF novels published by Stefan Wul in 1957: *La Peur géante [Gigantic Fear]* (Wul 1994) and *Oms en Série [Oms in Series]* (Wul 1972). The last option resonates with Pierre Boulle's well known *La Planète des singes [Planet of the Apes]* (Boulle 1963).

It would seem these options were already present in the sociopolitical environment; or, as Foucault would have had it, there existed "conditions of possibility" for these options to be conceived (Foucault 1992, 13). Thus, de Gaulle gives a factual speech concerning what Wul and Boulle express by writing SF novels. Free from the need of rigorous verisimilitude, these SF novels enrich the image of the Algerian War as they reflect and illustrate the sociopolitical structures implicit in de Gaulle's options.

The action in *La Peur* takes place in 2157.[5] The story begins with an apparently inconsequential phenomenon: the freezing point of water drops to -15 °C and normal refrigerators stop making ice. A few days later, water simply stops turning to ice no matter how much the temperature drops. All ice turns to water, the polar caps melt, and two planet-wide tsunamis move towards the equator ravaging everything in their paths. Six months later, water stops evaporating. This causes drought in the areas the tsunamis didn't flood. We then learn that a highly advanced hitherto unknown intelligent sea species, the *torpèdes* [electric rays], is responsible for modifying the properties of water. Apparently, these attacks are a reaction against worldwide land reclamation projects in which humans have dried out large areas of seafloor and forced sea species to move to deeper water. The *torpèdes* are simply trying to recover what has been taken from them. The parallel is unmistakable: Algerians want Algeria back.

This leads us to review how Algeria became French. On April 27, 1827, in a diplomatic incident related to money, Hussein Dey, ruler of Algiers *"perdit patience au cours d'un entretien avec le consul de France à Alger, Pierre Deval, lui donnant alors un 'coup d'éventail'"* [lost patience with the French consul in Algiers, Pierre Deval, during an interview, and hit him with a "hand-held fan"] (Peyroulou "Conquête" 2012, 24). To retaliate against this insult, Prime Minister Joseph de Villèle ordered a blockade of the Algerian coast. By January 27, 1829, King Charles X realized the blockade was useless. On August 3, 1829, Admiral La Bretonnière ordered the fleet to lift the blockade.

Nevertheless, by 1830, the government of Charles X was close to collapse. At the head of the government, Jules-Auguste de Polignac thinks a military victory could restore the regime. On June 14, 1830, a 40,000-strong French expeditionary force disembarks at Sidi-Ferruch, 20 kilometers west of Algiers. Nevertheless, Charles X abdicates on August 2, 1830, and exiles himself in England. Louis-Philippe, his successor, inherits in Algeria *"une terre qu'il n'avait pas briguée"* [a land he had not sought] (Peyroulou "Conquête" 2012, 25). Then, on February 24, 1848, Louis-Philippe also abdicates the throne and leaves for England. A short provisional government led by Alphonse de Lamartine declares the beginning of the Second Republic. After a turbulent time of temporary governments, street protests and repression, Louis Napoleon Bonaparte is elected President in December 1848.

Throughout Louis-Philippe's reign, the French army had been relentlessly eliminating all resistance in Algeria. The country was ready for colonization. Then, in November 1848, the constitution of the Second Republic stated that Algeria was part of France: *"Le territoire de l'Algérie et des colonies est déclaré territoire français, et sera régi par des lois particulières jusqu'à ce qu'une loi spéciale les place sous le régime de la présente Constitution"* [The territory of Algeria and the colonies is declared French territory, and will be governed by specific laws until a special law places them under this Constitution].[6] Unlike other French colonies, Algeria became indistinguishable from metropolitan France as it was organized *"sur le modèle métropolitain,*

*doté de départements, eux mêmes divisées en arrondissements et en com-
munes"* [on the metropolitan model, with departments, themselves divided
into districts and municipalities] (Peyroulou "Conquête" 2012, 33).

In hindsight, the incorporation of Algeria into France seems to be an
unintended consequence of unrelated geopolitical imperatives: Charles X
attempt to distract French public opinion from his deteriorating reign, the
ensuing lack of purpose about Algeria—*"L'État français occupait Alger, mais
sans plan de colonisation"* [The French state occupied Algiers, but without
a settlement plan] (Blais 2012, 54)—and the Second Republic's desire to
keep Algeria different from Ancient Régime colonies in order to avoid *"leur
héritage esclavagiste"* [their pro-slavery heritage] (Blais 2012, 56). Once
French Algeria comes into existence, France takes her to her bosom only to
learn, little by little, over more than a century, that having Algeria as part of
France is simply impossible.

The essential problem was that, in Algeria, self-determination and territorial integrity, both solid republican concepts, couldn't coexist. Through
discrimination, racism and denial of rights, French colonialism slowly
but surely caused the formation of a non–European Algerian population
that didn't want to be French: *"de plus en plus d'Algériens ne désiraient pas
être français, mais algériens"* [more and more Algerians did not want to be
French but Algerian] (Peyroulou "Historie" 2012, 319). Self-determination
dictated that such non–European Algerian people should have their
own country. Unfortunately, for this to happen, French territorial integrity had to be broken and, Algeria, officially part of France, had to be
given to them: *"Le drame était qu'on ne pouvait donner l'Algérie aux Ara-
bes sans l'enlever aux Pieds-Noirs"* [The tragedy was that we could not give
Algeria to the Arabs without taking it away from the Pieds-Noirs] (Roy
1982, 137).

Stefan Wul's *La Peur* solves the self-determination/territorial integrity dilemma by having non–European Algerians become French and
somehow harmoniously melting with the European Algerian population.
This harmony is abundantly shown as the novel starts with a presentation of a solid friendship and camaraderie between the hero, Bruno Daix,
"[un] géant blond" [(a) blond giant] and Pol Nazaire *"[un] homme de cou-
leur"* [(a) colored man] (Wul 1994, 9). Next comes the amicable and cor-
dial relationship between Bruno Daix and Driss Bouira, whose gray eyes
"se plissaient au-dessus de ses pommettes berbères" [creased over his Ber-
ber cheekbones] (Wul 1994, 13). Soon enough, Bruno Daix finds the person who will become his romantic interest, a Chinese journalist named
Kou-Sien. This allows Bruno to expound on the unbreakable link between
France and Algeria. Upon meeting Bruno, Kou-Sien asks him: *"On dit que
Paris est la tête de l'Afrance ... qu'est donc In Salah ? In Salah en est le cœur."*

[It is said that Paris is the head of the Afrance.... What is In Salah? In Salah is the heart] (Wul 1994, 27). Later, their conversation turns to the bridge joining the ports of Marseille and Algiers. Bruno refers to these cities waxing lyrically: "*Marseille, la mère, et Alger, la fille*" [Marseille, the mother, Algiers, the daughter] (Wul 1994, 28). As we can see, this demonstration of Afrench unity nevertheless reveals, even at this level of wishful thinking, the underlying power hierarchy where metropolitan cities are head and mother, while Algerian cities are just heart and daughter.

In particular, Wul masterfully consummates this Algerian/French marriage of sorts by having a territorial integrity based on actual geographic territorial continuity. In other words, the Afrance, the union of Algeria (Africa) and France, not only extends "*de Dunkerke à Tamanrasset*" [from Dunkirk to Tamanrasset] but does so as a single land mass (DeGaulle 1959). Not content with building the Marseille-Algiers bridge, Afrance has desiccated the Western Mediterranean by building "*le verrou de Gibraltar*" [the lock of Gibraltar,] a dam between Morocco and Gibraltar, and "*le barrage sicilotunisien*" [the Sicilio-Tunisian dam] a dam between Tunisia and Italy (Wul 1994, 69). Finally, the former seabed has been covered with wheat, and presumably other crops, in irrigated fields that reach the horizon. Instead of a sea that separates Algeria from France, life giving wheat fields join them. All that's left of the sea is a small lake in the middle called Lac Latin. This quintessentially science-fictional feat allows Wul to explore a reality where Algeria is truly and undeniably part of France.[7]

However much Wul wanted this unbroken land to be an expression of harmonious unity, the brutal reality of the Mediterranean seafloor shows us a basin quickly descending to depths of several thousand meters where the land would be so tortured by sunlight and atmospheric pressure that, in comparison, Death Valley would be a spring picnic destination. In his short story "Down in the Bottomlands," Harry Turtledove presents a more realistic description of a desiccated Mediterranean former seafloor that can only be reached by mule train, like the Colorado River at the Grand Canyon (Turtledove 1993).

But Afrance's prowess at controlling the sea does not end with desiccating the Western Mediterranean. It has also conquered the dessert by building a network of underground canals "*qui amènent, dessalée, l'eau des côtes mauritaniennes*" [which brings, desalinated, water from the Mauritanian coasts] (Wul 1994, 92). These underground canals are also how the Afrench army, stationed far from the coast, is able to reach the sea and attack the *torpèdes*.

Interestingly enough, Wul's 1957 pure SF desalination plants have been made a reality. In 2014, it was announced that Israel had "constructed five desalination plants over the past 10 years to put the country in an enviable position in the region. It now has more than enough water for its citizens and is able to share the rest with its neighbors" (Fitchette. 2015).

Some view Israel as one of the many examples of a powerful nation invading territory and making it their own to the detriment of its previous inhabitants. Wul's arguments for France taking over Algeria to make the Afrance resonate strongly with Zionist discourse. For example, Zionists argue that "they have a stronger claim to sovereignty over the country because they have exploited its agricultural potential more efficiently than the Palestinians could have done" (George 1979, 89). This resonates with Wul's textual world as Pol Nazaire describes how the Afrance conquered the desert: "*Territoire surcultivé parce que surinsolarisé, surindustrialisé parce que c'était le seul moyen de réussir quelque chose là où tout ne pouvait être qu'artificiel*" [An overcultivated territory because of sunlight abundance, an overindustrialized territory because it was the only way to achieve something where everything could only be artificial] (Wul 1994, 94).

But the most telling resonance between Afrance and Israel manifests itself when Nazaire says "*Il n'était pas question de superposer avec précaution une civilisation moderne à de vieilles et encombrantes structures*" [It was out of the question to cautiously superimpose a modern civilization over old and cumbersome structures] (Wul 1994, 94). In the Algerian desert, before either France or Afrance arrived, the "old and cumbersome structures" were the way of life of the Algerian people, as Todd Shepard explains: "From the assimilationist perspective, what prevented [non–European Algerians] from becoming citizens was their attachment to … 'particularisms,' 'communities,' [and] backward, feudal or religious traditions. [This] attachment to group 'difference,' with *backward* social *structures*—like Qur'anic Law—encouraged, prevented Algerians from becoming … citizens" (Shepard 2011, 301). Wul's total lack of references to Algerian culture suggests that the Afrench simply plowed under said culture.

Once he shows Afrance to be a physical geographic unit, Wul reinforces its national cohesion by pitting it against the *torpède* common enemy. Furthermore, Algeria is shown to be critically important to save the nation and mount a counterattack because metropolitan France has been devastated by the flood: "*Paris a été aplati comme une galette*" [Paris has been flattened like a pancake] (Wul 1994, 63). Thus, the government regroups in the Algerian city of In Salah, which just happens to be located about 850 km from the nearest coastline, and some 300 m above sea level.

Six months later, as the world begins to recover from the flood, flying saucers suddenly begin to appear "*[p]resque partout dans le monde, au dessus des mers et des zones inondées*" [almost everywhere in the world, over seas and flooded areas] (Wul 1994, 75). The *torpèdes* strike again by turning all water vapor into liquid water: "*L'eau est condamné à la forme liquide, elle est incristallisable et inévaporable*" [Water is condemned to be liquid, it will turn to neither ice nor vapor] (Wul 1994, 76). Shortly afterwards, "*[p] lusieurs centaines des disques volants lumineux apparurent au-dessus d'In Salah*" [several hundred luminous flying disks appeared above In Salah] (Wul 1994, 80). Thus, Wul incorporates the 1960s UFO sighting phenomenon to his textual world: "*Il y a bien longtemps que leurs soucoupes vinrent nos rendre visite. On supposait que ces engins venaient d'une autre planète. Nous étions loin de nous douter qu'ils sortaient de la mer*" [It was a long time ago that their flying saucers came to visit us. We supposed that these machines came from another planet. We were far from suspecting that they were coming from the sea] (Wul 1994, 87). In any case, the appearance of UFO's over In Salah triggers, much like a nuclear war scenario, a civil and military retreat underground. But this is not simply a matter of running to air raid shelters. Underground In-Salah, other desert cities, and large areas of the countryside, there are completely functional urban environments where people can comfortably live while the war against the *torpèdes* rages above. Bruno reassures Kou-Sien: "*Tout le monde est en sécurité*" [Everyone is safe] (Wul 1994, 86).

Interestingly enough, the military organization getting ready to fight the *torpèdes*, where Bruno Daix holds the rank of captain, is aptly called *the secret army*: Daix explains to Nazaire: "*Cette armée a été montée, il y a trois mois, dès qu'on sut à quel ennemi on avait affaire*" [This army was organized three months ago, as soon as we knew the enemy we were dealing with] (Wul 1994, 85). Of course, rather than the dreadful pro–French Algeria *Organisation armée secrète [Secret Army Organization]*, Wul's secret army is most likely inspired by the secret army of the French *Resistance* set up by Jean Moulin during World War II.

In summary, the Afrance is not only capable to defend itself, and protect its population indefinitely and with ease while helping the rest of the world, but it can also attack. Wul explains that this is due to the "*puissance colossale de ce pays*" [colossal power of this country] (Wul 1994, 92), which has been brought about by the implementation of what Wul calls a "simple" concept: organization: "*Quoique très durement éprouvée, l'Afrance était relativement indemne par rapport aux autres…. Son potentiel économique et ses réserves immenses lui permettaient de faire face aux besoins énormes de toute l'humanité. C'était pour elle un **simple** problème d'organisation*" [my bold italics] [Although she was hit very hard, Afrance was relatively unscathed compared to others…. Her economic potential and her immense reserves enabled her to meet the enormous needs of all humanity. For her, it was a *simple* organizational problem] (Wul 1994, 67).

The concept of organization as the key to prosperity is echoed in

Servan-Schreiber's *Le Défi américain*: "*nous n'assistons pas à un déborde-ment de dollars qui ne trouverait pas à s'employer aux États-Unis... mais... au déploiement sur le sol européen d'un **art de l'organisation** auquel nous demeurons étrangers*" [my bold italics] [we are not witnessing an overflow of dollars for which there would be no use in the United States ... but ... the deployment on European soil of an art of organization to which we remain foreign] (Servan-Schreiber 1967, 23).

If Wul knew about the importance of organization at the time he wrote *La Peur*—ten years before Servan-Schreiber presented it in his book—it is highly likely that de Gaulle also had this concept in mind when, in his 1959 radio address he warned that, in case of secession, "*[les Algériens] **organ-iseraient** sans [la France] le territoire où ils habitent, les ressources dont ils peuvent disposer, le Gouvernement qu'ils souhaitent*" [my bold italics] [(Algerians) would organize without (France) the territory where they live, the resources they can dispose of, the government they want] (De Gaulle 1959), and he clearly meant they would or could not do it well, as he states "*Pour ma part, je considère qu'un tel aboutissement serait invraisemblable et désastreux*" [For my part, I consider that such an outcome would be implausible and disastrous] (De Gaulle 1959). In *La Peur* Wul presents a reality where, by staying together, French and Algerians have avoided all the dire consequences predicted by de Gaulle and, instead, Afrance stands tall as a prosperous superpower. In other words, *La Peur* reflects the *franci-zation* option; that is, total assimilation.

However, Wul seems to recognize that such total assimilation is unre-alistic, that part of the population is truly inassimilable. Thus, he makes the *torpèdes* correspond to an inassimilable Algerian population made alien by its unwillingness and/or inability to become French. Then, *La Peur* shows how "inassimilables" can be dealt with.

The French/Afrench parallel is anchored in Algerian history. Through-out the occupation of Algeria, the French Army pushed inassimilable pop-ulations of Algerians further and further south into the desert, just like the Afrance pushed the *torpèdes* deeper and deeper into the sea: "*le peuple des torpèdes [s'est] replié toujours plus loin, [s'est] adapté aux grandes profond-eurs, où il est à peu près tranquille*" [the electric ray people (have) retreated ever further, (have) adapted to the great depths, where they are more or less in peace] (Wul 1994, 106). But then the *torpèdes* decimate humanity with their water attack and the only option is extermination: "*C'est eux ou nous*" [It's them or us] (Wul 1994, 94).

First the enemy is dehumanized by presenting it as beings who are not only physically frightening, but also evil and incompatible with humanity: "*La bouche en V paraissait petite et cruelle, mais les yeux surtout distillaient une intelligence diabolique, effrayante parce qu'elle semblait très différente, étrangère à l'intelligence humaine"* [The V-shaped mouth seemed small and cruel, but the eyes especially distilled a diabolical intelligence, frightening because it seemed very different, foreign to human intelligence] (Wul 1994, 88).

In addition, no attempt is made to communicate with them. In spite of the fact that Kou-Sien discovers that *"[c]es êtres communiquent par des variations d'influx magnétique"* [(t)hese beings communicate by magnetic impulse variations] (Wul 1994, 125), she never reaches the point where she can actually have a basic conversation with them. Kou-Sien's self-stereotyping when she says *"les chinois sont particulièrement doués pour la cryptologie.... Notre langue natale nous entraîne journellement à ce genre de difficultés"* [Chinese people are particularly good at cryptology.... Our native language makes us face this kind of difficulty daily] (Wul 1994, 120), would seem to point out that, if the best communicators on the planet, the Chinese, can't communicate with the *torpèdes*, then there is no point in trying to communicate with them at all.

After exploring the *francization* option in *La Peur*, Wul addresses the *close union* option—*"le gouvernement des Algériens par les Algériens ... appuyé sur l'aide de la France et en **union étroite** avec elle"* [my bold italics] [the Algerian government by the Algerians ... supported by France and in a close union with France] (De Gaulle 1959)—in *Oms en série*. Note that *La Peur géante* is first published in April 1957 and *Oms en série* in November 1957. This means that Wul is studying these options approximately two years before de Gaulle actually formulates them in September 1959.

Oms takes place on Ygam, a planet dominated by draags, an amphibian species which has established itself completely on land thanks to mutations introduced by their scientists: *"Aujourd'hui, ils sont amphibies, grâce aux mutations obtenues par le savant Zarek"* [Today, they are amphibians, thanks to the mutations made by the scholar Zarek] (Wul 1972, 26). Humans live on Ygam as pets and are called *oms*, a shortened version of *hommes* [men].

The pivotal fact in the novel is an unplanned situation. Tiwa, a young draag girl is given a pet om. She names him Terr. In order to keep Terr from escaping, Tiwa wears a bracelet which allows her to apply a pulling force on Terr's collar. Being of school age, Tiwa must listen to her teaching headphones a number of hours per day. She likes to do this while holding her pet om on her lap. An unintentional wireless connection between Tiwa's headphones and Terr's magnetic collar allows Terr to listen in on Tiwa's lessons and become educated: *"les paroles et les images tombaient dans son subconscient comme des graines dans la terre vierge"* [words and images fell into his subconscious like seeds on fertile ground] (Wul 1972, 24). Soon Terr escapes from his mistress and carries away the teaching headphones.

His knowledge allows him to become the leader of a united population of free oms.

This unintended knowledge transfer from owner to pet parallels a similar, inevitable and colonization-induced colonizer-to-colonized knowledge transfer. The colonizer justifies its attempt to increase its wealth and power at the expense of the colonized through a "*mission civilisatrice*" [civilizing mission] (Verdès-Leroux 2001, 60), rationalization that makes him feel "colonialism [is] self-evidently virtuous, morally unimpeachable, even ethically imperative" (Thomas 2011, ix). As the colonized becomes more and more "civilized" he acquires and/or reinforces colonizer ideals—freedom, equality, fraternity, justice, democracy, self-determination, etc.—that run counter to the exploitative, discriminatory, authoritarian, etc., policies imposed by the colonizer. Sooner or later, the colonized rise.

For example, Ghandi studied in London where, of all things, he "became a member of the executive committee of the London Vegetarian Society" (Nanda 2019). Among his fellow vegetarians, he met:

> socialists and humanitarians such as Edward Carpenter, 'the British Thoreau'; Fabians such as George Bernard Shaw; and Theosophists such as Annie Besant. Most of them were idealists; quite a few were rebels who rejected the prevailing values of the late–Victorian establishment, denounced the evils of the capitalist and industrial society, preached the cult of the simple life, and stressed the superiority of moral over material values and of cooperation over conflict. Those ideas were to contribute substantially to the shaping of Gandhi's personality and, eventually, to his politics [Nanda 2019].

The story of Algerian independentist leaders may look comparatively less colorful but it still illustrates the point. For example, Ahmed Ben Bella "successfully completed his early studies at [a] French school and continued his education in the neighboring city of Tlemcen, where he first became aware of racial discrimination and also mingled with the fringes of the nationalist movement" (Merle n.d.); Ferhat Abbas "received an entirely French education at Philippeville (now Skikda) and Constantine and at the University of Algiers…. Disillusioned by the French in 1938, he organized the *Union Populaire Algérienne*, which proposed equal rights for French and Algerians while preserving the Algerian culture and language";[8] and Messali Hadj was enrolled "*dans une école primaire française [à sept ans]. Son père refuse l'école coranique, car selon lui, en apprenant le français, son enfant pourra se défendre vis-à-vis des Français pour demander ses droits*" [in a French primary school (at age seven). His father refuses the Koranic school because, according to him, by learning French, his child will be able to defend himself against the French in order to demand that his rights be respected] (Wikiwand, n.d.). Nevertheless, the education of these leaders illustrates the same point: the colonized learn revolutionary ideas from the colonizer.

By the time de Gaulle declares that he will direct his three questions to Algerians as individuals because *"depuis que le Monde est le Monde, il n'y a jamais eu d'unité, ni à plus forte raison de souveraineté algérienne"* [since time immemorial, there has never been an Algerian unity, let alone a greater reason for Algerian sovereignty] (De Gaulle 1959), he's only technically correct. It is true that throughout history none of numerous invaders turned Algeria into a nation, but France made Algeria administratively French in 1848. Thus, in addition to providing revolutionary ideas to Algerians—ideas cast in the fire of the French Revolution—France engaged in nation-building and set the foundations of an Algerian unity and an Algerian state.

In *Oms,* Wul presents a hero initially at a clear disadvantage with respect to his would-be followers, who rank quite low in terms of the organization capability extolled by Servan-Schreiber. Oms are organized only as independent tribes competing for meager resources.

Fleeing his Draag home, Terr runs first into Brave, the leader of the "bande du Gros Arbre" [Gros Arbre tribe] (Wul 1972, 36) one of three om tribes living in a park. Oms survive by stealing supplies. Terr's ability to read labels increases their theft efficiency and improves his standing in free om society. The next step in Terr's ascent comes from what we could call his sense of *"fraternité"*: he reads a sign that says *"Parc fermé demain— Désomisation"* [Park closed tomorrow—Desomization] (Wul 1972, 51). He warns Brave and tells him they have to warn the other tribes. In Brave's less evolved social worldview, the idea is preposterous: *"T'es fou ! Belle occasion d'en être débarrassés ! La bande du Buisson Rouge a le meilleur coin du parc. Nous prendrons sa place une fois l'alerte passée"* [You're crazy! This a great opportunity to get rid of them! The Buisson Rouge tribe has the best corner of the park. We will take their place once the alert is over] (Wul 1972, 52). Against Brave's order, Terr attempts to warn the Buisson Rouge tribe. In the process, he manages to get caught, which allows him to meet the Buisson Rouge tribal leader: *"[une] vieille ome noire aux membres secs [et] á la chevelure blanche et crépue"* [(an) old black Om woman with thin arms (and) white frizzy hair] (Wul 1972, 55). Terr impresses the Old Woman with his reading knowledge and she allows him to go back to his tribe. Knowledge doesn't have to be spread very wide to cause effects in a society.

In the end, both tribes[9] leave the park independently. However, the Gros Arbre tribe runs into two Draags who attempt to kill them: *"Liquidons-en quelques-uns avant que les autres ne s'enfuient"* [Let's kill some of them before they run away] (Wul 1972, 63). As Oms fight back, the Buisson Rouge tribe joins the fray. One Draag is killed, the other one flees. Brave also dies. The Old Woman takes over the now united tribes.

Wul is taking us step by step towards the formation of a large, complex and powerful society feeding its growth from the very forces that attempt to eliminate it. The next time we see oms, they have built an underground city in an abandoned draag seaport: "*Dans un réseau the canalisations souterraines et d'anciens égouts, une ville cachée avait installé ses rues, ses unités d'habitation et ses bâtiments publics. Une ville d'oms. De trois millions d'oms.*" [In a network of underground pipes and old sewers, a hidden city had built its streets, housing units and public buildings. A city of oms. Three million Oms.] (Wul 1972, 77). Here we see what could be called a certain penchant for abandoned underground waterworks in Wul. In *La Peur*, after the initial defeat, humans take shelter underground in "*un ancien réseau qui pompait le liquide des nappes souterraines, au siècle précédent. Ces nappes sont aujourd'hui épuisées. De là, tous ces couloirs et toutes ces salles qui sont autant d'anciennes conduites et d'anciens réservoirs. Il n'y avait plus qu'à les équiper*" [an old network that pumped groundwater in the previous century. These aquifers are now exhausted. That's where all these corridors and rooms—just old conduits and reservoirs—come from. We only had to make them habitable] (Wul 1972, 92).

Terr is planning an Om exodus from Draag lands and Wul provides him with convenient solutions through extreme terraforming that makes desiccating the Mediterranean Sea look simple. On Ygam, in addition to two natural empty and untouched continents, Draags inhabit four apparently terraformed continents:

> *Les quatre continents retouchées par les draags sont de forme triangulaire équilatérale et de dimensions égales. Deux sont placés à égale distance l'un de l'autre dans l'hémisphère A, les deux autres son placés à égale distance l'un de l'autre dans l'hémisphère B. Leurs pointes sont dirigées vers les pôles, leurs bases regardent l'équateur* [The four continents modified by Draags are equilateral triangles of equal dimensions. Two are equidistant from one another in hemisphere A, the other two are equidistant from each other in hemisphere B. Their points are directed towards the poles, their bases towards the equator] [Wul 1972, 23].

There's a little geometry problem with Wul's Ygam geography. If the continents are equilateral triangles, they don't have bases, only sides. They don't have points, either; they have vertices, and since none is privileged, the phrase "*leurs pointes sont dirigées vers les pôles*" [their bases are directed towards the equator] is ambiguous.

Unlike Algerians, who were trying to expel an occupier, Oms can unobtrusively colonize one of Ygam's two conveniently empty continents that "*servent de réserve aux espèces inferieures*" [serve as a reserve for inferior species] (Wul 1972, 23).

Also conveniently, for the advancement of the story, the Old Woman dies and bestows all her power onto Terr: "*Tu sens, petit ? Mon énergie qui coule de mes bras ? Elle va dans les tiens. Je te la donne. Elle me quitte.*" [You feel it, little one? The energy flowing in my arms? It's going into yours. I give it to you. It's leaving me.] (Wul 1972, 81). When Terr announces the death of the Old Woman: "*La Vieille est morte*" [The old woman is dead] (Wul 1972, 82), the crowd falls silent. Then, after a few moments, an Om woman shouts from the crowd "*Vive l'Édile !*" [Long live the Aedile!] (Wul 1972, 82). Then Terr reassures his people that their salvation is not lost "*la Vieille est morte en m'adjurant de réussir l'Exode*" [the Old Woman died making me promise to succeed in our Exodus] (Wul 1972, 82). Maybe these words are not as well balanced as *le roi est mort, vive le roi* [the king is dead, long live the king], but it is a sign that om society has gone from random disorganized tribes in parks to a nation with a strong leader and a purpose of biblical proportions.

In particular, Terr's speech after the Old Woman's death resonates lightly with de Gaulle's Appeal of 18 June 1940, inasmuch as the purpose of both speeches is to reassure the people that the setback they have suffered is not final. By June 18, the French army had been defeated and a newly formed French government had announced its willingness to surrender. Countering this, de Gaulle announces that not all is lost: "*le dernier mot est-il dit ? L'espérance doit-elle disparaître ? La défaite est-elle définitive ? Non!*" [the last word, has it been said? Should hope disappear? Is defeat definitive? No!] (De Gaulle n.d.).

Although this speech is considered the birth of the French Resistance, it wasn't heard by many people, given the circumstances: "It was broadcast on the BBC, an English radio station, practically unannounced, and given by an obscure brigadier general only recently appointed junior minister" (De Gaulle n.d.). In addition, it was not directed to the people in general but to military personnel and people involved in the war effort: "*de Gaulle s'adresse avant tout, et de manière explicite, aux militaires (officiers et soldats) et aux spécialistes des industries de l'armement (ingénieurs et ouvriers) en les appelant à appuyer l'effort de guerre du Royaume-Uni*" [de Gaulle specifically and explicitly addresses the military (officers and soldiers) and weapons industries specialists (engineers and workers) by calling them to support the United Kingdom's war effort] (De Gaulle n.d.).

However, in *Oms*, Terr's speech better reflects the mythical proportions the Appeal of June 18 has taken. Terr is given, of all things, only a *téléboîte* (an Om walkie-talkie) to give his speech, but he feels he's reaching his people: "*il sentait sa voix s'adresser par les ondes à des milliers d'oms penchés sur leurs récepteurs dans toute la ville, et plus loin, aux sentinelles des postes avancés jalonnant les pistes. Plus loin encore, peut-être, son discours allait réveiller l'énergie des unités de pillage en action dans les villes draags*" [he felt his voice address through the air thousands of Oms leaning over their receivers throughout the city, and further on, the advanced posts sentries along the roads. Further still, perhaps, his speech would awaken the energy of the looting units in action in Draag cities] (Wul 1972, 83). This is only the beginning. Wul seems to be, little by little, turning Terr into an Om version of Charles de Gaulle.

As the novel goes from its first to its second part, the reader wonders how is it that two apparently small Om tribes living in a park manage to build a three-million-inhabitant underground coastal city on continent South A. There are certainly enough Oms on Ygam to populate such city. An Om specialist, Maître Sinh, states that "*Le nombre d'oms sans collier approche de trente millions, sur notre continent*" [The number of collarless Oms approaches thirty million on our continent] and then he adds: "*Il y a … près de deux cent millions d'oms sur notre planète*" [There are … nearly two hundred million Oms on our planet] (Wul 1972, 71). Therefore the question is, how did Oms manage to build this city in the short period of time in which "*les draags ont tout juste réussi à voter cette petite loi de désomisation*" [Draags have just managed to vote on this little *desomization* law?] (Wul 1972, 86).

Early in *Oms*, Wul describes Tiwa's happiness after seeing the newborn om litter from which she will choose her own pet Om: "*Elle était heureuse ; dans quelques jours, les petits oms sauraient marcher.*" [She was happy; in a few days, the little Oms would be able to walk.] (Wul 1972, 16). Delany's SF reading protocol must be applied here. Human children start to walk at about one year of age. How does an Om newborn get to walk in a few days?

In a direct author-intervention paragraph, Wul attempts to explain: "*Il est vrai qu'un seul jour de la grosse planète Ygam équivalait a quarante-cinq jours d'une petite planète nommée Terre, monde très lointain d'où les oms étaient originaires.*" [It is true that one day on big planet Ygam was equivalent to forty-five days on a small planet called Earth, the very distant world where Oms originated] (Wul 1972, 16). Unfortunately, Wul's explanation is thoroughly flawed as none of the stated facts—Ygam is larger than Earth, Ygam's rotation period is 45 Earth days—addresses the fact that what Wul really needs is for Oms to live/think faster than Draags in order to learn and catch up with their masters' advanced technology and social organization … and then successfully rebel against them, resist them and confront them.

Since we have never been able to determine and compare how fast species live/think, other than playfully express time periods in *cat years* or *dog years*, Wul had no way to scientifically support oms' faster thinking/living rate. The closest available scientifically valid theory was general relativity: time passes slower in higher gravitational fields. This was well illustrated in a recent SF film. In Christopher Nolan's film *Interstellar*, the ship *Endurance* goes through a wormhole and arrives near a planetary system centered on a black hole called Gargantua. The ship goes into orbit safely away from Gargantua to avoid its high-intensity gravitational effects. Three crew members take a lander to Miller's Planet, a water world orbiting very close to Gargantua. In the few hours the lander group spends on Miller's Planet, the crew member left on *Endurance* ages 26 years. Although Miller's Planet has normal Earth gravity, its proximity to Gargantua relative to the ship's proximity dilates time. Aboard *Endurance*, scientist Romilly says to pilot Cooper: "Every hour we spend on that planet will be maybe ... seven years back on Earth" (Nolan 2014). Fifty years after publication of *Oms en série*, *Interstellar* provides a scientifically valid way to have time pass more slowly on a planet.

However, none of this applies to Draags and Oms because both species live on the same planet and, therefore, they are exposed to the same gravitational field. Nevertheless, Wul seems to have applied his own faulty rule of proportional size—large planet, long day, large Draags—to imply, first, that time elapses faster for Oms than Draags because Draags are bigger and/or they have evolved on a stronger gravity planet[10] and, second, that since time elapses faster for oms, oms can live/think faster. In retrospect, it would have been easier to indicate that—rather than a physical—this is a biological phenomenon, adopt a speculative approach, and simply state that there is no reason to assume all species live/think at the same rate and that oms just happen to live/think faster than Draags.[11]

The faster life/thought rate of oms is fundamentally important for the story, and Wul explains it clearly in Terr's words:

> [I]l faut un quart de lustre à un draag pour atteindre l'âge adulte. Il ne faut qu'une année à un om.... Quand j'ai quitté les draags ... ma petite maîtresse était une fillette. Elle est encore une fillette aujourd'hui.... Et moi, je suis un om à barbe blonde. J'ai eu six enfants.... Nous vivons à un autre rythme et c'est notre principal atout [it takes a Draag a quarter lustrum to reach adulthood. It takes an Om only a year.... When I left the Draags ... my little mistress was a little girl. She is still a girl today.... And I am a blonde bearded Om. I have had six children.... We live at another pace and this is our main asset] [Wul 1972, 86].

In the end, Oms manage to leave en masse their underground city on continent South A, board the three colony ships they have built, and set sail towards "le Continent Sauvage" [the Wild Continent] (Wul 1972, 118), one of Ygam's uninhabited continents. "*Cap à l'est, [trois navires] emportaient dans leurs flancs tout l'espoir d'une race en rupture de chaînes.*" [Heading east, (three ships) carried all the hope of a race breaking chains] (Wul 1972, 101). They leave just in time because Draags have already located their city and plan to neutralize them.

In particular, Wul uses here his preferred solution to quash non-recoverable populations. While in *La Peur*, the joliba virus takes away the *torpèdes'* intelligence, in *Oms*, the Draag plan is "*prétexter une épidémie et rendre obligatoire la vaccination des oms contre une maladie fantôme. À la faveur de ce mensonge nous pourrions nos pas tuer les oms, mais détruire certains centres cérébraux pour enlever toute intelligence*" [under the pretext of an epidemic, make it compulsory for Oms to be vaccinated against a phantom disease. Thanks to this lie, rather than kill Oms, we could simply destroy part of their brain in order to remove their intelligence.] (Wul 1972, 100). By the time we get to Boulle's *La Planète des singes*, the loss of intelligence happens spontaneously to the ruling class rather than as a result of a successful pacification.

In any case, when Oms leave South A, *Oms en Série* stops resonating with the Algerian War. As long as Oms were organizing their rebellion on Draag territory, parallels could be established between their rebellion and the Algerian resistance to the French government. The resonance ends when Wul starts describing both Om efforts and sacrifices—first, to cross the ocean, and then to go from South A's coast to the *Continent Sauvage's* highlands to build their city—and Draag reactions to the alleged Om exodus.

All through Terr's ascendance, Draags show remarkable social inertia in the sense that they refuse to accept that Oms have become a problem. When Maître Sinh warns North A's First Aedile that Oms are no longer just a population of pets, the leader reassures him: "*tranquillisez-vous un peu ... la conquête des draags par les oms n'est pas pour demain !*" [calm down a little ... the conquest of Draags by Oms is not going to happen tomorrow!] (Wul 1972, 76). The next warning is for South's A First Aedile, who has obtained photos of the underground city on South A's old port. Again the First Aedile minimizes the threat and tells Sinh: "*Vous poussez les choses au noir.*" [You make things look darker than they are.] (Wul 1972, 99). After some previously blurry images are processed and cleaned up, Sinh warns all four First Aediles in plenary session: "*Les oms ont choisi ... le port le plus proche du 'Continent Sauvage.' Et les trois objets énigmatiques sont des vaisseaux.*" [Oms have chosen ... the closest port to the "Wild Continent." And the three enigmatic objects are ships.] (Wul 1972, 126). The Aediles finally decide to act and set up a force field around the old port to trap Oms before exterminating them. They don't think Oms could leave by sea. "*Des demain, les oms seront dans l'impossibilité de sortir de leur cité ! Il leur restera la mer, plaisanta quelqu'un*" [Starting tomorrow, Oms will be unable to leave their city! Their only way out will be the sea, joked someone], (Wul 1972, 128) which is exactly what Oms do. However they leave behind cloth cutouts of giant fish as a distraction. Draags think these cutouts are what Maître Sinh's saw in air reconnaissance images and that Oms have simply left through deep tunnels. Still, just to be on the safe side, the old port is sterilized with hard radiation. Draags go back to their complacency: "*Tranquillisez-vous [Maître Sinh] il n'en reste plus un [des oms]*." [Calm down (Master Sinh), there are no (Oms) left.] (Wul 1972, 131). Maître Sinh insists but he's chastised by South A's Édile: "*Le Conseil vous a accordé deux désomisations par mois et la destruction du port. Ne lui demandez pas d'autres excentricités*." [The Council has granted you two desomizations per month and the destruction of the port. Do not ask for more eccentricities.] (Wul 1972, 131).

Leaving him no option, Maître Sinh organizes a secret air reconnaissance mission and sends a pilot to the *Continent Sauvage's* highlands. The pilot brings back images of a teeming Om city with vehicles, tanks, and assorted manifestations of technology. Oms see the Draag spy flying sphere as it swoops down on them taking pictures. In a hastily called meeting, Terr calms Council members: "*les draags savent que le continent est peuplé de milliers d'oms. Ils savent que nous avons des chars, et comme il est impensable que nous ayons passé l'océan à la nage ou sur des bateaux primitifs, ils savent que nous sommes capables de construire des bâtiments*" [Draags know that the continent is populated by thousands of Oms. They know we have tanks, and since it's unthinkable that we have crossed the ocean swimming or on primitive boats, they know we can build ships] (Wul 1972, 156). Then he announces their defense plan: a force field.

Armed with new photographic evidence, Maître Sinh convinces Draag Aediles to initiate a general *desomization* campaign in Draag territory. Aediles also finally agree to send in a volley of ICBM's to destroy the Om city on the highlands. The Algerian War resonance restarts in *Oms en Série* as Wul describes a nation defending itself against its former masters.

In spite of the brutality of *desomizations* in Draag continents, Oms' main problem is to resist the impending intercontinental ballistic missile attack on Om city. This is where the name of the novel comes from. In order to withstand this attack, Oms set up a defensive force field partly powered by electricity drawn from human muscle mass. Thousands of Oms lie together connected in an electrical series circuit to power this defensive force field. Here Wul describes Oms sacrificing themselves for the cause, a civilian population resisting the enemy in every way possible.

Their efforts bear fruit as the force field makes missiles fall harmlessly into the ocean. Then Draags send marine infantry to invade the *Continent Sauvage*, but Oms have enlisted the help of Ygam's fauna in their war effort. A species of giant birds lay their eggs on one of the *Continent Sauvage's* coasts and lets ocean currents carry them to Draag continents. Oms take failed eggs, empty them, fill them with explosives, and set them on the current. These explosive eggs run into Draag ships and sink them. Then the force field keeps the few ships that manage to get through from making landfall.

All of these failed strategies end up convincing Draags that Oms are not only practically invincible but also a threat to Draags, given their capacity to innovate and build on Draag culture and technology. Sav, one of Terr's advisers, tells him: "*Après leur premier échec, dû a notre télébarrage, [les draags] vont nous prendre par des adversaires dangereux et nous pourrons peut-être obtenir une paix basée sur la coexistence.*" [After their first failure, due to our force field, (Draags) will consider us dangerous opponents and maybe we will be able to agree to a peace based on coexistence.] (Wul 1972, 177). Based on this, Terr suggests to Draags: "*pourquoi poursuivre une guerre inutile alors que vous avez tout à gagner à collaborer avec nous*" [why continue a useless war when you have everything to gain from working with us] (Wul 1972, 183).

Draags accept, and Terr, magnanimously, reassures them: "*Il n'y aurait plus de race maîtresse, mais deux races égales, qui travailleront côté à côté, en se faisant mutuellement bénéficier de leur progrès.... Je prévois pour nos deux races un avenir extraordinaire.*" [There would be no longer a master race, but two equal races, which will work side by side, mutually benefiting from their progress.... I predict for both races an extraordinary future.] (Wul 1972, 189). This full equality, cooperation and mutual benefit differs from what de Gaulle would propose to Algerians two years later with the *close union* option: "*gouvernement des Algériens par les Algériens appuyé sur l'aide de la France*" [government of Algerians by Algerians supported by France] (De Gaulle 1959). For De Gaulle, French and Algerians are not "*deux races égales*" [two equal races]. Instead, France is a "superior race" that graciously accepts to continue helping an "inferior race" that has gone independent. This reflects the deeply-seated paternalistic colonial notion that, since the colonized are less capable than the colonizer, they need the colonizer's help to thrive. However, as Oms base their culture on Draag culture, Wul plays somewhat indirect homage to the colonizer concept of "civilizing mission."

Notwithstanding clear differences between the French and Draags as they relate to their respective "inferior societies"—France went into Algeria seeking to expand its colonial empire, Draags arrived on Earth as explorers; France took Algeria from the Ottomans and installed itself as the ruling power, Draags only took a few Oms as pets back to Ygam—there are also similarities.

First, when they come into contact with Algerians and Oms, both contacted societies lack statehood or nationhood. Algerians are organized in tribes that maintain a more or less stable relationship with the Ottoman occupier: "*l'Empire Ottoman règne en maître, mais son autorité n'atteint pas certaines zones placées sous le contrôle de deys et féodaux locaux.... Des région entières demeurent dissidents avec des tribus à peine sortis d'un état médiéval."* [the Ottoman Empire reigns supreme, but its authority does not reach certain areas under the control of local authorities and feudal lords.... Entire regions remain dissident with tribes just now emerging from a medieval state.] (Ferracci 2012. 27). For their part, Oms live like ants, as Maître Sinh explains:

> *Ils vivaient dans des vastes agglomérations de terriers cimentés, ou chacun avait sa place. Ils constituaient des sociétés d'environ un million d'individus. Une hiérarchisation étroite y maintenait une discipline sans défaut, automatique. On y choyait les reproductrices, dont le seul travail était d'enfanter. À sa naissance, chaque bébé subissait une sélection qui le destinait à la reproduction, au travail ou au combat. Ils avaient un langage rudimentaire* [They lived in vast conglomerations of cemented burrows, where each one had their place. They constituted societies of about one million individuals. A narrow hierarchy maintained a faultless, automatic discipline. Reproducers whose only job was to give birth were pampered. At birth, each baby underwent a selection that destined him/her to reproduction, work or combat. They had a rudimentary language] [Wul 1972, 72–3].

Maître Sinh goes on to explain that Spraw *"un savant du dernier lustre"* [a scientist from the previous lustrum], suggested that:

> *les oms avaient connu autrefois une civilisation plus brillante, analogue à la nôtre, mais qu'il fallait voir dans sa perfection même la raison d'une sclérose progressive, d'une fixation du mode de vie. Étroitement emprisonnés dans leur loisirs et leurs règlements,* **les oms n'auraient plus éprouvé le besoin de penser** [my bold italics] [Oms had had a more developed civilization, analogous to ours, but it was necessary to see in its very perfection the reason for a progressive *sclerosis*, a fixation of the way of life. Tightly imprisoned in their leisure and regulations, *Oms would no longer have felt the need to think*] [Wul 1972, 73].

In other words, although they had a full civilization, humans lost it due to their own perfection and now they are only good for pets, never mind being stateless and nationless.

Second, France starts its "civilizing mission" on Algerians but, as it tends to happen with colonization, the civilization brought by the colonizer carries the seeds that destroy the colonial system. Benjamin Stora explains this in very simple words: *"certains de ces ... nationalistes [algériens] ont eu à apprendre l'histoire de la République. Ils ont entendu parler des droits de l'homme, des grands principes de la Révolution de 1789. Or ils n'ont pu que constater l'écart entre ces grands principes et la réalité quotidienne, profondément inégalitaire, de l'Algérie"* [some of these ... (Algerian) nationalists learned about the history of the Republic. They heard about human rights, the great principles of the Revolution of 1789. And they couldn't help but notice the gap between these great principles and the deeply unequalitarian daily reality of Algeria] (Stora 2012, 22). This inevitably led to Evian.

Although they were not Algerians but Martinicans, Aimé Césaire and

Frantz Fanon are excellent examples of colonized learning from the colonizer, and then turning against them.

> In the 1930s, while studying in Paris, [Césaire] became one of France's most well known poets and elaborated, along with Léopold Sédar Senghor and Léon Damas, the idea of negritude.... He worked to make his poetics of blackness speak to other experiences of oppression as well as to awaken people who denied the humanity of those, such as Africans, whom they oppressed.... [Fanon] studied in metropolitan France, practiced medicine in French Algeria, and then worked for Algerian independence in Tunis and Ghana [Shepard 2006, 61–2].

For their part, Draags, quite unwittingly, caused a somewhat similar phenomenon. Maître Sinh explains that Draag intervention, the very fact that Draags turned humans/Oms into individuals, pets or otherwise, eliminated the unthinking collectivism that stunted their intelligence: *"Nous avons ... détribalisé l'om, nous l'avons rendu à son individualité.... Nous l'avons sorti de l'impasse de l'instinct pour le replacer sur la route du progrès."* [We have ... destribalized Oms, we have returned them to their individuality.... We have taken them out of the impasse of instinct and put them back on the road of progress.] (Wul 1972, 75). As a consequence, Oms flee Draag households in exponential droves: *"Au mois du Lion 713 : cent trois pertes d'oms. Au mois de l'Oiseau : cent quarante-cinq pertes. Mois du Poisson : deux cent dix. Ensuite, de mois en mois, nous avons successivement : deux cent vingt-sept, trois cent deux, sept cent vingt et un ... pour arriver au mois dernier ... mille deux cent trente-six déclarations de perte."* [In the month of Lion 713: one hundred and three Om losses. In the month of Bird: one hundred and forty-five losses. Fish Month: two hundred and ten. Then, from month to month, we have successively: two hundred and twenty-seven, three hundred and two, seven hundred and twenty-one ... to arrive at last month ... one thousand two hundred and thirty-six reports of om losses.] (Wul 1972, 75). This common but individually generated behavior towards freedom is the precursor to the recovery of statehood, which will be triggered by an enlightened Promethean/Mosaic/de Gaullian Terr who first recovered his own individualism and intelligence, then took Draag knowledge to his fellow Oms, and finally led them to a promised land where he built an Om nation.

Finally, there are other similarities between the Franco-Algerian and the Draag-Om relationships. For example, Muslim demographic pressure in Algeria had become a concern fairly early in the 20th century. *"Depuis les années 1930, la croissance de la population algérienne est prise au sérieux par la plupart des observateurs, qui la considèrent même une menace."* [Since the 1930s, the growth of the Algerian population has been taken seriously by most observers, who consider it even a threat.] (Tengour 2012, 469). When the Draag-Om agreement is finally signed, Maître Sinh admits this concern: "*Vous êtes beaucoup plus rapides que nous. Certes, nous vivons plus longtemps, mais vous vous multipliez très vite.*" [You are much faster than we are. Of course, we live longer, but you multiply very fast.] (Wul 1972, 188). Terr reassures him by telling him that the agreement "*prévoit une large association de nos deux civilisations*" [provides for a broad association of our civilizations] (Wul 1972, 189).

As we all know, Algerians chose the *secession* option, which resonates with Pierre Boulle's *La Planète des singes*.

In *La Planète*, while taking a vacation traveling through space in their own ship, Jinn and Phyllis find a bottle containing a manuscript written and then thrown into space by Ulysse Mérou, the only survivor of an expedition to planet Soror. The story starts in 2500 and describes how Mérou and two other human explorers find a society in which humans are animals and apes are people. Mérou survives because he manages to communicate with the apes. In the end, aided by two chimpanzee scientists, he returns to Earth with his Sororian human companion, Nova, and their son, Sirius. Unfortunately, the same evolutionary process has taken place on Earth in his absence, and Mérou and his family leave Earth in search of a more welcoming planet. This is the end of the story as read by Jinn to Phyllis. Then, in the last paragraph of the novel, Boulle lets the reader know that Jinn and Phyllis are in fact chimpanzees.

The most salient aspect of *La Planète* is the fact that Sororian humans lose their intelligence while apes acquire it. Cornelius, an enlightened chimpanzee scientist, shows Mérou a woman in whom chimpanzee psychiatrist Hélius "*a réussi à réveiller ... non pas seulement la mémoire individuelle mais la mémoire de l'espèce*" [has managed to wake up ... not only individual memories but the memory of the species] (Boulle 1963, 171). Under treatment, the woman channels the voices of several people to describe the rise of apes thousands of years before. She reveals that apes begin to speak, reject human authority, imitate humans, make humans serve them, evict them from their homes and eventually take over their cities. Then, she gives a limited explanation of why Sororian humans lost their society and their intelligence: "*Ce qui nous arrive était prévisible. Une paresse cérébrale s'est emparé de nous.*" [What happens to us was predictable. A cerebral laziness has taken over us.] (Boulle 1963, 173).

Boulle does not directly specify the cause of this cerebral laziness. Unlike him, Wul gives in *Oms* a detailed explanation of human intelligence loss: "*Il existe un grand danger pour une société évoluée: la sclérose.... Quand une civilisation atteint son point de perfection, elle devient une gigantesque machine, incapable de progrès, et dont tous les membres ne sont plus que des rouages sans pensée.*" [There is a great danger for an advanced society: sclerosis.... When a civilization reaches its point of perfection, it becomes a gigantic machine, incapable of progress, and all of its members become nothing but unthinking cogs.] (Wul 1972, 188). This is the ant-like state in which draags find human society when they stop by Earth to pick up oms as pets.[12] In *La Peur*, Wul has Bruno Daix explain that, although Afrench science and technology brought society to a point of perfection where "*chaque citoyen [n'avait] plus à travailler ... que deux heures par mois*" [each citizen had to work ... no more than two hours a month], the government left the workload at "*trois heures par jour pendant cinq jours par semaine*" [three hours a day five days a week] (Wul 1994, 92) to avoid "*les dangers terribles courus par notre civilisation. Outre le fait qu'un homme n'exerçant son métier que deux heures par mois, deviendrait rapidement inhabile, faute d'entrainement, les **loisirs forcés** se transformeraient en supplice générateur de **paresse***" [my bold italics] [the terrible dangers our civilization would be exposed to. In addition to the fact that a man exercising his trade only two hours a month would quickly lose his skills for lack of training, the *forced leisure* would become a *laziness* generating ordeal.] (Wul 1994, 93).

In summary, humans lose their intelligence when their society reaches a certain point of perfection, but the effect is not inevitable. The Afrench avoided it by keeping a workload above the technically indispensable.[13] Ygam humans recovered from it because Draags took them away from their ant-like existence on Earth. Unfortunately, Sororian humans descended below ant-like levels of organization and became nothing but unthinking animals.

However, Sororian humans could recover their intelligence, as Mérou reports on his trip back to Earth: "*Sirius [Mérou and Nova's child] parle couramment et **Nova presque aussi bien** * [my bold italics]. *Elle a appris en même temps que lui.*" [Mérou and Nova's child Sirius speaks fluently and Nova *almost as well*. She has learned at the same time he has.] (Boulle 1963, 188). On the other hand, Earth humans arriving on Soror may also lose their intelligence, as shown by Dr. Antelle, the brilliant scientist who conceived and led the expedition to Soror. Antelle became an unthinking animal in a matter of months after arriving on Soror.

It could be argued that Antelle had already been showing a tendency to reject humans. Mérou recognizes this as they leave Earth: "*Je soupçonnais même que la perspective d'échapper aux hommes de sa génération était un attrait supplémentaire pour le professeur. Il avouait souvent que ceux-ci le lassaient.*" [I even suspected that the prospect of escaping the men of his generation was an added attraction for the professor. He often confessed that they tired him.] (Boulle 1963, 13). He later adds that, although Antelle's rejection of society had not reached the level of misanthropy, "*il déclarait souvent qu'il n'attendait plus grand chose (des hommes)*" [he often declared he didn't expect much from (men)] (Boulle 1963, 14). Furthermore, upon arriving on Soror 350 years into the future and 643 light years into extraterrestrial space, Antelle seems disappointed to learn that Soror is inhabited by humans: "*'Soror est donc habitée par des humains,' murmura le professeur Antelle.... Il y avait une nuance de déconvenue dans sa voix.... Il haussa les épaules.*" ["Soror is inhabited by humans," mumbled Professor Antelle.... There was a nuance of disappointment in his voice.... He shrugged.] (Boulle 1963, 23). In the end, Antelle is placed in a comfortable individual cage and, upon visiting him, Mérou reports: "*Il ne répond à aucune de mes sollicitations et se conduit toujours comme un parfait animal.*" [He does not answer to any of my requests and always behaves like a perfect animal]. (Boulle 1963, 138). Cornelius uses Antelle's case to suggest to Mérou: "*Vous voyez bien que l'esprit peut se perdre, comme il peut s'acquérir.*" [You can see that the mind can be lost, just as it can be acquired.] (Boulle 1963, 180).

Published in 1957, *La Peur* and *Oms* are "what if" novels where Wul could speculate what would happen if Algerians chose *francization* or *close union*. Published in 1963, *La Planète* faces a *fait accompli* and therefore takes on allegorical undertones to show what happened when Algerians chose *secession*. This is why finding resonances between Wul's novels and the Algerian War is more straightforward than finding them between *La Planète* and the Algerian War.

Since no group actually loses its intelligence at the expense of another as Algeria moves towards independence, it becomes necessary to find out the Algerian War counterpart to *La Planète's* intelligence; that is, the characteristic lost by one group and gained by the other. In order to do that, the groups involved in the Algerian conflict must be identified.

Formally, when the war starts in 1954, there has been only one group in Algeria and France since 1848: the French. In actuality, there have been at least three: Algerians, metropolitan French and Algerian French (Pieds-Noirs). Neither one nor three groups make for an easy correspondence with *La Planète's* clearly defined two groups: Sororian humans and apes.

Since Boulle attributes Sororian human loss of intelligence to the advent of a cerebral laziness, it seems reasonable to search for a specific characteristic lost by one of the three groups defined above.

First, metropolitan French people were becoming less and less interested in governing Algeria in spite of appearances. "'Public opinion' was far more skeptical than leaders of opinion about the legitimacy, the realism or the cost of keeping Algeria French" (Shepard 2006, 55). Specifically, the number of people in favor of keeping the *status quo* in Algeria went down quickly between 1955 and 1957: "*en octobre 1955, 47% ; en avril 1956, 40% ; en septembre 1957, 36%*" [in October 1955, 47 percent; in April 1956, 40 percent; in September 1957, 36 percent] (Verdès-Leroux 2001, 20). By the time the Evian Accords are finalized, "*82% des Français se diront satisfaits*" [82 percent of French people said they were satisfied] (Verdès-Leroux 2001, 21). Since the *status quo* was that France governed Algerian departments, progressive loss of support for that *status quo* indicates a loss of the will to govern Algeria.

This was a sudden and rather inexplicable new development because, for a long time, the French had tried to turn Algerians into full French citizens. First, they made Algeria part of France in 1848. Then they attempted, in vain, to impose on Algerians numerous forms of assimilation, coexistence, integration, etc. In the end, France never achieved its goal because, in spite of its numerous rationalizations, it never wanted Algerians to be French. What seems to have made them finally abandon what de Gaulle called "*fictions juridiques*," [legal fictions], and accept that "*jamais l'Algérie n'a été française*" [Algeria has never been French] (Peyrefitte 1994, 2:140) was the vision of a part-Muslim metropolitan France.

For example, Peyrefitte reports that, in March 1959, de Gaulle told him:

> *Les musulmans, vous-êtes allé les voir ? Vous les avez regardés, avec leur turbans et leur djellabas ? Vous voyez bien que ce ne sont pas des Français.... Si nous faisions l'intégration, si tous les Arabes et Berbères d'Algérie étaient considérés comme Français, comment les empêcherait-on de venir s'installer en métropole.... Mon village ne s'appellerait plus Colombey-les-Deux-Églises, mais Colombey-les-Deux-Mosquées* [Muslims, have you gone to see them? Have you watched them with their turbans and djellabas? You can clearly see that they are not French.... If we did the integration, if all the Arabs and Berbers of Algeria were considered French, how would we prevent them from coming to live in France?.... After that, my village would not be called *Colombey-Two-Churches*, but *Colombey-Two-Mosques*] [Peyrefitte 1994, 1:52].

Second, Algerians were, obviously, very willing to govern Algeria, and they saw independence as the only way to achieve it. De Gaulle himself stated so, should Algerians chose secession: "*[Les Algériens] organiseraient sans [la France] ... le **Gouvernement** qu'ils souhaitent* [my bold italics]" [(Algerians) would organize without (France) ... the *government* they want] (De Gaulle n.d.).

Not all Algerians had always desired independence. For example, Ferhat Abbas, who went on to become one of the key figures of the independentist movement, believed at some point that France would eventually grant all Algerian inhabitants indistinguishable French citizenship. Thus in 1936, he wrote: "*je ne mourrai pas pour la patrie algérienne, parce que cette patrie n'existe pas... Nous avons, une fois pour toutes, écarté les nuées et les chimères pour lier définitivement notre avenir à celui de l'œuvre française dans ce pays.*" [I will not die for the Algerian homeland, because this country does not exist.... We have, once and for all, dismissed clouds and chimeras to definitively bind our future to what France has done in this country] (Abbas 2002, 100). However, in 1943 he published the *Manifeste du peuple algérien* [Manifesto of the Algerian People] where, considering the instability of Algerian Jews French citizenship—established in 1870 by the Government of National Defense, withdrawn in 1941 by the Vichy government, and then restored in 1943 by the Committee for National Liberation—he stated: "*La nationalité et la citoyenneté algériennes offrent au musulman algérien plus de sécurité, et donnent une plus claire et plus logique solution au problème de son évolution et son émancipation*" [Algerian nationality and citizenship offer Algerian Muslims more security, and give a clearer and more logical solution to the problem of his evolution and his emancipation] (Abbas 1943). In other words, rather than Algerian independence, Abbas was interested in Algerian self-government; that is, he was interested in Algerians governing themselves either as full citizens of the French state or, when that proved to be unreliable, as full citizens of an Algerian state. Of course, other than Abbas, as early as the interwar period, there had been forces fully committed to independence, such as the *Association des Oulemas* (Islamic Reform Movement), whose motto was "Islam is our religion, Arabic is our language, Algeria is our country" (Shepard 2006, 38).

Third, the Pieds-Noirs had no problem ruling themselves as full French citizens of French Algeria. Unlike French expatriates in French colonies, who knew they were on foreign soil, the Pieds-Noirs fully believed they lived in their own homeland after the 1848 constitution created the three French Algerian departments. Furthermore, since France would not allow Algerians to fully govern themselves, the Pieds-Noirs had to govern Algerians in collaboration with metropolitan French.

There is no sign that the Pieds-Noirs ever lost the will to govern Algeria. Instead, Algerian independence took that will away from them. Algerian independence also meant that, in addition to no longer governing Algeria, they had to choose between being governed by Algerians or losing their homeland. An estimated 800,000 chose to leave and lost their homeland in 1962 and the following years. For example, in August 1962, the French office for repatriates reported to have registered "506,644 individuals between 1 January and 12 August 1962" (Shepard 2006, 215). Needless to say, the idea of leaving Algeria was extremely difficult to handle: "*C'était impensable pour un Pied-Noir de penser … jamais, penser à une autre terre que l'Algérie, ça ne traversait même l'esprit*" [It was unthinkable for a Pied-Noir to think … never, think of a land other than Algeria, it did not even cross their mind].[14] An estimated 200,000 chose to stay behind and be governed by Algerians. Only a few hundred remain today.

In the end, France lost the will to govern that Algeria gained, Thus, when comparing the Algerian War of Independence to *La Planète,* the will to govern corresponds to intelligence.

Although, as stated earlier, Boulle does not explain why Sororians suddenly developed their *cerebral laziness,* interactions between Cornelius and Mérou suggest that apes acquired intelligence either through imitation or natural evolution. Concerning imitation, Cornelius comments "*Vous m'avez dit aussi que les singes possèdent chez vous un esprit d'imitation très développé*" [You have also told me that apes on your planet have very well developed imitation skills], to which Mérou answers, "*ils nous imitent dans tout ce que nous faisons.... C'est au point que le verbe singer est pour nous synonyme d'imiter*" [they imitate us in everything we do … to the point that the verb *to ape* is for us synonymous with to imitate] (Boulle 1963, 141). Cornelius' conclusion is "*à la longue, l'esprit peut s'incarner dans le geste*" [in the long run, the mind can be embodied in the gesture].[15] Concerning evolution, Cornelius suggests that the ascent of apes is a natural event. "*Cet événement était inscrit dans les lignes normales de l'évolution. L'homme raisonnable ayant fait son temps, un être supérieur devait lui succéder, conserver les résultats essentiels de ses conquêtes, les assimiler pendant une période de stagnation apparente, avant de s'envoler pour un nouvel essor*" [This event was inscribed in the normal lines of evolution. Rational man having had his day, a superior being had to succeed him, preserve the essential results of his conquests, assimilate them during a period of apparent stagnation, and then spread his wings and take flight] (Boulle 1963, 161).

Coincidentally, Cornelius' natural event hypothesis resonates with the words of a Pied-Noir witness: "*Il y avait une évolution historique inéluctable et c'était normal qu'on arrive à que ce pays soit indépendant*" [There was an inescapable historical evolution and it was normal that this country would become independent].[16] Furthermore, it can be argued that Cornelius' hypothesis resonates with none other than the concept of decolonization, the *natural evolution event* proposed by some historians as the triggering mechanism for the eventual independence of Algeria.

French historian Henri Fonfrède coined the term *decolonization* in 1836 in reference to Algeria, but it "disappeared from circulation by the 1850s" (Shepard 2006, 56). The term resurfaced in Europe between world wars. According to Shepard, French historian Charles-Robert Ageron outlined how "during the interwar period, the word 'decolonization' was invested with racist understandings that the world was witnessing the historically inevitable process of Western decadence" (Shepard 2006, 56).

According to Ageron, German economist Moritz Julius Bonn "*prophétisait même dans son livre* **Crumbling of Empire** *(1939) qu'on ne tarderait pas à assister non seulement à l'écroulement de l'Empire britannique, mais aussi à celui de tous les empires coloniaux*" [prophesied even in his book

Crumbling of Empire (1939) that it wouldn't be long before we witnessed not only the collapse of the British Empire, but also the collapse of all colonial empires] (Ageron 2004). In other words, decolonization was not really a natural evolution event brought about by a European "supremely rational interpretation of world events" (Shepard 2006, 55), but simply a racist attempt to insulate Europe from its colonies in order to avoid being "overrun" by them.

Pieds-Noirs also concur: "*Trente ans après, si on raisonne bien, comment la France aurait-elle pu intégrer trente millions de musulmans ?... Algérie Française, ça veut dire que vingt millions ou trente millions d'individus, avec la carte nationale française, demain, ils peuvent venir s'installer ici*" [Thirty years later, if we think about it, how could France have integrated thirty million Muslims?.... French Algeria means that twenty or thirty million people can come settle here tomorrow with their French national card].[17]

All of this indeed resonates with *La Planète*: "*Ces singes ... ils se multiplient sans cesse ... ils deviendront presque aussi nombreux que nous.... Ils deviennent arrogants. Ils soutiennent notre regard.*" [These apes ... they multiply constantly ... they will become almost as numerous as we are.... They become arrogant. They stare back.] (Boulle 1963, 172).

Thus, as the world approached the middle of the 20th century, Europe started shedding colonies: India (1947), Palestine (1948), Indonesia (1949), Libya 1951, Morocco (1957), etc. Decolonization was more difficult in Algeria because, legally, Algeria was not a colony but actually part of France. For example, when comparing Algeria and Tunisia, Pierre Mendès France says of Algeria: "*Ici, c'est la France, là, c'est un pays étranger étroitement associé au nôtre et que nous protégeons*" [Here, this is France, there, that is a foreign country closely associated with ours that we protect] (Mendès France 2001, 423).

The fate of the Pieds-Noirs and the fate of Sororian humans show some resonance too. For the Pieds-Noirs, the metropolitan French loss of the will to govern Algeria meant the loss of their homeland, and they didn't even have the possibility of an exodus to a *Continent Sauvage* as oms did. Fortunately, the Pieds-Noirs who left in 1962 and shortly afterwards managed little by little to blend into metropolitan French society: "*Les Pieds-noirs, en général, ont bien réussi, parce qu'ils ont quand même du cœur au ventre ; l'adversité a été souvent un aiguillon*" [The Pieds-Noirs, in general, have been very successful because, anyway, they have guts; adversity has often prodded them].[18] However, according to other witnesses, the blending was incomplete: "*Nous, en France, nous ne sommes pas des Français comme les autres.... La seule intégration que nous ayons complètement réussie, c'est notre intégration économique.*" [We in France, we are not

French like the others…. The only integration we have achieved completely is our economic integration].[19] And notwithstanding their eventual integration, the Pieds-Noirs were not welcome in France when they began arriving in large numbers, as exemplified by mayor of Marseille Gaston Defferre's famous words: *"Que les Pieds-Noirs aillent se réadapter ailleurs"* [Let the Pieds-Noirs go readapt themselves somewhere else] (Cardinali 2012, 9).

The approximately 200,000 Pieds-Noirs who stayed in Algeria risked death and could be killed individually in score-settlings or in large numbers in events such as the *"fusillade de la rue d'Isly"* [shooting of the *rue d'Isly*] (Daum 2008) in Algiers or the massacre of Oran, where the French Army failed "to stop the … killing of Europeans … by 'Muslim' rioters" (Shepard 2006, 213). However, once the Algerian nation began to stabilize, life went on more or less as usual. For some Pieds-Noirs, quality of life improved because *"[L]'Algérie, en manque de cadres, a … souvent offert aux pieds-noirs restés de belles carrières"* [Since it lacks executives, Algeria has … often offered beautiful careers to the Pieds-Noirs who stayed] (Portes 2012).

In the end, the fate of the Pieds-Noirs seems to have been certainly better than the fate of Sororian humans, who became animals to be hunted for sport and used as guinea pigs in neurological experiments. On the other hand, the fate of the *Harkis*, who didn't even have a country to be repatriated to, bespeaks one of the most unjust abandonments and betrayals of a people. Nothing resonates with the *Harkis* in *La Planète*.

Finally, *La Planète* leaves us with the image of a couple of gorillas driving a Jeep at Orly to meet Mérou upon his arrival 700 years after he left for Betelgeuse. Mérou then realizes Earth humans have suffered the same fate as their Sororian counterparts. There's obviously no equivalence between the Algerian War and this aspect of *La Planète*, unless we consider the possibility that one day France will become part of Algeria, a sort of *France Algérienne*. After all, geographically speaking, Algeria is larger than France.

In the end, it becomes clear that, at the time these novels were written, the concept of *sclerosis*—defined in medical pathology as "a hardening or induration of a tissue or part, or an increase of connective tissue or the like at the expense of more active tissue—"[20] had been transferred to a social context to describe a condition affecting societies when they reach a certain point of sophistication. Societal sophistication per se is not harmful as long as people can continue to find worthy challenges that keep them struggling to achieve goals. The actual goals achieved are less important than the process of achieving them. This is as simple as the saying "if you don't use it you lose it."

These novels show the idea that, by eliminating obstacles and hardships and creating an ever increasing amount of leisure time, technological and organizational advances eliminate the drive to strive at the individual level, which, in turn, causes stagnation at a societal level. However, the technology and organization levels that worried these authors and intellectuals in mid–20th century is dwarfed by our current levels. In other words, if their fears had been founded, all Western societies would be fully stagnant by now. The factor these authors and intellectuals seem to have overlooked is that, as they allow societies to reach a given set of goals, technology and organization create a new set of goals. For example, shoe factories all but eliminated shoemaking as a trade, but offered former or would be shoemakers shoe factory jobs. Then automated shoe factories eliminated shoe factory jobs, but offered former or would-be shoe factory workers shoemaking software engineering jobs.

In this context, and only assuming that the concept of sophistication-induced societal sclerosis is valid, which it is not, it seems possible to suggest the following correspondence between de Gaulle's stated options and societal sclerosis. *Francization* implies France would keep itself from societal sclerosis by striving to homogenize French and Algerian societies. *Close union* implies a less vitalizing effect for France since Algeria's own priorities would not necessarily match France's priorities. *Secession* implies France would have no help from Algeria to keep its societal sclerosis at bay.

In hindsight, *secession* was obviously best for Algeria since an independent Algeria no longer had to dedicate its energies to treat France's imagined societal sclerosis. In the grand scheme of history it would seem that the Algerian War of Independence had a happy ending.

Notes

1. Asimov explains: "Mary Shelley was the first to make use of a new finding of science [Galvani's discovery of the reaction of muscle tissue to electricity] which she advanced to a logical extreme, and it is that which makes *Frankenstein* the first true science fiction novel" (Asimov 1981, 183).

2. "Fantasy, also spelled phantasy, imaginative fiction dependent for effect on strangeness of setting (such as other worlds or times) and of characters (such as supernatural or unnatural beings).… Science fiction can be seen as a form of fantasy, but the terms are not interchangeable, as science fiction usually is set in the future and is based on some aspect of science or technology, while fantasy is set in an imaginary world and features the magic of mythical beings." (Editors of *Encyclopedia Britannica*, "Fantasy," accessed February 19, 2019, https://www.britannica.com/art/fantasy-narrative-genre.)

3. "*Après avoir involontairement fermé les yeux, je les rouvris, et je vis que l'agent lumineux s'échappait d'un demi-globe dépoli qui s'arrondissait à la partie supérieure de la cabine.*" [After involuntarily closing my eyes, I opened them again, and I saw that the luminous agent was coming from a frosted glass half-globe at the top of the cabin.] (Verne, *Vingt mille lieues*, accessed February 18, 2019, http://www.gutenberg.org/files/54873/54873-h/54873-h.htm.)

4. "What is the Culture? What do we believe in…? Surely in freedom, more than anything else. A relativistic, changing sort of freedom, unbounded by laws or laid-down moral codes, but—in the end—just because it is so hard to pin down and express, a freedom of a far

higher quality than anything to be found on any relevant scale on [Earth]" (Banks 1991, 161).

5. In science fiction novels, placing the action in the future by adding whole centuries is a well-known technique. For example, the action in Louis-Sébastien Mercier's *L'An 2440, rêve s'il en fut jamais* (Montreuil: Burozoïque, 2010) takes place 700 years after Mercier's birth year: 1740. Wul places *La Peur géante's* action 100 years after the publication year.

6. French Constitution of 1848, art. 109, accessed February 18, 2019, http://www.conseil-constitutionnel.fr/conseil-constitutionnel/francais/la-constitution/les-constitutions-de-la-france/constitution-de-1848-iie-republique.5106.html.

7. Interestingly enough, during the 1970s, scientists working in the Deep Sea Drilling Project, "the first of three international scientific ocean drilling programs that have operated over more than 40 years" ("Deep Sea Drilling Project Reports and Publications," *About DSDP. Deep Sea Drilling Project*, accessed September 24, 2017, http://deepseadrilling.org/about.htm.) discovered, under the Mediterranean seabed, minerals that could only form in the open air, thus demonstrating that the Mediterranean basin had been dry. It turns out that 5.96 million years ago, "a tectonic closure in the general region of the modern Strait of Gibraltar" (McKenzie 1996, 614) isolated the Mediterranean from the Atlantic Ocean. The rivers emptying into the Mediterranean, mighty as they might have been, were no match for evaporation, and so the Mediterranean became increasingly salty and eventually dried out, except for "large salty lakes recharged by rivers flowing through deep canyons"4 (McKenzie 1996, 613). It was not until 5.33 million years ago that "Atlantic water poured across the Gibraltar arc and into the Mediterranean basin" (McKenzie 1996, 613) due to a "dramatic rise in sea level" (McKenzie 1996, 614).

8. Editors of *Encyclopedia Britannica*, "Ferhat Abbas. President of Algeria," accessed September 27, 2017, https://www.britannica.com/biography/Ferhat-Abbas.

9. The third tribe mentioned by Brave turns out to be nothing but "des vagabonds, même pas organisés, des idiots" (Wul 1972, 52).

10. Denoël editors appear to attempt to explain this on the back cover of the 1972 edition by stating that on Ygam "le temps s'écoule quarante-cinq fois plus lentement que sur la Terre" (Wul 1972, back cover).

11. In addition to failing to scientifically validate the higher life/thought rate of oms, Wul's thoroughly unscientific explanation creates its own problem. Although Ygam is purportedly larger than Earth, oms behave on it as if they were in an Earth normal gravitational field.

12. Maître Sinh explains that these mindless earthlings have become enemies with ants, which he describes as "un insecte géant organisé de manière similaire vivant, lui aussi, dans des cités rudimentaires" (Wul 1972, 73). In that sense, Wul could have written a novel called *Planet of the Ants*. The fact that Sinh indicates that, before draags arrived, ants were *giant insects,* suggests that ants have evolved to become larger and powerful enough to confront unintelligent humans. This brings to mind Brian Aldiss' novel *Hothouse*, where humans have become smaller because they barely live past reproductive age on an Earth totally covered in vegetation, except the oceans (*Planet of the Plants?*). In *Hothouse*, ants have also become larger, but they don't fight humans.

13. One must assume that this workload is not only the minimum necessary to reduce leisure to levels that won't cause societal sclerosis but also varied enough to avoid levels of automation that atrophy creative thought.

14. Witness quoted in Verdès-Leroux 2001, 359.

15. Boulle, *La Planète* (1963), 141.

16. Witness quoted in Verdès-Leroux 2001, 359.

17. Witness quoted in Verdès-Leroux 2001, 468.

18. Witness quoted in Verdès- Leroux 2001, 386.

19. Witness quoted in Verdès- Leroux 2001, 382.

20. Random House Webster's Unabridged Dictionary (V3.0 for 32bit Windows™ systems, 1999), s.v. "sclerosis."

Works Cited

Abbas, Ferhat. 1943. "L'Algérie devant le conflit mondial. Manifeste du peuple algérien." Accessed September 28, 2017. https://texturesdutemps.hypotheses.org/1458.

_____. 2002. "La France, c'est moi." *L'Entente franco-musulmane*, February 23, 1936. Quoted in Charles-André Julien. *L'Afrique du Nord en marche. Algérie-Tunisie-Maroc 1880–1952*. Paris: Omnibus.

Ageron, Charles-Robert. 2004. "Décolonisation." *Encyclopedia Universalis*. Accessed September 29, 2017. https://www.universalis.fr/encyclopedie/decolonisation/.

Asimov, Isaac. 1981. "The First Science Fiction Novel," in *Asimov on Science Fiction*. Edited by Isaac Asimov, 181–3. Garden City, NY: Doubleday.

Banks, Iain, M. 1991. "The State of the Art" in *The State of the Art*. London: Little, Brown and Company.

Blais, Hélène. 2012. "Pourquoi la France a-t-elle conquis l'Algérie?," in *Histoire de l'Algérie à la période coloniale, 1830–1962*. Edited by Abderrahmane et al. Paris: Barzakh. 52–7.

Boulle, Pierre. 1963. *La Planète des singes*. Paris: Julliard.

Cardinali, François. 2012. Foreword to *L'exode des pieds-noirs: 1962–2012*. Paris: Maule.

Dard, Olivier. 2012. "Qui ont été les membres de l'OAS?," in *Histoire de l'Algérie à la période coloniale, 1830–1962*. Edited by Abderrahmane et al. Paris: Barzakh. 640–3.

Daum, Pierre. 2008. "Trois événements traumatisants." *Le Monde Diplomatique*. May. http://www.monde-diplomatique.fr/2008/05/DAUM/15871.

De Gaulle, Charles. 1959. "Allocution radio-télévisée prononcée au palais de l'Elysée le 16 septembre." Accessed January 20, 2017. http://fresques.ina.fr/de-gaulle/fiche-media/Gaulle00043/allocution-radio-televisee-prononcee-au-palais-de-l-elysee-le-16-septembre-1959.html.

_____. n.d. "Appel du 18 Juin." Accessed September 27, 2017. https://fr.wikisource.org/wiki/Appel_du_18_Juin.

Deep Sea Drilling Project. n.d. "Deep Sea Drilling Project Reports and Publications." *About DSDP. Deep Sea Drilling Project*. Accessed September 24, 2017. http://deepseadrilling.org/about.htm.

Delany, Samuel R. 1980. "Generic Protocols: Science Fiction and Mundane," in *The Technological Imagination: Theories and Fictions*. Edited by Teresa de Lauretis, Andreas Huyssen, and Kathleen Woodward. Madison: Coda Press.175–193.

Encyclopædia Britannica Editors. 2018. "Ferhat Abbas. President of Algeria." Accessed February 20, 2019. https://www.britannica.com/biography/Ferhat-Abbas.

Ferracci, Jean-Baptiste. 2012. *L'adieu: 1962. Le Tragique exode des français d'Algérie*. Paris: Editions de Paris.

Fitchette, Todd. 2015. "Desalination Makes Desert Nation Water-Independent." *Western Farm Press*, May 04. Accessed February 27, 2017. http://www.westernfarmpress.com/blog/desalination-makes-desert-nation-water-independent.

Foucault, Michel. 1992. *Les Mots et les choses*. Paris: Gallimard.

French Const. of 1848. Art. 109. http://www.conseil-constitutionnel.fr/conseil-constitutionnel/francais/la-constitution/les-constitutions-de-la-france/constitution-de-1848-iie-republique.5106.html.

George, Alan. 1979. "'Making the Desert Bloom.' A Myth Examined." *Journal of Palestine Studies*. 8, no. 2. Winter. 88–100. Accessed February 20, 2019. www.jstor.org/stable/2536511.

Gould, Stephen Jay. 1983. "Evolution as Fact and Theory," in *Hen's Teeth and Horse's Toes: Further Reflections in Natural History*. New York: Norton. 253–262.

Heinlein, Robert A. 1977. "Science Fiction: Its Nature, Faults and Virtues," in 1959 *Turning Points: Essays on the Art of Science Fiction*. Edited by Damon Knight. New York: Harper & Row. 3–28.

MacLean, Heather. 1994. "Science Fiction and Surrealism: A Reader's Dream." PhD Dissertation. Charlotte: University of North Carolina.

Malmgren, Carl D. 1991. *Worlds Apart: Narratology of Science Fiction*. Bloomington: Indiana University Press.

McKenzie, Judith A. 1996. "From Desert to Deluge in the Mediterranean." *Nature*, August 12, 1996.

Mendès France, Pierre. 1986. "Intervention à l'Assemblée Nationale." *Gouverner c'est choisir, 1954–1955, volume 3 of Oeuvres complètes.* Paris: Gallimard. Quoted in Jeannine Verdès-Leroux. 2001. *Les Français d'Algérie de 1830 à aujourd'hui: une page d'histoire déchirée.* Paris: Fayard.

Mercier, Louis Sébastien. 2010. *L'An 2440: rêve s'il en fut jamais.* Montreuil: Burozoïque.

Merle, Robert. n.d. "Ahmed Ben Bella. President of Algeria." Accessed September 27, 2017. https://www.britannica.com/biography/Ahmed-Ben-Bella

Nanda, B.R. 2019. "Mahatma Gandhi. Indian Leader—Sojourn in England and Return to India." Accessed February 20, 2019. https://www.britannica.com/biography/Mahatma-Gandhi/Sojourn-in-England-and-return-to-India.

Nolan, Jonathan, and Christopher Nolan. 2014. *Interstellar—The Complete Screenplay with Selected Storyboards.* London: Faber & Faber.

Peyrefitte, Alain. 1994. Vol. 1 of *C'était de Gaulle.* Paris: Editions de Fallois, Fayard.

_____. 1994. Vol. 2 of *C'était de Gaulle.* Paris: Editions de Fallois, Fayard.

Peyroulou, Jean-Pierre. 2012. Introduction to "1919–1944: L'Essor de l'Algérie algérienne." *Histoire de l'Algérie à la période coloniale, 1830–1962.* Edited by Abderrahmane et al. Paris: Barzakh. 319–346.

Peyroulou, Jean-Pierre, et al. 2012. Introduction to "1830–1880: La Conquête coloniale et la résistance des Algériens." *Histoire de l'Algérie à la période coloniale, 1830–1962.* Edited by Abderrahmane et al. Paris: Barzakh. 19–44.

Portes, Thierry. 2012. "Ces Français qui n'ont jamais quitté Alger la Blanche." *Le Figaro Premium.* March 16. http://www.lefigaro.fr/international/2012/03/16/01003-20120316 ARTFIG00639-ces-francais-qui-n-ont-jamais-quitte-alger-la-blanche.php.

Random House Webster's Unabridged Dictionary. 1999. V3.0 for 32bit Windows™ systems. s.v. "sclerosis."

Roy, Jules. 1982. *Étranger pour mes frères.* Paris, Stock.

Servan-Schreiber, Jean-Jacques. 1967. *Le Défi américain.* Paris: Denoël.

Shepard, Todd. 2006. *The Invention of Decolonization: The Algerian War and the Remaking of France.* Ithaca: Cornell University Press.

_____. 2011. "Thinking Between Metropole and Colony." *The French Colonial Mind.* Edited by Martin Thomas. Lincoln: University of Nebraska Press. 298–323.

Stora, Benjamin. 2012. *La Guerre d'Algérie expliquée à tous.* Paris: Éditions du Seuil.

Suvin, Darko. 1979. *Metamorphoses of Science Fiction: On the Poetics and History of a Literary Genre.* New Haven: Yale University Press.

Tengour, Ouanassa Siari. 2012. "1945–1962: vers l'Indépendance." *Histoire de l'Algérie à la période coloniale, 1830–1962.* Edited by Abderrahmane et al. Paris: Barzakh. 465–493.

Thomas, Martin. 2011. Preface and Acknowledgments of *The French Colonial Mind.* ix–x. Lincoln: University of Nebraska Press.

Turtledove, Harry. 1993. "Down in the Bottomlands." *Analog Science Fiction and Fact.* January.

Verdès-Leroux, Jeannine. 2001. *Les Français d'Algérie de 1830 à aujourd'hui: une page d'histoire déchirée.* Paris: Fayard.

Verne, Jules. (1878) 2017. *Vingt mille lieues sous les mers.* Accessed February 18, 2019. http://www.gutenberg.org/files/54873/54873-h/54873-h.htm.

Wikiwand. n.d. "Messali Hadj." Accessed September 27, 2017. http://www.wikiwand.com/fr/Messali_Hadj

Wul, Stefan. 1972. *Oms en série, 1957.* Paris: Denoël.

_____. 1994. *La Peur géante, 1957.* Paris: Denoël.

Napoleonic Conquest and Chinese Absorption

Dialectics of Territorial Expansion in Jack London's "The Unparalleled Invasion"

JULIE HUGONNY

> Madam, I have not disappeared. I am very tiny. I am a germ. A rare disease. I am called *malignalitaloptereosis* ... and you caught me, Mim!—Reitherman 1963

> I like Chinese,
> I like Chinese,
> There's nine hundred million of them in the world today,
> You'd better learn to like them, that's what I say.—Python 1989

In 1904, the countries of Russia and Japan both laid claim to the territories of Manchuria and Korea, sparking a conflict that was to last for 18 months and be known as the Russo-Japanese war. Russia's rationale for wanting to annex the area was the need for a warm-water port on its eastern coast. Vladivostok being situated on the 43rd parallel North, it was frozen for most of the year and only fully operational in the summer. As for Japan, it simply sought to secure the area it had taken from China just ten years prior, during the First Sino-Japanese war of 1894–1895.

In February 1904, Japan began hostilities with a surprise attack on the Russian fleet stationed in Port-Arthur, Manchuria. For a year and a half of raging hostilities, Japan won every single battle against its opponent, and in May 1905, it decisively won the war at the battle of Tsushima, humiliating Russia with eight sunk battleships and over 500 casualties. This crushing victory, Japan's second consecutive military success, reinforced Japan's reputation as a Pacific fighting force to be reckoned with, and caught the eye of European nations. The news of this unexpected outcome reso-nated through Asia and the world and astounded western countries who saw it as a veiled threat to their own safety. As a matter of fact, since the Sino-Japanese war had been an exclusively Asian conflict, Japan's undis-puted victory over Russia marked the first time an Asian country defeated a major European power.

Jack London, a war correspondent in Manchuria at the time and a prime witness to the hostilities, keenly understood the worldwide impli-cations of this new state of power. His short story, "The Unparalleled Inva-sion" is a parable on the consequences of threatening the hegemony of Western countries over the world.

"The Unparalleled Invasion" presents itself as a future historian's account of the events of a fictionalized 20th century. It relates how Japan, having internalized the "machine civilization" (London 1993, 1236) of the West, namely its means of progress and modernization, passes it on to China in the hopes of improving it to better control it. But China, now able to keep its growing population alive, soon bursts out of its frontiers and engages in a slow territorial expansion into the neighboring coun-tries. Alarmed at this sudden awakening, Western states such as France and England try to wage war on China, but to no avail: their military weapons do not measure up to China's demographic power, and their armies, how-ever large, get swallowed up by the new giant. Realizing the futility of using conventional weapons against this unconventional enemy, they resort to a merciless form of germ warfare, effectively wiping out China's entire population.

The tale, published in 1910, follows similar fictional works denouncing the perceived risks associated with the growing Chinese population and the subsequent increase of Chinese immigration to the U.S. In *The Yellow Peril, Chinese-Americans in American Fiction, 1850–1940*, William F. Wu, defines the trend as follows:

> [The] *Yellow Peril* [is] the threat to the United States that some white American authors believed was posed by the people of East Asia. As a literary theme, the fear of this threat focuses on specific issues, including possible military invasion from Asia, per-ceived competition to the white labor force from Asian workers, the alleged moral indecency of Asian people and the potential genetic mixing of Anglo-Saxon with Asians, who were considered a biologically inferior race by some intellectuals in the nineteenth-century [Wu 1982, 1].

Invasion and engulfment, the swallowing of the white West in a demo-graphic takeover wasn't, then, an image of London's invention. Follow-ing Stuart Creighton Miller's analysis of the phenomenon in *The American Image of the Chinese, 1785–1882*, Wu explains this sudden anxiety regard-ing Asian workers in the U.S. workforce by an increased awareness of Asia as a whole, following the development of mass media in the 1840s and its subsequent coverage of Asian affairs for the rest of the century. The authors of those works of fiction highlighted, among other simplistic reasons for their race-based fears, the irredeemable differences between Chinese people and white Americans of European descent. Their works and the apprehensions they stoked led to real-life social and political consequences. For Wu, the Chinese Exclusion Act of 1882, which, for the first time in the U.S., stopped all immigration from one specific country, "revealed a genuine fear of immigration, specifically from China, and this fear was based on culture and race, not just on politics and economics" (Wu 1982, 30).

In his chapter titled "Early Novels of Chinese Invasion," Wu highlights the manner in which writers of alarmist yellow peril fiction most commonly describe Chinese immigrants, as "a solid unit" (Wu 1982, 39) "a group, with no individual characterization" (Wu 1982, 31). In Pierton W. Dooner's 1880 novel, *Last Days of the Republic*, they are "a monolithic mass with a single, common ambition" (Wu 1982, 35) for power, which makes them "invincible and insupportable" (Wu 1982, 35).[1] In Robert Woltor's *A Short and Truthful History of the Taking of Oregon and California by the Chinese in the Year A.D. 1899* they "act as one large organism […] in automatic concert without visible leaders" and display a certain "quality of mindlessness, a puppet-like mass obedience" (Wu 1982, 33). Wolton himself doesn't hesitate to refer to them as an "Asiatic swarm" (Wu 1982, 34).[2] Lastly, at the turn of the century, Oto Mundo's *The Recovered Continent: A Tale of the Chinese Invasion* depicts a Chinese "war of expansion into Southeast Asia, against the holdings of England and France, and into Russia" (Wu 1982, 37) and features the headline: "FOUR HUNDRED MILLION CHINESE ARE POURING LIKE A FLOOD OVER EUROPE!" (Wu 1982, 38).[3] This alarmist vision of Asians flooding Europe via Russia is, still according to Wu, reminiscent of the Mongol invasion which, in the 13th century, "swept across Asia into Eastern Europe, conquering all they faced" (Wu 1982, 10). For him, even though the Mongols decided to settle in Russia and spared Western Europe, "the surprise and power of th[eir] initial onslaught had made a deep impression on the European chroniclers of the day" (Wu 1982, 10) and would remain in the Western collective memory for centuries.

London's short story thus appears to be in the line of descent of those works, not only for its subject, the demographic threat the Chinese pose on their neighboring countries and the world, but also for the way he describes them, as a shapeless, hive-minded mass bent on territorial expansion.

As a matter of fact, London's short story has been read by critics such as John N. Swift in his article "Germ Warfare, Eugenics and Cultural Hygiene," and Stephen Hong Sonn in "Alien/Asian: Imagining a racialized future," as a straightforward expression of London's racism towards

Asia. But it is, to me, an oversimplification of London's relationship with race. Critics often quote a damning statement he made at a socialist meeting party, where he was reported to have said: "I am first of all a white man and only then a socialist" (Swift 2002, 67–8). John Raskin, in the introduction to "If Japan Wakens China," even goes so far as to say that, although London did manage, in the course of his writing career, to see the world from the eyes of a dog in *The Call of the Wild*, "his ability to empathize did not extend to non-white races" (Raskin 2008, 220). This is a gross misunderstanding of London's intentions as a writer, and we need to address this question before we delve into the tale itself.

Admittedly, "The Unparalleled Invasion" borrows freely from two of London's most racially problematic essays: "The Yellow Peril," written in Manchuria in 1904, and "If Japan Wakens China," published in *Sunset* in 1909. In "The Yellow Peril," written during his stint as an observer of the Russo-Japanese war, he chronicles his travels through Korea and Japanese-occupied China, and depicts Asian "types" in sweeping generalizations:

> The Korean is the perfect type of inefficiency—of utter worthlessness. The Chinese is the perfect type of industry. [...] [The] Japanese [is] a race of mastery and power, a fighting race through all its history, a race which has always despised commerce and exalted fighting [London 1910, 274–279].

More tellingly, and much like his late 19th-century predecessors, he describes the differences between the East and the West as unbridgeable and portrays China as a clear threat to the Western world, in dismally racist terms:

> [T]he menace to the Western world lies, not in the little brown man [Japan], but in the four hundred millions of yellow men [China], should the little brown man undertake their management [London 1910, 281].

This threat of a thriving, bustling and ever-expanding China, led by a triumphant Japan is in fact the premise of "The Unparalleled Invasion." In "If Japan Wakens China," he insists on the impossibility of a deep understanding between Western countries and Japan, claiming they are "soul-strangers [...] unutterably alien, absolutely without any kinship or means of communication" (London 2008, 222).

But London's relationship with Asian nations is much more complicated than a cursory reading of these essays might suggest. First of all, he did explore non-white subjectivities in short stories such as "The Mexican," "The Chinago" and "The Whale's Tooth," which all depict, in the words of Jeanne Campbell Reesman, "whites [...] as diseased, evil, foolish or alcoholic wastrels" (Campbell-Reesman 2009, vi). In "The Chinago," for instance, a Pacific Islander named Ah Cho is wrongly accused of murder for the resemblance of his name with the true perpetrator's, Ah Cho. The French and the British officials who conduct his trial and subsequent execution realize the mistake but do not stop the proceedings, as the company they work for needs a scapegoat. The tale is told from the point of view of Ah Cho, a hardworking and peaceful man who watches with silent contempt weaker men invoking wasted time and lost money to send him knowingly to the gallows. The chilling conclusion of the investigation: "Let's put the performance through just the same. It is only a Chinago" (London 1993, 1416) expose the white men as profoundly inhuman or criminally bureaucratic. The dismaying ending of the narrative, cutting off abruptly as Ah Cho is guillotined, is a clear indictment of Europe's practices toward indigenous people, and an "attack [on its] racist, capitalist and imperialist values" (Campbell-Reesman 2009, vi).

Already perceptible in his fictional works, London's personal interest in Asia also shines in his reports from the Russo-Japanese front. For Daniel Metraux, "his Korean and Manchurian dispatches show considerable sympathy for ordinary Asians" (Metraux 2009, vii). His contempt is reserved for authority of any kind, regardless of the country from which said authority emanates. His chronicles abound in small mutinies against the people in charge: one account has him fighting Japanese officials who want to confiscate his camera for snapping a picture of a secret fortified place. In another one, he refuses to wait in line to meet Pak-Choon-Song, a Korean magistrate, and breaks protocol by walking right up to him.

London thus seems to have bristled at any form of authority, and encouraged similar behavior from any lowerclassman: as he makes his way forcefully to the Korean magistrate, London looks back at his translator, Manyoungi and contemplates the possibility of a future rebellion in the young man:

> Manyoungi was standing and being shouldered by the crowd. [...] In his head was the ferment of a new idea, the Western idea of the rights of man. In his head were mutiny and revolt. In his head, though dimly perhaps, were the ideas of Revolutionary France [Metraux 2009, 249].

Grounding our reflection in his written words, we can thus safely assume that, contrary to what he allegedly once claimed, Jack London was a socialist first, and only then a white man.

Even in "The Yellow Peril," arguably its most bluntly-termed essay, he credits the Chinese with the power to take over the world, and does so in fairly appreciative terms: "the Chinese [...] is an efficient worker, makes a good soldier, [and is] deft, intelligent, and unafraid to die. [...] Under capable management, he will go far," (London 1910, 281) he writes. He also acknowledges Japan's leading role in this possible takeover, musing: "the Japanese is prepared and fit to undertake this management" (London 1910,

281). Later, he describes the 45-million Japanese as "splendid fighting animals, scientific and modern" (London 1910, 282).

Of course, even his praise is tinged with a sense of his own superiority. Conscious of his own bias, he closes his argument on a note of self-awareness, and writes:

> [I]t must be taken into consideration that the above postulate is itself a product of Western race-egotism, urged by our belief in our own righteousness and fostered by a faith in ourselves which may be as erroneous as are most fond race fancies [London 1910, 288–9].

Acutely aware to be a product of his time and place (and turn-of-the-century California was particularly prejudiced against Pacific workers as we saw), he denounces the West as self-righteous and egotistical, essentially blind to the rest of the world. "The Unparalleled Invasion" is a case in point, not of his own racism, but of his denunciation, through cynical satire, of the racism that saturates the Western mindset. Pervasively ironic, and operating under the safe cover of a science-fiction parable, "The Unparalleled Invasion," reveals that the West is afraid, and follows the worldwide effects of this fear to their most logical and most chilling consequences.

The story is told from the point of view of Walt Mervin, an historian we can safely assume is a white and Anglo-Saxon, and thus embodies that race-egotism London was warning us against. Mervin's enthusiastic description of the eventual genocide of a whole nation is much too callous, and his obliviousness to his own prejudices much too appalling to reflect London's opinions. As Lawrence I. Berkove puts it, "it is impossible to believe that London would identify with a historian so obviously shallow and ethnocentric" (Berkove 1992, 34). Moreover, the tale was published in *The Strength of the Strong*, a collection of short stories whose eponymous narrative exemplifies the idea that history is written by victors, and is therefore a tale not to be trusted.

The "Unparalleled Invasion" is thus constantly working on two levels. On the first level, we have the historian's false objectivity in depicting China as a threatening force whose sole purpose is the consumption and annexation of territories, a convenient tale naturally leading to his rationalization of the massacre of its population as a necessary evil. On the second level, watermarked throughout the text in scathing irony, lies Jack London's criticism of those very notions. This criticism, nestled in the heart of Walt Mervin's account, is particularly obvious in three points: in the description of an alien threat; in the notion of a "Napoleonic dream" (London 1993, 1238); and in the celebration of the "sanitation" (London 1993, 1245) of China.

An Alien Threat

From the first sentence of the story, China is described as irremediably alien, almost non-human, or at least not part of what Walt Mervin associates with humankind, since he alludes to "trouble between the world and China" (London 1993, 1234) at a date when China itself represents two thirds of the world population. This *us versus them* mindset allows him to casually exclude China from the community of humans.

All through the short story, and in keeping with the imagery created by the yellow peril fiction of the 1880s, Eastern countries in general—and China in particular—are characterized by their excess, their animalized devouring power. Japan's agents "swarm" (London 1993, 1236) the Chinese Empire to modernize it. China itself, described as a "colossus" (London 1993, 1237) and as Japan's "gigantic protégé" (London 1993, 1237) is eventually "awakened" (London 1993, 1237) from its slumber. Having entered the industrial revolution, China's growing population "spills" (London 1993, 1239) indiscriminately over the neighboring counties and "flows on" (London 1993, 1239) despite summons to stop. When attacked by irate Western countries, it first simply "withdraw[s] like a turtle in its shell" (London 1993, 1239), then responds by "swallow[ing] up" armies in its "cavernous maw" (London 1993, 1239). Its "rampant" (London 1993, 1239) population is conjectured to be soon a billion and a half, and is described as an "over-spilling monstrous flood of life" (London 1993, 1239). China is a force of nature, a young and unruly titan still in its infancy, a monstrous toddler destroying everything it touches, an unstoppable leviathan with a boundless appetite. As a comparison to this unthinking entity, France is seen "mak[ing] a stand," "call[ing] a halt," and "assembl[ing] a force" (London 1993, 1239), so many precise, rational and deliberate actions highlighting by contrast China's troubling lack of control. Tough they seem to be in line with Robert Woltor's "swarm," and Oto Mundo's "flood," London's images are much too hyperbolic and much too numerous to be taken seriously. This periphrastic frenzy, this conscious effort to name every stereotype and touch on every metaphor is an ironic exaggeration aimed at poking fun of the Western paranoia concerning a possible Asian takeover.

For John N. Swift, Walt Mervin's account "deploys a freewheeling, highly conventional vocabulary of Anglo-Saxon anxiety." But I wouldn't qualify it as he does, as an "openly sexual anxiety" (Swift 2002, 60). Of course, industrious Japan and expanding China are both referred to in the feminine, but so is Russia. Furthermore, the increase of the Chinese population is not described as the usual threat of a promiscuous, corrupt, predatory and heavily feminized Orient. In fact, the iconography prevailing at the time, featuring the welfare mother and the prostitute as the two figureheads of the eastern (feminine) threat to western (masculine) morality, are nowhere to be found in this story. On the contrary, steering away from any gendered personification of the country, London keeps China's population a number. The Chinese do not reproduce, breed or procreate, they multiply abstractly. Their migration is a block, a force, a marching army of working, toiling civilians.

The West is nonetheless afraid—not of China's demographic growth or even of its economic takeover, though they both play their part in anticipating what John N. Swift calls the "precariousness of white racial supremacy" (Swift 2002, 60). The West is afraid of the radically different mindset of Eastern nations, of the impenetrable motives behind their actions. In "The Yellow Peril" London reports that, upon being asked what she thought of the Japanese, an American woman living in Tokyo answered: "It seems to me that they have no soul" (London 1910, 286). He clarifies:

> This must not be taken to mean that the Japanese is without a soul. But it serves to illustrate the enormous difference between their souls and this woman's soul. There was no feel, no speech, no recognition. This Western soul did not dream that the Eastern soul existed, it was so different, so totally different [London 1910, 286].

These deep, irreconcilable differences in spirit—in "soul" as the American lady puts it, make the idea of an Eastern subjectivity unfathomable to the Western mind, even one immersed in Asian culture. Japan, however, maybe more receptive to new ideas or strategically more inclined to open-mindedness, proved perfectly capable of understanding the West. From the end of the 1860s to World War II, Meiji–era Japan not only assimilated Western ideas of progress, but also put them to work to modernize the country. By borrowing from European ideas and embracing what Jack London terms the "machine civilization," Japan jump-started its own industrial era, and set off to defeat both China and Russia at the turn of the century.

Jack London has no satisfying explanation for Japan's adaptability, and resorts to consider it an exception among Asian countries:

> Now the Japanese race was the freak and paradox among Eastern peoples. In some strange way Japan was receptive to all the West had to offer. Japan swiftly assimilated the Western ideas, and digested them, and so capably applied them that she suddenly burst forth, full-panoplied, a world-power [London 1993, 1235].

Here, the transformation of Japan from an ordinary Asian country to a Westernized world power is described in terms of progression on the scale of living organisms: from the "reception" and "assimilation" (London 1993, 1235) of ideas, two passive terms one could apply to plants metabolizing sun and water, to "digestion" (London 1993, 1235), a basic and unconscious animal function, Japan acquires agency: it "capably applies" (London

1993, 1235) the ideas the West has bestowed upon it, showing—at last—intellectual process. The culmination of this progression from plant-like entity to fully-realized human is, of course, its readiness to wage war. Like Athena, coming out fully armed from Jupiter's thigh, Japan reveals its military power and territorial ambitions over its neighbors, thus consecrating its Westernization. This new aggressive streak earns Japan a place in the "comity of nations" (London 1993, 1234) among like-minded world powers.

But if Japan has managed to understand Europe enough to take advantage of its means of modernization and enter its colonization game, China remains recalcitrant. It doesn't have the same flexibility, the same power of adaptation to Western thought as Japan does, and there is no connection possible between China and Europe. In "The Unparalleled Invasion," London takes up the same terminology found in his essays, in order to describe the unbridgeable mental gap between China and the West: "their thought-processes were radically dissimilar. […] The fabrics of their minds were woven from totally different stuffs. They were mental aliens" (London 1993, 1234–5). Gridlocked in mutually-exclusive mindsets, the East and the West's attempts at communication repeatedly hit a "blank, incomprehensible wall" (London 1993, 1234).

Borrowing from Western practice just enough to sustain its population, China declines to engage in conventional warfare with in turn, France, England, Russia, and the USA. This refusal to play along, this noncompliance to the rules of the world as defined by western countries, is the offense that demands retribution.

The Napoleonic Dream

China slowly overruns Korea, Indo-China, Burma and the Malay Peninsula, and then advances on to Southern Siberia, Nepal, Bhutan, Afghanistan, Persia, and Turkestan, sparking outrage and declarations of war from every major European power in the process. But China does not colonize those countries for their wealth in raw materials or their strategic position, as a European country would. It needs space, and thus spills over its own frontiers, indiscriminately. Far from draining the resources of the conquered country to increase the motherland's economic power, it claims the territory as a necessary extension of the motherland itself and gets to work on it. Its strategy starts with infiltration by early Chinese immigrants, then comes the "brushing away of all opposition by a monster army of militia-soldiers" (London 1993, 1239), and finally, the implantation of families at the ready. Those families, in turn, are only asking for one thing: the ability to work, illustrating once more what London theorized in "The

Yellow Peril": "the Chinese is the perfect type of industry. [...] Work is the breath of his nostrils. [...] Liberty to him epitomizes itself in access to the means of toil. To till the soil and labour interminably [...] is all he asks of life" (London 1910, 274).

The absolute outrage of European countries might seem a little over-played, since China does not appear to have designs on them quite yet. Of course, it is advancing Westward, but remains far. What scares Europe most of all is a number: in 1970, a certain Burchaldter warns the world that there are more Chinese people on Earth than there are white people. By the time China has reached Central Asia, he has revised his estimate and claims there are now two Chinese for every white person. It is at that very moment, which unsurprisingly coincides with China's annexation of Indo-China, that France sees its patience run thin and attacks the new giant, only to lose its entire army to China's civilian militia.

As Lawrence Berkove points out, part of the problem is that China is taking over countries that are already colonized by European powers:

> The narrative [...] quietly underplays the fact that of th[e] countries [China is occu-pying], only Siam was independent: Indo-China had already been taken over by the French, Burma and the Malay Peninsula by England, and Siberia by Russia. The West-ern nations were Napoleonically imperial; China's empire was driven by the need for *lebensraum* [Berkove 1992, 36].

The only asset China threatens directly is the economic prevalence European countries gained by colonizing other nations, but then again, maybe it is precisely what hurts the most. What those countries do not see—or hypocritically choose to ignore—is the inherent contradiction of their situation, as they condemn China for the theft of their own colonies, in the name of the self-determination of nations.

But beyond the loss of their economic interests, slowly eaten away at by China, what makes it a threat is a fundamental ideological difference. As Walt Mervin himself notes, once awakened, the country mystifies the world, because "contrary to expectation, China [does] not prove warlike. She ha[s] no Napoleonic dream, and [is] content to devote herself to the arts of peace" (London 1993, 1237–8). In fact, despite its modernization, passed on to it by Japan, and despite its unprecedented demographic power, China is not bent on world domination.

The expression "Napoleonic dream" is the key to understand this rift between East and West, and the uneasy in-between status of Japan. Jack London introduces the phrase in "The Yellow Peril," where he describes Japan's incredible talent for taking in and using Western means of progress:

> Equipped with the finest machines and systems of destruction the Caucasian mind has devised, [...] this rejuvenescent Japanese race has embarked on a course of conquest,

the goal of which no man knows. The head men of Japan are dreaming ambitiously, and the people are dreaming blindly, a Napoleonic dream [London 1910, 274–5].

For Jack London, by familiarizing itself with Western ideas, Japan has internalized the drive for conquest that urged European countries to colonize the rest of the world, as evidenced by its takeover of Manchuria and Korea. This "Napoleonic" ambition of an Empire, built from military strategy and ensuring territorial conquest, seems to be a very contagious idea, as it also affects Russia: "the Slav, too is dreaming greatly" (London 1910, 280). London writes. For him, the Russo-Japanese war of the early 20th century is no more than the butting heads of two adjacent nations with the same dream.

In "If Japan Wakens China," London recognizes that Europe is still very much basking in the afterglow of its fulfilled Napoleonic dream, the great adventure of colonization:

We English-speaking peoples are in the midst of our great adventure. We are dreaming as all race-adventures have dreamed. And who will dare to say that in the Japanese mind is not burning some colossal Napoleonic dream? And what if the dreams clash? [London 2008, 223].

London imagines a plausible scenario: building on its victory over Russia, and backed up by a now-thriving Chinese population, Japan might then turn its endeavors toward Europe, first by superseding it economically, then militarily.

It is true, it is only an economic clash, but economic clashes always precede clashes at arms. And what then? Oh, only that will-o'-the-wisp, the Yellow peril. But to the Russian, Japan was only a will-o'-the-wisp until one day, with fire and steel, she smashed the great adventure of the Russian and punctured the bubble-dream he was dreaming. Of this be sure: if ever the day comes that our dreams clash with that of the Yellow and the Brown, and our particular bubble-dream is punctured, there will be one country at least unsurprised, and that country will be Russia. She was awakened from her dream. We are still dreaming [London 2008, 223–4].

Still building on the idea of the white man's race-egotism, shining through his misplaced confidence in his own superiority, London imagines the West's surprise when Asian troops come crashing. "The Yellow Peril" is a warning to European countries, foreseeing a rude awakening if they don't snap out of their self-absorption and start paying attention to what is happening around them. This prediction is backed up by the example of Russia, an Indo-European, continent-sized empire, who had to bend the knee to Japan, a new warrior and unlikely challenger. London warns that in the search of its own great "race-adventure," Asia will not hesitate to "smash" other countries, "puncture" the bubble of obliviousness they live in, and wake them up from their blissful daydreaming. "The Yellow Peril," this seemingly racist diatribe, turns out to be just the opposite: it is both a tribute to what Asia can—and will—accomplish, and an indictment of Europe's dangerous navel-gazing.

But at least, an Asian Napoleonic endeavor is a recognizable force to Western countries, and, despite its victory over Russia, Japan is too weak to constitute a real threat to the world. Moreover, despite its efforts, it cannot count on China's help: once prosperous, China gently dismisses the Japanese emissaries present on its territory and refuses to follow Japan in its dream of world conquest. More disquieting, when attacked by military powers such as France or the UK, it takes the hit (it can afford to, for any attack is a bee sting for a population of 500 million and counting), but does not retaliate, a never-before-seen tactic that baffles the West. Worse, it keeps growing and spreading.

With its demographic strength and lack of military ambition, China puzzles Japan, Russia and the West, all Napoleonically inclined countries. Its *modus operandi*, a slow and steady swallowing of land, is unprecedented in the history of war, and its overarching purpose remains a mystery for all.

To add insult to injury, the Chinese government does not seem at all fazed by the threats of war of the West and only asks to be left alone. When summoned by the comity of nations, Li Tang Fwung, the head of China replies:

> What does China care for the comity of nations? [...] We are the most ancient, honourable, and royal of races. We have our own destiny to accomplish. It is unpleasant that our destiny does not tally with the destiny of the rest of the world, but what would you? [...] You cannot invade us. [...] Send your navies. We will not notice them. Send your punitive expeditions, but first remember France [...] Send a million [men]; send five millions, and we will swallow them down just as readily. Pouf! A mere nothing, a meagre morsel [London 1993, 1240].

In this unacceptable display of complacency and self-centeredness— doubled with a disquieting readiness to consume everything thrown at it—China not only shrugs off Europe's threats, but boasts in its own dismissive way, to be justified in doing so, as Europe is effectively helpless against it. Upon hearing Li Tang Fwung's words, "the world [is] nonplussed, helpless, terrified" (London 1993, 1241) according to Walt Mervin, who conflates again "the world" with "the Western world." Dismissed as an inconvenience, their summons relegated to the rank of unpleasantness one can simply ignore, Western countries have never be treated so cavalierly. Everything they know about power and influence is being challenged by this humongous country who just asks to be left alone and—most frustratingly—claims to care about its own destiny before theirs. It is truly by refusing to engage with the West, by expressing disinterest in military engagement, the only language the West knows, that China marks itself as a power to destroy.

In a way, China is a creation of the West, a creature much like Frankenstein's own, and potentially as destructive. Through Japan's intercession, the West gave China the means of modernization it now uses to sustain its population. As a matter of fact, long before Japan, Western countries had themselves tried to modernize China, but to no avail. The opening of the narrative tells us that "the Western nations had tried to arouse China, and they had failed. Out of their native optimism and race-egotism they had therefore concluded that the task was impossible, that China would never awaken" (London 1993, 1234). Once more, grandstanding Western countries cannot imagine anyone succeeding where they have failed and chalk off China as a lost cause. To their surprise, Japan turns out to be a superior teacher and achieve the wished-for development of China. But Western countries didn't foresee that, once awakened, China would make use of its free will and refuse to obey them. By claiming instead the intrinsic value of its own life, China expresses a desire to exist on its own terms. Just like in Mary Shelley's novel, the West's creation refuses to be its creature and the elation of the scientist bringing inert matter to life quickly gives way to the anguish of losing control over it.

Indeed, China is Victor Frankenstein's worst nightmare come true: like the West, the young man is afraid of his creature multiplying and he fears "a race of devils [that] would be propagated upon the earth [...] at the price, perhaps, of the existence of the whole human race" (Shelley 1993, 144). The idea of a new, more resilient race that would short-circuit the evolutionary process and supersede the Western man is echoed by Walt Mervin's insistence on dissociating "China" and "the world." To him, the Chinese are simply not part of humanity. This newfound extinction anxiety challenges the status of the white man as the center of the world, and he needs to protect his supremacy at all costs.

For Colleen Lye, in *America's Asia. Racial Form and American Literature, 1893–1945*, the U.S. was at the time starting to get the measure of Asia's potential.

> At a time when American politicians and intellectuals [...] were lamenting America's transformation into a "business civilization" at the expense of its "warrior" qualities, the potential combination of a martial Japan and an industrious China appeared to symbolize a magical and maximal merging of what in America were seen to have become polarized tendencies [Lye 2005, 16].

Operating the synthesis of two seemingly contradictory mindsets— or at least of two qualities Western countries couldn't reconcile, the East places itself in a situation of "both heir and rival to a decaying West" (Lye 2005, 16–7).

"And so perished China"

The solution to this evolutionary threat comes from Jacobus Laningdale, an unassuming and obscure scientist who single-handedly defeats the giant country the Western way: with smarts and science. Jacobus Laningdale is the Western fantasy of a providential man: he is an everyman, an unassuming figure with no great authority or charisma, but he is a scientist and ultimately a savior. His solution is simple and deadly, and immediately ratified by the heads of the greater Western states.

Their plan is easily put into practice and deceptively simple: they send out planes over China, to release seemingly empty glass tubes over its densely inhabited territory. Those glass tubes are revealed to contain all the epidemics known to man, and turn China's demographic strength into a weakness.

> Had there been one plague, China might have coped with it. But from a score of plagues no creature was immune. The man who escaped smallpox went down before scarlet fever. The man who was immune to yellow fever was carried away by cholera; and if he were immune to that, too, the Black Death, which was the bubonic plague, swept him away. For it was these bacteria, and germs, and microbes, and bacilli, cultured in the laboratories of the West, that had come down upon China in the rain of glass [London 1993, 1244].

Walt Mervin's didactic tone (he helpfully reminds us that the common name of the Black Death is the bubonic plague) and his rhetorical effects of repetition and amplification mimic the organized chaos the West has unleashed on China. Epidemics are described, not as a force of nature striking blindly wherever it falls, but as Europe's allies in this fight: tiny, obedient soldiers; a new, less unruly western creation designed to bring monstrous China to its knees. For John N. Swift,

> [E]nacting a grim *lex talionis*, biology answers biology; the West appropriately responds to the plague of uncontrollable reproduction with the managed biotechnology of germ warfare [Swift 2002, 61].

The unparalleled invasion is an unparalleled infection. With technological advances unhindered by any kind of moral qualms, the West wins, this time for good. In a chilling display of elation, Walt Mervin revels in describing the poetic justice of this extreme form of reckoning.

> China had laughed at war, and war she was getting, but it was ultra-modern war, twentieth century war, the war of the scientist and the laboratory, the war of Jacobus Laningdale. Hundred-ton guns were toys compared with the micro-organic projectiles hurled from the laboratories, the messengers of death, the destroying angels that stalked through the empire of a billion souls [London 1993, 1245].

The rational lab-grown science of the West thus defeats the demography run amok of the East. But this rational science serves a vindictive and irrational purpose: the West doesn't seek to curb China's population, to control its growth or keep it within its frontiers, but to take revenge on a nation who dared defy it. Walt Mervin's biblical tone is jubilant, triumphant with the pride of being the judge, jury and more cathartically, the executioner. He portrays science, wielded by the West, as the instrument of retribution for China's reproductive *hubris*, but fails to see that what it has exacted is a revenge in no common measure with the slight.

On this point, *The Sword in the Stone*, a 1963 Walt Disney production, offers us a surprising but revealing parallel. Merlin and Madam Mim engage in a battle of magic, in which they turn into various animals and try to overpower each other. The rules are simple, and only include two caveats: "no disappearing" and "no make-believe things, like a pink dragon" (Reitherman 1963).

One after the other, they assume the form of increasingly bigger animals, such as a bird, a rabbit, a cat, a walrus and a crocodile. Angry at losing the advantage, Mim becomes a purple dragon, taking advantage of the loophole written in the phrasing of the rule—no *pink* dragon. Caught into her claws, Walrus-Merlin seems to disappear—another forbidden move. In a voice seemingly coming from thin air, he explains he's gone microscopic: "Madam, I have not disappeared. I am very tiny. I am a germ, a rare disease. I am called *malignalitaloptereosis* … and you caught me, Mim!" (Reitherman 1963).

Having figuratively as well as literally caught the virus, Mim immediately develops chills, headaches and erupts in blotchy red patches, and is soon reduced to a sad, bedridden purple dragon. Merlin wins the fight.

China is in a similar position as Mim: by growing bigger, it imposes size, its own strength, as the leading parameter of the fight, and expands to the point of breaking all measure. Like Mim, it is ultimately defeated by the minuscule serving the rational. In both tales, locked in an unwinnable logic of escalation, the victor is the one who thinks outside the box, shifting the parameters of the argument from brawns to brains. Of course, we can see poetic justice in the fact that the decisive trump card is at the exact opposite of size. But in Disney fashion, Mim deserves her fate, a mortifying but non-lethal one, because she cheated, and Merlin deserves his victory because he did not.

In London's short story, the world has not agreed on rules for war and territorial expansion. Of course, there is the Napoleonic way to go about it, which is the traditional, European way, tacitly ratified by countries influenced by the western ideas; but China, having no army and no navy, is the one actually finding ways around the resources it doesn't possess. In a world lacking written, agreed-upon rules, growing out of proportions can be seen as a fair move, and a brilliant one, both in its unexpectedness and in the helplessness in which it quickly leaves its opponents. In a strict sense, in unleashing death on the Chinese territory, Western heads of state are not strictly cheating either. But by committing the genocide of five hundred million people, they crossed an implicit moral line. Stumped by China, they had to face the humiliating realization that not only their armies—their pride and joy for centuries—were useless, but also that the Napoleonic dream was maybe not as universal as they had thought, that it had become an outdated way of thinking. This lesson in humility, this forced shift from their perspective to China's, is ultimately what leads them to exact such a conclusive vengeance.

The figure of the soft-spoken Jacobus Laningdale, savior of the Western world and killer of China, is strangely similar to another quiet man of great power in London's writings: Percival Stultz, aka Goliah, from the eponymous story, published in 1909 in *Revolution and Other Essays* along with "The Yellow Peril."

In this other tale, set in the future 1920s, a man named Goliah reaches out to heads of state and summons them to disarm and relinquish all power to him, for the good of Mankind. Of course, no one takes him seriously, until he kills all the noncompliant governing entities, and vaporizes their fleets and weapons with a mysterious, invincible force named *Energon*. Faced with a madman wielding the ultimate weapon, the world disarms, kings abdicate and rulers step down from their positions. As promised, Goliah acts as a benevolent dictator: he offers Energon to the world and resolves the energy crisis, bringing about safety, prosperity, joy and laughter, as was his plan. Goliah, the elusive "scientific superman and world-tyrant" (London 1993, 1220) then yields to popular demand and reveals his true identity. Percival Stultz thus comes out of the shadows, a bespectacled little man with a bald patch and a weakness for salted pecans. After an initial reaction of disbelief upon learning the disappointing identity of the formidable Goliah, people learn to love the man behind the mask, "for his simplicity and comradeship, and warm humaneness" (London 1993, 1221).

Goliah is a best-case scenario of the socialist superman: despite his unlimited power, Stultz conducts surgical strikes to take out the exact number of lives necessary to ensure happiness for the rest. As Jonathan Berliner points out, in most of London's writings, "mere brute force is villainy" (Berliner 2008, 68). What makes Stultz a great man is the restrained use of his otherwise absolute power, backed up by the ingenuity to create Goliah, a larger-than-life fictional character whose evocative name makes him fit to wield the superpower of Energon.

Jacobus Laningdale, the inventor of the plague tubes, sets out to be a Stultz-like character. He is "a very obscure scientist" with a head "very

like any other head" (London 1993, 1241). Laningdale's position as a professor in the laboratories of the health department of New York City,
another crowded and bustling place, allows him to think of the Chinese
issue in terms of health hazard, similarly to Stultz, whose work as an engineer and night classes in sciences lead to the discovery of Energon. But far
from fleshing out the character of Jacobus Laningdale with personal details
such as like Stultz' twinkling eyes and communicative laughter, the text
approaches the character clinically. Laningdale is little more than an idea,
a clever idea pushing its way to realization, as a parasite would control its
host to the destination of its choice. The text develops the description of
Laningdale's ordinary head with: "in that head was evolved an idea. Also,
in that head was the wisdom to keep that idea secret" (London 1993, 1241).
After a period of incubation in Jacobus Laningdale's mind, the idea is then
communicated to other people in viral terms: after his initial talk with the
U.S. President, "the secret that he carried began to spread, but it spread only
among the heads of Governments" (London 1993, 1241). It is a controlled
virus, carefully kept away from the public and only handled by specialists,
scientists and politicians who know the safety protocol. This secrecy, which
keeps the public, the reader, and above all the people of China in the dark,
make for a swifter and a more spectacular outcome. The mystery surrounding the undisclosed but almost self-willed idea, followed by the equally
puzzling rain of empty glass tubes, and lastly the revelation of their deadly
contents all participate in the slow increase in tension, violently resolved in
Walt Mervin's ecstatic depiction of the Chinese purge. The reader is placed
in the same apprehensive state in both short stories, expecting and dread-
ing the outcome with equal intensity. But whereas "Goliah" limits casualties and closes on universal happiness, "The Unparalleled Invasion" ends in
a carnage poorly disguised as a victory.

Thus, despite their similarities, the two situations and the two men
couldn't be more different: where Stultz quite naively intends to bring back
joy and laughter in the world, Laningdale coldly applies the most efficient
formula in his arsenal in order to solve a mathematical problem, without
consideration for the life of a billion non-white humans.

"And so perished China" (London 1993, 1245), says Walt Mervin. The
fable draws to an end, its clear moral: do not defy the West. For John Reider,
"war […] restores order and teaches the natives a lesson. The lesson, ultimately, is the superiority of the whites over the non-whites" (Reider 2008,
41). This "superiority" of the West first lies in its ingenuity, for one has to
admit unleashing plagues on an overcrowded continent is an effective way
of clearing it of its inhabitants—but it also lies in its readiness to take the
logic of escalation to its extreme in order to win an argument. By carrying
out the genocide of the Chinese people, the West cuts the Gordian knot of

the questions previously raised: that of a population growing excessively, but also that of diplomacy between world powers with a different mindset. It also sends a clear warning to all the other emergent countries, by revealing just how far exactly it is ready to go to preserve its supremacy.

China is left to fester, its bodies unburied and its population unmourned. "Brave" (London 1993, 1245) expeditions sent to reconquer the land simply shoot the survivors on sight. A nation, once two-thirds of the world population, is quite literally wiped off the surface of the Earth and evacuated from the story. A "vast and happy intermingling of nationalities settles down in China" (London 1993, 1245) to populate its now empty land.

These new settlers are only the last wave of a score of invasions and conquests, both physical and ideological, happening in the story. First came the spreading of European ideas of progress and conquest throughout Eastern nations, advancing from Russia to Japan and to some extent, China. Then came the unprecedented expansion of China's population as the unforeseen consequence of its modernization, and the uncontainable wave of Chinese immigrants into adjoining countries. Next, appeared Jacobus Laningdale's contagious idea, making its progress from Laningdale's mind to the heads of states, and spurring them into action. The plague of epidemics that ensues, yet another conquest of land akin to an epidemiologic Napoleonic dream, is only the prelude to the final invasion—that of western human groups, peacefully sharing a land cleared of its native population.

Of all these attacks, conquests, incursions and annexations, the rain of diseases and their dissemination through the land is the only event of the story to be referred to as "the unparalleled invasion," in keeping with the image of each bacillus as an obedient soldier of the West. Needless to say, the growth and spreading of the Chinese population beforehand was itself wholly unprecedented in the history of mankind, as even Walt Mervin, admits wonderingly that "never was there so strange and effective a method of world conquest" (London 1993, 1240). But the nuance of impressive achievement, of awe-striking endeavor contained in the term "unparalleled" is of course, reserved for the doings of the West. What seems to really make an impression on the historian is not that a nation going on a billion strong managed to feed and clothe all its citizens, but rather than another one managed to kill them all.

The last wave of territorial conquest crowning this accomplishment takes us back to an old form of colonization, that of an appropriation of foreign land by Western immigrants. This return to known and comforting Western models of occupation erases the Chinese foray into new patterns of territorial expansion from history—or at least relegates it to an anomaly—and reasserts the authority of Western paradigms.

Indeed, the territory formerly known as China being now empty and available to the international community, people of all nations happily settle on it, in a "tremendous and successful experiment in cross-fertilization" (London 1993, 1245). This description is made in biological terms reminiscent of the ones used to explain a new super-bacteria born from the crossbreeding of diseases in the tubes, a collateral damage of the whole operation: "a new plague-germ had originated, that in some way or other a sort of hybridization between plague-germs had taken place, producing a new and frightfully virulent germ" (London 1993, 1244). After unleashing many forms of death on China, and creating in the process a superbug, Europe releases its many people on the territory in very much the same way, but reaps this time a "splendid mechanical, intellectual, and art output" (London 1993, 1245). But this rational, utopian society depicted as a new golden age of humanity only superficially resembles Goliah's happiness and laughter. What this new pan–European nation in the middle of Asia will develop, sooner or later, is what we have isolated as its most repulsive and most salient trait so far: the ability to commit acts of utmost violence under the pretext of efficiency, a virulent strand of what Lawrence Berkove calls "national and ethnic aggressiveness, [which is] never more inhuman than when it is augmented by intelligence but concealed by lofty rationalization" (Berkove 1992, 38).

The cheerful tone of Western triumphalism Walt Mervin uses to describe the mixed incoming of Europeans on former Chinese land only imperfectly hides a dark omen. The Great Truce that allowed Western countries to carry out the biological bombing of China shows signs of cracking. The presence of China, a common enemy, once held Europe together in a unified front. Its disappearance has created a power vacuum and reopened old wounds as France and Germany, both superlatively Napoleonic nations, fight once again over no other than Alsace. But countries like France and Germany are the first ones to know how far they are both ready to go in their fight for national supremacy, and the successful killing of 800 million Chinese people has only unlocked new potential for a creative use of epidemics. A worldwide convention is called in a hurry, and "all nations solemnly pledg[e] themselves never to use against one another the laboratory methods of warfare they had employed in the invasion of China" (London 1993, 1245). The apparent earnestness of the wish for peace and the professed universal concern of all nations for a lasting peace bring them to pledge an oath that isn't without side-glances at each other. In the wake of the realization of their own power, Western countries themselves seem to see the very breaking of this non-aggression pact as only a matter of time.

Indeed, the peace will not last. According to Lawrence Berkove "every reader of this story at all familiar with history is fully aware of how bogus and futile such non-aggression pledges have always been" (Berkove 1992, 38). The mere fact that the situation between France and Germany requires a pact of this nature is a sure giveaway of its tenuous strength. The story ends on this oath, with no comment or follow-up on the subsequent events, underlining its ominousness. To quote Lawrence Berkove's analysis once last time, "what started out as Mervin's glorification of one of the West's finest hours ends, unintentionally, as an exposure of its duplicity" (Berkove 1992, 38).

"War is today the final arbiter in the affairs of men, and it is as yet the final test of the worthwhile-ness of peoples" (London 1910, 269). Jack London wrote in "The Yellow Peril." Whether those words are meant to ring with wistfulness, resignation or irony, they appear less as his personal opinion than an acknowledgment of the state of the world as he sees it in 1904.

This is in part why he wrote this strange little tale, half parable and half warning. In "The Unparalleled Invasion," London anticipated, not only the emergence of China as an economic and demographic superpower, but also as a contender for world power and a disruptive challenger to the Western way of thinking. But he also predicted the increasing use of biological weapons in war—a practice that took its first modern steps in World War I, just a few years after the publication of *The Strength of the Strong*.

More importantly, he saw unprecedented power wielded by the West over Eastern nations, with no hesitation, no restraint and no remorse. The choice of science-fiction, a genre born of fantasy and logic, and the unusual format of a fictional historical entry mixing both realistic events and a strong emotional presence, show enough that London considered his premonition to be both an extreme and a plausible one. Sadly, he was proven right, not in the immediate Great War, but 40 years later, as the United States dropped the atomic bomb on the Japanese cities of Hiroshima and Nagasaki on 6 and 9 of August 1945.

London's astonishing foresight on the extent of Western countries' potential for brutal panic when cornered, and his unrelenting irony regarding the legitimacy of their actions, prove that he believed the most destructive force on Earth to be none other than the Western way of thinking.

Notes

1. Dooner quoted by Wu.
2. Woltor quoted by Wu.
3. Mundi quoted by Wu.

Works Cited

Berkove, Lawrence I. 1992. "A Parallax Correction in London's 'The Unparalleled Invasion.'" *American Literary Realism*, 1870–1910, Vol. 24, No. 2 (Winter), 33–39.

Berliner, Jonathan. 2008 "Jack London's Socialistic Social Darwinism." *American Literary Realism*, Vol. 41, No. 1 (Fall), 52–78.

Campbell-Reesman, Jeanne. 2009. *Jack London's Racial Lives: A Critical Biography*. Athens: University of Georgia Press.

Clarke, F. 1996. "The Origins of Future War Fiction." *Science Fiction Studies*, Vol. 23, No. 3 (Nov.), 546–548.

Hong Sonn, Stephen. 2008 "Alien/Asian: Imagining the Racialized Future." *Melus*, Vol. 33, No. 4 (Winter), 5–22.

London, Jack. 1910. *Revolution and Other Essays*. New York: Macmillan.

_____. 1914. *The Strength of the Strong*. Project Gutenberg.

_____. 1993. *The Complete Short Stories of Jack London, Vol.2*. Stanford: Stanford University Press.

_____. 2008. *The Radical Jack London: Writings on War and Revolution*. Berkeley: University of California Press.

Lye, Colleen. 2005. *America's Asia. Racial Form and American Literature, 1893–1945*. Princeton, NJ: Princeton University Press.

Metraux, Daniel. 2009. *The Asian Writings of Jack London: Essays, Letters, Newspaper Dispatches, and Short Fiction*. Lewiston, NY: Edwin Mellen Press.

_____. 2009. "'Beware the Monkey Cage': Jack London and the Yellow Peril." East-West Connections: *Review of Asian Studies*, Vol. 9(1), p. 44 (20).

Monty Python. 1989. *Monty Python Sings*. Virgin.

Raskin, Jonah. 2008. *The Radical Jack London: Writings on War and Revolution*. Berkeley: University of California Press.

Reider, John. 2008. *Colonialism and the Emergence of Science Fiction*. Middletown: Wesleyan University Press.

Reitherman, Wolfgang, Dir. 1963. *The Sword in the Stone*. Disney. Film.

Shelley, Mary. 1993. *Frankenstein or the Modern Prometheus*. London: William Pickering.

Swift, John N. 2002. "Jack London's 'The Unparalleled Invasion': Germ Warfare, Eugenics, and Cultural Hygiene." *American Literary Realism*, Vol. 35, No. 1 (Fall), 59–71.

Wu, William F. 1982. *The Yellow Peril: Chinese Americans in American Fiction, 1850–1940*. Hamden, CT: Archon Books.

PART III

Cold War and Post–9/11

Waging Metaphorical Warfare in Feminist Dystopian and Utopian Writing[1]

NAOMI R. MERCER

In the 1970s feminist utopian texts, many authors carried the Cold War and its threat of nuclear annihilation to its logical conclusion by depicting post-apocalyptic societies that seized the opportunity to build egalitarian communities.[2] In contrast, some of the dystopian novels of the 1980s and beyond reproduced traditional gender roles in extremis. While texts from both the utopian moment during the Second Wave feminist movement and dystopian turn that occurred during the backlash against feminist gains (Fitting 1990, 141) show us possibilities and warnings for our future as a result of physical warfare, many of these novels also depict a metaphorical war against pervasive kyriarchal systems of oppression—most recently manifested in the current political climate as the "War on Women." However, I argue that the metaphorical warfare carried out in these texts demonstrate that the War on Women is just as insidious and catastrophic as nuclear holocaust—and has been ever-present in American culture from the post–World War II era. We see feminist dystopian and utopian writers' responses to the War on Women most frequently portrayed in feminist utopian and dystopian writing as metaphorical warfare on misogynist cultures.

For more than a century, the utopian genre has functioned as means for women to imagine futures in which women are the equals of men and recognized as fully human. Frequently, the trends in feminist utopian writing have closely matched the political climate of American society, including periods of feminist activism and the subsequent resistance to the "perception" of advancements toward women's equality, resulting in "backlashes" against women (Faludi 1991, xix).[3] During the 1970s, at the height of the women's movement, feminist utopian writing proliferated as well, from Marge Piercy to Sally Miller Gearheart to Suzy McKee Charnas. Feminist authors interrogated ideas of worlds with equality and often without men, endorsing the theory that women could only gain true freedom and complete personhood in men's absence. The resurgence of a backlash in the 1980s and the heightening of Cold War militarization wrought changes in the feminist movement, and new texts emerged to challenge the idea of separatism as well as continuing to confront kyriarchal norms in American society.

While women struggled for equality and their own empowerment, men wrestled with, and resisted, negotiating their traditional presumptions to power, particularly through violence and warfare. Conversely, however, male writers did not participate in the feminist trend in utopian writing other than depicting futuristic male-dominated societies that reproduced, sometimes viciously, kyriarchal norms. Female-dominated societies in texts written by men fared no better. Male authors' lack of participation in imagining egalitarian utopian communities during the 1970s and 80s, with the notable exception of Samuel R. Delaney's *Trouble on Triton* (1976), may indicate resistance to the changes proposed and agitated for by the Second Wave of feminism and the real changes going on in women's lives. This lack of participation may also merely indicate another facet of a more universal reaction against the feminist movement as it gained momentum in U.S. society. This reaction has resulted in the rise of Men's Rights Activists (MRAs), who are primarily white men bent on jealously guarding their gender entitlement,[4] and has also morphed into the War on Women in American society, seen in rape culture and the multitudes of legal actions aimed at curtailing women's rights, particularly reproductive rights and bodily autonomy.[5]

Justine Larbalestier's *The Battle of the Sexes in Science Fiction* (2002) is a survey of war between the sexes type of stories in science fiction from 1926 through the end of the 20th century. Using Joanna Russ's *"Amor Vincit Foeminam"* as a spring board, Larbalestier notes that science fiction has a long-standing tradition of "engagement with feminism, sexual difference, and sex and sexuality" (Larbalestier 2002, xi). Larbalestier, following from Russ, contends that this "sex war" between genders, which fiction authors generally reduce to a gender binary, "posits as a solution to this conflict that women accept their position as subordinate to men" (Larbalestier 2002, 1). Larbalestier's critical accounting of "the battle of the sexes" focuses primarily on anti-feminist types of stories, to include gender-role reversal scenarios that, unless halted, do not have optimistic indications for humanity's future. *The Battle of the Sexes in Science Fiction* is an important contribution to science fiction criticism, especially since Larbalestier traces the historical roots of the "debates about the place of women in the field" of science fiction (Larbalestier 2002, xii), the "formation of contemporary feminist science fiction," and establishes that gender concerns have always-already inhabited the genre (Larbalestier 2002, 2). Moreover, as Russ argues in "*Amor Vincit Foeminam*," these "battles," this war between men and women, are constituted more by the "long one-sided massacre" of women in service to "male supremacy" (Larbalestier 2002, 13). In that vein, I am inclined to view this "sex war" as journalist Valerie Tarico has succinctly labeled it instead: an assault on women rather than a war at all. Tarico explains that "[i]n wars, both sides are armed. Soldiers are comrades whose loyalty to each other trumps all else. They are taught to dehumanize their enemies. They come home heroes. They get medals." Assault, on the other hand, is the realm of perpetrators and victims who frequently cannot or will not fight back. Assault consists of the actions of individuals enabled by systemic oppression toward their victims and is clearly "one-sided" in nature (Tarico 2015). Labels notwithstanding, however, the alliteration of "War on Women" is much more catchy and well-known in the media. While I grant Tarico's point that the term "war" elides to some extent the nature of the "long, one-sided massacre" of gender relations in U.S. society, I want to also acknowledge how feminist science fiction engages in metaphorical warfare, how some writers envision women as fighting back, and how the texts themselves do just that. I also recognize that these texts perpetuate gender essentialism by ascribing violent tendencies primarily to men, or write against such gender essentialism.

My purpose, unlike Larbalestier's, is less broad. I am interested in how the feminist utopian and dystopian novels, from the 1970s to the present moment, treat warfare. I take a two-pronged approach to this topic. First, I explore some texts, such as *A Door into Ocean* (1986), *The Wanderground: Stories of the Hill Women* (1976), *Outlander: Captivity* (1989), and *Les Guérillères* (1971), that depict, or at the very least mention, war between the utopian (or dystopian) community and some other entity that attacks the community on the basis of gender or gendered assumptions. Second, and here my two-pronged approach becomes significantly intertwined, I examine how these texts and the communities they depict respond to the ideological War on Women on a metaphorical level, engaging the issue of male aggression.

"Death-dealing rays": Physical Warfare in Feminist Utopian Writing

In addition to her argument in "*Amor Vincit Foeminam*," Russ contends in "Recent Feminist Utopias" that "the violence that does occur in these stories … is that of ideological skirmish, natural disaster, social collapse, and/or something that may have occurred in the past but is not happening in the present.... None are dramatically full-scale shooting wars and none are central to the plot of the story" (Russ "Recent" 2000, 75–6). Perhaps one of the most notable exceptions to Russ's claims that the feminist utopian writing of the 1970s tends to wage ideological warfare rather than physical warfare is Monique Wittig's *Les Guérillères*. Wittig's *elles* do engage in physical war and use conventional weapons to kill their (male) oppressors, yet in their battles, the women seem to have all the strategic advantages. More intriguing is their use of unconventional weapons: baring their breasts as a sign of aggression (Wittig 1971, 99–100); dancing and stamping their feet in war games that seem to be more predicated on fun than killing anyone (Wittig 1971, 99) while their "victim[s] writhe on the ground" (Wittig 1971, 120); confiscating rifles and other armaments (Wittig 1971, 85) and burying them (Wittig 1971, 127); and using mirrors to communicate that also have "death-dealing rays" (Wittig 1971, 120). When men look in the mirrors that *elles* hold up, seeing the reality of who they are as oppressors becomes the "death-dealing ray" that reflects the men back at their actual size rather than as their egos and entitlement have previously projected men to themselves. The women's violence also takes the form of destroying the language of kyriarchy and writing it anew. In fact, as feminist utopian scholar Frances Bartkowski observes, "the women warriors learn the 'ancient text' of history the better to overthrown them" (Bartkowski 1989, 42). In effect, *elles* use the "master's tools"—language and (strategically applied) violence—to "dismantle the master's house." However, the women use acts of violence in order to end the "battle of the sexes" permanently, so that "all trace of violence must disappear from this earth" (Wittig 1971, 127).

Because of the presence of the metaphorical war waged through the dismantling of and reinvention of language without its kyriarchal baggage, Wittig's text wages war on multiple levels. The "death blood blood burn death war war war..." (Wittig 1971, 64) warning of the horrific conditions of physical war echoes in the women's redefinition of childbirth as inherently warlike. For example, "[w]hen the child is born the midwife begins to utter cries like women who fight in battle. This means that the mother has conquered as a warrior and that she has captured a child ... women with mouths wide open, screaming, squatting, the child's head between their thighs" (Wittig 1971, 72). The ultimate goal to end violence, the reinvention of language to encompass women's experiences, and the use of mirrors and other unconventional weapons exhibit a multi-faceted utopian impulse. Jamie Davis's essay, "Utopia in Blood," makes a similar observation: "although Wittig does deploy highly graphic depictions of war itself in *Les Guérillères*, and mangled corpses, calls to arms and sinister and bloody battles do abound in the text, these marks of destruction are not blemishes, but ultimately indicate, much to the contrary, signs of hope" (Davis 2002, 27). All of these metaphorical warfare maneuvers in *Les Guérillères* combine to offer alternatives to fighting back against the War on Women.

Joanna Russ's hybrid utopian-dystopian novel, *The Female Man* (1975), reveals, over the course of the narrative, that the utopian Whileaway resulted from physical warfare waged by the segregated "Womanland" against "Manland." Jael tells Joanna, Janet, and Jeannine that "there was only one war left" (Russ "Female" 2000, 164) and she means to see an end to the 40 years of gender warfare. Other than Jael's slaughter of the "boss" she had a mission to assassinate, this gender war is somewhat peripheral and distant in the text until the last chapter of the novel. In these last scenes, Jael tells an unbelieving Janet that the plague in Whileaway's history that had destroyed men was actually Jael's gender war that "gave [Whileaway] a thousand years of peace and love and the Whileawayan flowers nourish themselves on the bones of the men we have slain" (Russ "Female" 2000, 211). It would seem that in Russ's imaginary, women waged the physical warfare to ultimately defeat men and establish a lesbian-separatist utopia; however, duels are common so perhaps Whileaway is not quite violence free without the presence of men.

The majority of the text, particularly when Janet first comes to Joanna's present-day reality of the 1970s, focuses on the physical and ideological warfare that men have been waging against women since time immemorial. The text pokes fun at the social constructions of masculinity and femininity, the privileging of male traits, names, bodies, etc., as superior. Yet the comedic tone is exceedingly serious in its commentary on the inequality of half the population—deadly serious once the reader learns of how millennia of subjugation of women eventually results in the violent annihilation of men. Feminist science fiction critic Dunja M. Mohr argues in *Worlds Apart: Dualism and Transgression in Contemporary Female Dystopias* that feminist dystopian writing demonstrates "the oppression of women [carried] to a logical extreme" (Mohr 2005, 36), which we readily see in the dystopias depicted in *The Handmaid's Tale* (1984), *Walk to the End of the World* (1974), *Swastika Night* (1937), *Native Tongue* (1984), and *The Terrorists of Irustan* (1999), among many others. Women in these dystopian settings have been reduced to the status of chattel, slaves, and minor children, completely controlled by powerful men. Yet I propose another logical extreme: that an oppressed group may rise up against their oppressors and seek revenge along with their own liberation. That revenge may very well result in not just the oppression of the original oppressors, but in their extermination.

"Absence" of Physical War After Catastrophe

Perhaps the possibility of extermination, or at least an apocalyptic holocaust that destroys the structure and engines of civilization, offers the best framework for rebuilding the world anew, particularly for societies to practice gender equality. Much of the feminist utopian writing from the 1970s predicates their utopian communities on rampant plagues, nuclear holocausts, environmental degeneration, and the widening economic gaps between those with money, and the power that accrues to it, and those without. Scholars John Beck and Mark Dorrian write that:

> any project that is able to rewrite catastrophe as survival opens up the possibility of a postcatastrophic utopia where the conditions of life, far from being at the mercy of toxic or violent agencies, can instead be engineered from the outset to expand rather than diminish the prospects for life. Even the most dread-infused project devised to escape certain death carries with it the germ of a genuinely apocalyptic utopianism inasmuch as it offers the creative possibility of a life beyond [Beck and Dorrian 2014, 133].

But major catastrophes also open up the possibility of dystopia. The 1980s dystopian turn, while admittedly following the political backlash against women's perceived gains in social and legal power at the time, is populated with communities that oppress women in much the same ways women have always been oppressed, but more explicitly, and that the 1970s utopian communities had seemed to overthrow. Beck and Dorrian also contend that even in "the darkest imaginings of a world on the threshold of annihilation, a yearning for renewal through containment and control can be discerned—a yearning that has, in turn, animated large-scale projects designed to circumvent catastrophe since at least the Cold War and that connects … the nuclear era with a much longer tradition of utopian wish-fulfillment underpinned by colonial violence and appropriation" (Beck and Dorrian 2014, 133). As I have argued elsewhere, traditional utopian writing by men tends to focus on control and conformity rather than egalitarianism (Mercer 2015, 1); this "yearning" for control of the Other results in the colonialism that Beck and Dorrian identify and the systemic and overt oppression of women that feminist dystopian writers recognize and attempt to subvert.

For example, in Margaret Atwood's *The Handmaid's Tale*, nuclear holocaust and the resulting environmental toxicity have produced widespread infertility. The fundamentalist and militarized state of Gilead has subsequently enacted the extreme subjugation of women through their confinement to the domestic sphere, state-sanctioned rape, and the valuing of women purely for their reproductive capacities. War rages somewhere beyond the confines of Cambridge, Massachusetts, where the protagonist of the novel, Offred, serves as a "Handmaid," but physical war is evident almost everywhere: if the men are not "Commanders" in the military and government, they are "Guardians" who are part of the uniformed police force and evidence of the conscription of all men into some sort of militarized service, if not direct combat. Offred mentions "Angels," or the combat soldiers, though she rarely sees them except at ceremonial gatherings such as a mass wedding, and the conspicuous absence of wounded or disabled Angels is most telling in their lack of presence in the small area to which Offred's paucity of freedom limits her. Perhaps more disturbing is the threat of the "Colonies" of "Unwomen": the areas on the periphery of Gilead where the regime sends infertile or otherwise troublesome women and gay men to work to their deaths in nuclear waste dumps.

Similar to *The Handmaid's Tale*, in Suzy McKee Charnas's novel, *Walk to the End of the World*, the world has been devastated by nuclear war and women have been reduced to slaves, used as breeders for the next generation of men and exploited for their labor while older men wield power and privilege in the Holdfast and younger men need only wait, suffering their own exploitation though less so than the "fems," until they come of age and join the elite class. The fems grow up in "kit pits" that enforce a survival-of-the-fittest divisiveness among the female children, and all fems subsist on the nutrition of "curdcakes" made from the breast milk of lactating fems. Some men keep fems as "pets," and all men revile the fems as sub-human even as they carry out their own sentences in the "breeding rooms," raping fems to impregnate them. If these conditions are not horrific enough, one male character goes even further and plots to use "throwback" or less desirable fems for food other than a small group to keep for breeding purposes (Charnas 1999, 205–6). While I have argued elsewhere that the utopian impulse tends to be much stronger in feminist dystopian writing than in feminist utopian writing (Mercer 2015, 3), the nightmarish qualities of the dystopian societies in these feminist texts are chilling and depressing commentary on the state of contemporary American society.

However, both Offred and the fem Alldera eventually escape Gilead and the Holdfast, respectively. Atwood leaves Offred's ultimate fate, other than the recording of her experiences as a Handmaid, ambiguous and unknown. Furthermore, the academic conference in the "Historical Notes" at the end of *The Handmaid's Tale* demonstrates that very little has changed in gender relations, despite drastic climate change, the rise and fall of regimes like Gilead, and the movement of people of color from the margins to the center. Alldera, however, finds the Riding Women and Free Fems in Charnas's sequel, *Motherlines* (1978). The utopian community of the Riding Women fits many of Russ's qualities of feminist utopias from her essay "Recent Feminist Utopias," such as communal living or focus on family units as the base of society; concern with ecology; lack of class distinctions; simple assumptions that gender stereotypes do not apply; sexual permissiveness; physical freedom to live and travel safely; freedom to pursue any kind of job regardless of gender; and female bonding and friendship (Russ "Recent" 2000, 73–80).

The Riding Women have skirmishes among themselves, mostly stealing horses as a rite of passage for young women, but do not engage the men of the Holdfast from their tribal, nomadic communities on the steppes beyond the wilderness area that separates them. More locally, the Riding Women are waging an ideological war with the Free Fems—fems who escaped the Holdfast but continue to reproduce kyriarchal structures in their microcosm of existence rather than copying the egalitarian patterns of the Riding Women or trying to join them. The Riding Women do not participate in the fems' revolt against the men of the Holdfast in *The Furies* (1994) but do maintain contact with the Free Fems and visit the Holdfast once the Free Fems have defeated the men. The Free Fems, unfortunately, reverse the power structure and turn men into slaves to exploit their labor and use for breeding purposes. The ideological warfare carries into the final book of the series, *The Conqueror's Child* (1999), when Alldera's daughter, Sorrel, attempts to reconcile with her mother and to find a middle ground between the misogyny of the Holdfast and the misandry of the Free Fems. Although a physical war takes place in the series, the ideological warfare is the central focus of the plotlines and the texts' argument for a society based on gender equality.

"Women's long revolution": Physical Warfare in Feminist Dystopian Writing

Even though in 2015 most women feminists value working with men and do not perceive men as a group to be the enemy, in this period, conceptually, a war between the genders seemed normal and gave rise to some of the Second Wave feminist movement's best fiction. The peripheral nature of physical warfare in feminist utopian and some feminist dystopian writing makes it easy to elide; yet where physical warfare is present, so too is ideological warfare. This is evident in various novels: *The Wanderground: Stories of the Hill Women* by Sally Miller Gearhart, *Woman on the Edge of Time* (1976) by Marge Piercy, *Outlander: Captivity* (1989) by B.J. Salterberg, and *A Door into Ocean* (1986) by Joan Slonczewski. Each of these novels contains a feminist utopic community, but the novels themselves are hybrids of utopia and dystopia which form an abiding part of the ideological wars waged inside and outside of the texts: the dystopian elements, so much like our own society and communities, threaten utopian possibilities and must be defended against.

Utopian societies in some of the feminist texts are more likely to wage ideological warfare with another group than to engage in physical warfare that results in deaths, injuries, and collateral damage to their communities and eco-systems. Ideological warfare tends to entail teaching other cultures and societies to put aside social constructions of gender, helping women and men to realize their full potential as human beings, and may involve inviting outsiders into the utopian community or converting them to the utopian ideals through community members' behavior when away from the utopian society. Frequently the relative isolation of the utopian community precludes their involvement in physical warfare, but sometimes the less-removed societies must invoke a self-defensive posture to stave off a physical attack by an invading force that is opposed to the communities' utopian precepts.

In *The Wanderground: Stories of the Hill Women*, this self-defensive posture takes the form of the women of the forests reinforcing their psychic network and connection to Mother Earth, as well as forging an alliance with gay men, to prevent the men of the cities from invading the women's preserve, capturing and enslaving them. The Earth itself has revolted against the misogyny and ecological pollution present in kyriarchal societies. Men find themselves confined to the cities and unable to exist in the woods in communion with nature. Women, on the other hand, can move freely in the wild and have learned to respect nature and the environment, to the point that they can reproduce parthenogenically and have developed psychic powers. Feminist science fiction scholar Natalie Rosinsky contends that "Gearhart's text differs from traditional depictions of gender warfare in its portrayal of [the Hill] women as 'resisters and watchers ... as defensive observors [sic]' rather than as warriors" (Bowman 1984, 79). Initially, the Earth's rejection of technology and environmental degeneration seems necessary for the women who escape to the wilds of the Wanderground to become confident, fully-realized human beings. Gay men, called "gentles" in the text, have acted as allies in the cities—helping women escape the cities and helping women from the Wanderground to covertly gather information about the status of women. The war they fight seems to not concern strikes or shows of force but rather a continual undermining of the men's power in the cities and their control of women.

However, one of the central questions of the novel concerns whether men and women can ever live together in harmony with each other and with nature. When the gentles also develop psychic powers, though their powers require a group of them touching in order to work while the women's psychic powers are solely exercised by individuals, some of the women do not want to accept the gentles as also being in communion with the Earth. Furthermore, operatives from the cities report that conditions are worsening for women still there while others spot men outside the cities in the borderlands where the men are able to rape women—a situation that seems to indicate the Earth's revolt has taken a negative turn. Nature had seemed to be on the women's side, but these factors indicate that segregation is still a bankrupt idea in American society.

Rather, now that women have had time and space to develop themselves, away from the social norms that constantly define them as inferior, the time seems nigh, much as in our own historical moment, for men and women to negotiate an egalitarian society that may no longer require gender segregation. Rosinsky views this development in the narrative as a "composite view of feminism in conflict" (Rosinsky 1984, 90). The ideological war, in *The Wanderground*, seems to go both ways: men, who have not changed substantively from traditional misogyny, and women who, more like younger feminists today, no longer internalize kyriarchal inferiority, must now navigate how to fully restore the Earth's ecological balance and permanently establish gender equality in the Wanderground and in the cities. Both sides must change, though clearly, *The Wanderground* acknowledges that men may have more dramatic changes to affect in their socialization, performance of masculinity, and exercise of power.

The utopian communities in *Woman on the Edge of Time* do present an exception among the 1970s texts in that community members volunteer for military service and engage in physical warfare with another society bent on destroying them, pointing prophetically to the engagement of women in combat in modern armies. In the era of feminist utopian texts, women did not often appear in popular culture as warriors, fighters, or killers.[6] In *Woman on the Edge of Time* specifically, the battle front appears quite far removed from the utopian communities, and the war largely does not interfere with everyday life—at least not until Jackrabbit, a particularly beloved character, dies during his military service. Piercy does not give the reader a glimpse into his life (or death) fighting against Mattapoisett's enemies, but rather shows his friends celebrating his life, mourning his death, and attempting to make meaning of it (Piercy 1976, 301–19).

While the text refers to military service as going "on defense" (Piercy 1976, 266), Connie comes to the realization that one of the strategies for winning what she thinks of as "Luciente's war" depends on her actions in the present in order to prevent "the other world that might come to be" (Piercy 1976, 295) and preserve the future Mattapoisett and other utopian communities. Connie ultimately kills the doctors and destroys the research they have conducted into forms of mind-control that would bring about not the reality of Mattapoisett, but a dystopian future where women are used as sex toys, surgically altered to fit an exaggerated feminine standard of beauty, and kept quiescent through psychotropic drugs. Yet these physical manifestations of war in the text do not give a complete picture of the metaphorical warfare also taking place.

A major component of utopian texts is parenthood as a universalized experience, not merely the realm of women as the expected, and frequently under-appreciated, childcare providers, but a process shared among communities' members. In cultural anthropologist Susan Lees' article, "Motherhood in Utopia," she presents two theories of maternity that emerge from her survey of 1970s feminist utopian texts. Lees notes that in the first theory, the utopian societies merely equalize the distribution of "tasks and responsibilities associated with caring for children and seeks to relieve women of the unjust burden they bear in this regard" (Lees 1984, 219) so that women and men are co-parents, or the community raises all children together in dormitories rather than in separate family units. The other theory posits that the utopian societies attempt to "universalize the social benefits of maternal experience" (Lees 1984, 219) by making everyone a parent or mother-figure. This is the case in *Woman on the Edge of Time* in which each child has three parents and two of them agree to nurse the baby, with the aid of hormones, no matter the biological gender of the parents.

In this theory, the utopian societies venerate what sociologist Pepper Schwartz labels "the siren call of motherhood" (Schwartz 1995, 161), or the intense bonding that mothers may experience with their infant children and the tendency to immerse themselves in caring for their children and ensuring their well-being. Piercy draws on Shulamith Firestone's *The Dialectic of Sex*, which brilliantly re-examines and reconstructs the basic theoretical building blocks of Marx and Freud to conclude that love is oppression and women would be more liberated without societal reliance on our wombs. In Piercy's Mattapoisett, the system of growing babies in "brooders," frees women from being "biologically enchained" and create a civilization with "no power for anyone" (Piercy 1976, 97). Lees argues that this approach to motherhood in utopian fiction includes men as equals so that they too can experience the intensity of the parent-child bond, and releases women from "sole responsibility" of caring for their children or the children of the community so that women and men have the freedom to pursue other interests. Most importantly, the real motivation behind this method lies in giving parents the "freedom to enjoy loving children" (Lees 1984, 219) removing the resentment factor because children no longer monopolize so much of one parent's, usually the mother's, time and energy.

In *Woman on the Edge of Time*, Luciente uses the phrase, "women's long revolution" (Piercy 1976, 97) to discuss how Mattapoisett society came about. This is a reference to the War on Women waged by kyriarchy: the war had to end with women fomenting a revolution—a revolution that took many years to come to fruition, so to speak, and free them from the tyranny of biology. In Piercy's imagined Mattapoisett, the War on Women ends in equality through freedom from biological imperatives and the destruction of traditional hierarchical systems but also points to the lack of equality in contemporary American society due to the existence of kyriarchal power structures that privilege (heterosexual, wealthy, white, cis-gendered, able-bodied) men. Yet, some of these ideas have moved from utopian novels into social reality as men too can take parental leave in some companies. To most women, biology is no longer a tyranny and women have more freedoms now than in the 1970s. However, the pro-woman hype rooted in woman-centered counterculture of the 60s and 70s morphed into a way to market consumer products as a means of enabling women's empowerment rather than actual empowerment.

In B.J. Salterberg's *Outlander: Captivity*, physical warfare between men and women is explicitly present in the text. At face value, this novel seems to depict merely a reversal of the 1930s pulp science fiction texts and 1950s B-movies such as "I Married a Martian from Outer Space," in which men capture women for breeding purposes. While the women's community in this 1980s text reproduces, to a certain extent, the separatism of 1970s feminist texts in its liminal qualities, i.e., containment within finite walls or boundaries and partial if not complete segregation of the sexes, the women train constantly for battle. The women leave their walled compounds in a mostly geographically protected area mainly to defend themselves from attacks by the male army. The narrative opens with Konnor, an officer from the army, realizing that he is a captive of the women's community. The women's community, recovering from a plague and other calamities, is greatly in need of fertile men and Konnor finds himself assigned to the household of Meagar and her women warriors. The narrative follows Konnor as he negotiates his place in the household and Meagar as she experiments with integrating a man from a misogynist institution that trains men to hate her kind into the women's society.

The women have developed a female-dominated society in reaction to male violence perpetuated against them. During a nuclear holocaust in their history, a group of women raped by the invading army found refuge in a valley with a woman who bred dogs. The women trained themselves and the dogs to defend the valley and became skilled warriors who periodically fended off attacks by the invading army, which remain camped on the plains below. Some of the women had children as results of their rapes, graphically raising some of today's concerns in conservative challenges to abortion and reproductive rights. The women raised the girls as warriors, leaders and decision-makers, and raised the boys as inferior beings in order to ensure that the boys would not develop aggressive tendencies nor ever try to force themselves on the women of the community.

The narrative reveals two distinct, yet interlocking, social constructions of women perpetuated in the army of men: that women are objects for men's pleasure, and that women who fight back and reject that objectification are evil, an attitude that makes women hesitant to declare their feminism even today. In the novel, the women's community has carefully cultivated its image as a group of Amazons, ensuring that women can defend themselves against rape and assault and engage in combat. The women also, in the beginning of their society, cultivated the fierce image they present to the army to strike fear into the psyches of their would-be attackers by castrating the men they killed and sending the mutilated bodies back to the army. Perhaps a comment on Freud's discussion of male castration anxiety and its absurdity, this aspect of the text literalizes the categorizing of women as "castrating bitches" when they seek equality. As a consequence of the women's actions in the novel, the army continues to circulate wild stories, especially among cadets in training, that claim the women will castrate the soldiers if they are captured and will mutilate their bodies before floating the corpses down the river for the army to retrieve and bury. This propaganda serves multiple purposes for the army by ensuring that the soldiers will fight to the death rather than face capture, keeps the soldiers from questioning too closely why the army does not overrun this sworn enemy but merely sends semi-annual raids of cadets and troublemakers against the women to winnow the cowards out of the army's ranks, and soldiers who fear the "vile ones" are less likely to grow sympathetic to them and defect to the women's community.

The army's treatment of the women in the surrounding concentration camps, which resembles the treatment of women in Bosnia and Kosovo and other historical realities and not solely in feminist imaginary, exemplifies the social construction that men are fierce soldiers with entitlements to women's bodies which can be bought and sold, used or tossed away as the whim takes them. The women of the camps, in contrast to the women's community, are not women to be feared but objectified. As Konnor tells Meager, "the women in those concentration camps, the women who work the canteens, are objects—no more—to be used, to satisfy a man's lust" (Salterberg 1989, 231). The army views all the women in the camps as prostitutes and controls them accordingly: they objectify the women, among which the officers, or those with higher status in the hierarchy, retain the privilege of first choice for sexual partners similar to accounts of Holocaust survivors subjected to rape by their Nazi captors.

From a legalistic standpoint, the women could whip Konnor into submission or kill him with impunity if Konnor proves recalcitrant or acts aggressively toward any of them once he becomes a member of their household. More importantly, the women possess the training, confidence in their abilities, and physical fitness needed to survive hand-to-hand combat situations against larger and stronger adversaries. The text does not presume that all women have the capability to become stronger than all men; instead, the text acknowledges that for the women to best the men of the army on the battlefield, not only must the women develop their physical strength but must also use their intellect and special techniques to defeat their opponents in the shortest amount of time.

In some respects, *Outlander: Captivity* also reproduces the gender-role-reversal of many of the texts that Larbalestier and Russ discuss in their scholarship. However, through the auspices of gender-role reversal, this text exposes the social constructions of American society that classify women as inferior human beings because of perceived physical weakness. Salterberg's novel is entirely feminist in that rather than re-establishing the status quo with either the "defeat" of the women's community through force or their "conversion" to femininity through sexual coercion at the end of the novel, Meagar's family manages to resocialize Konnor into accepting gender equality. Significantly, Meagar's family undergoes resocialization themselves by beginning to treat the men in their household as more like human beings than breeding stock. The metaphorical warfare performed in the text through resocialization of women and men demonstrates the workings of kyriarchal ideology and feminist theory's subversion of misogyny.[7]

Physical warfare is a feature, too, of Joan Slonczewski's *A Door into Ocean*; however, the physical warfare ends as a result of ideological warfare—strangely enough, psychological warfare that the oppressors impose on themselves. Valans, the kyriarchal aggressors of the utopic Sharers or women's community on Shora withdraw out of fear that the women, who have developed superior technological advances in biology and other natural sciences, will release a plague on their army, and may have already done so. The Sharers, of course, have no such intentions, but the Valan leaders' trepidations of taking a virus back to their home planet and unleashing a plague on an unwitting populace forces them ultimately to seek peace—a peace that they had disrupted in the first place due to their own greed and thirst for power.

The actual ideological warfare waged in the text is one of pacifism against military and any other kind of violence. The Sharers have developed a society where all action is shared; thus, anything a person does to someone else has repercussions for the person doing the action. Even in their language, Sharers lacks subjects and objects making power relationships impossible. The Valan military leaders who invade Shora do come to understand that the Sharers see themselves as part of a web that encompasses all of biological life (and the Sharers come to understand that stone or other inorganic material is not necessarily "dead"). One of the military leaders wisely observes, "Sharers never take *any* action toward you which they would not gladly accept for themselves"[8] (Slonczewski 1986, 349), but still fundamentally misunderstands that Sharers also see the invaders as part of the web and thus would not actively harm them. Instead, the military leaders believe that they have no place in the web of life and Sharers view them as useless. As a result, the Valans project their own murderous intentions, or "sickness," onto the Sharers, thinking that the Sharers will commit genocide through a biological plague.

The non-hierarchical nature of Sharer society also contributes to the success of its non-violent stance. One of the Valan generals believes that by capturing and breaking the will of the Sharer he identifies as the "leader," he will destroy the Sharers' resistance to the invasion. Realgar is wrong on two counts: he cannot break a Sharer who is willing to die rather than engage in violence, and the Sharers' decentralized organization is not vulnerable to the loss of any one person. Sharers assure their succession of leadership because they distribute leadership horizontally—everyone is a leader and takes part—rather than vertically, leaving major decisions in the hands of the most powerful few.

A Door into Ocean presents, in many ways, an iconic feminist utopian community in the Sharers. The text itself is a hybrid between the utopic community and the dystopian advent of the Valans threatening that community with destruction through military invasion. The physical warfare in the text ultimately is less important than the ideological warfare that the text itself wages: that human beings are part of the web that unites all living things, including the eco-system of the planet we inhabit. *A Door into Ocean* serves as a metaphor that demonstrates how the relationship between humans and the environment is crucial for the deconstruction of binaries and the advancement of gender equality.[9] In *A Door into Ocean*, the War on Women is simultaneously literal, through the war on women/Sharers, and figurative, through the argument the text makes for eco-feminist egalitarianism against millennia of kyriarchal oppression, colonial aggression, and worldwide pollution.

The War on Women is simultaneously literal and figurative, in much the same ways, in Starhawk's *The Fifth Sacred Thing* (1993). In this hybrid text, a military force threatens the utopic community of San Francisco in a future, drought-ridden California. The utopic community practices pacifism and connection to the environment and all life forms like the Sharers in *Door*, and with many of the same elements of spiritual connection (the "fifth sacred thing" is spirit; air, fire, water, and earth are the other four). *The Fifth Sacred Thing* also explores the themes of non-violence in the face of catastrophic climate change and how the exercise of power leads to gender inequality and other kinds of oppression. The denizens of San Francisco slowly begin to win over individual soldiers from the invading army, through ideological warfare, until the army units eventually turn upon each other and either flee or destroy themselves in the chaos of mutiny.

The ideological components of the novel show concern that a reversal of power—turning their community into a matriarchy—is not truly egalitarian. This community is a representative democracy—representative of people as well as of concepts and values. Their council also includes a representative from a tribe of misfits who do not live in the city proper and do not necessarily espouse the same values of environmentalism and pacifism—yet this tribe has a voice and can express their dissent or agreement in the process of reaching consensus with the other council members. The inhabitants of San Francisco come to understand, over the course of the novel, that they must reach out to groups in more oppressed and vulnerable positions outside of their community as well as continue to refine their own governance. When their community first formed, only women representatives were elected to the defense committee—after millennia of wars and violence perpetrated primarily by men, the community wanted change. The text demonstrates that not only does kyriarchy explicitly damage women, but is perhaps just as damaging, in less overt ways, to men as the perpetrators of violence. However, they come to realize that excluding men categorically from the most powerful part of their council is biological essentialism that reproduces kyriarchal oppression, albeit on a small scale, and the community resolves to rectify their past mistake. The War on Women cannot, by default, become a war on men at any level.

The utopic community in *Raising the Stones* (1990) is based, simply enough, on empathy and understanding through connection, and shows utopia as a continual process of refinement and contribution to common knowledge through that connection, therefore rejecting violence. The Voorstoders who invade Hobbs Land with a stolen, programmed army of pseudo-flesh, weaponized cyborg soldiers are combated by organic rockets propelled out of the temples on Hobbs Land. Ironically, after being coated with fungus spores released from the rockets, the Voorstoders and their cyborg army are transformed into trees dotted over the landscape (Tepper 1990, 450). This outcome integrates quite well with Tepper's eco-feminism and the text's argument for the inter-connectedness of intelligent species with each other as well as their environment. The physical warfare is a very small part of the actual plot, but the ideological war in the text takes place primarily in response to the War on Women in contemporary American culture.

In *Raising the Stones*, Tepper depicts several societies and elicits the subtle and overt sexism in each. The Voorstoders are a fundamentalist death cult who treat women as chattel or "*merely processes by which followers may be created*"[10] (Tepper 1990, 422). Voorstoders reduce women to their reproductive capacities as a necessary evil of their culture: "*kept private, kept quiet, kept healthy until they have borne children, and then they may be disposed of*"[11] (Tepper 1990, 422). The High Baidee, another religious denomination, seem more egalitarian on the surface. However, feminist theological critiques of rabbinic commentaries on the Torah, Christian theological treatises, and explanations of Muhammad's *hadith* argue that (male) religious leaders' interpretations reproduce their own prejudices against women. Similarly, the (male) High Baidee Scrutators, or priests, insist upon interpretations that may reflect their own biases more than any "divine" revelation. This results in not only literalized interpretations of their prophet's words—whose galactic mission was to eradicate misogyny, a mission the High Baidee seem to have abandoned—but also religious hypocrisy. As the text rather scathingly makes evident: "The prophetess had declared it a sin to believe in absolute truths, but the Scrutators claimed that didn't apply to religious truths, of which they had manufactured a good supply over the centuries" (Tepper 1990, 156). The Scrutators thus justify their own rule-breaking within their religious faith and can continue to dictate religious doctrine based on literal interpretation with impunity and no input from dissenting groups, such as women.

While the inherent misogyny of the High Baidee and Voorstod societies is glaringly apparent in the text, the Hobbs' Land inhabitants seem to have achieved a degree of gender equality. Their society is matrilineal and people appear to have equal opportunities for work and leadership regardless of gender. However, Hobbs Land, at the beginning of the novel, appears to have residual kyriarchal issues, including gender, that may not be completely resolved by the end of the narrative despite Hobbs Land's utopian qualities. Writer and critic Sylvia Kelso points out what she views as "some inadvertent endorsements of gender and economic status quos" (Kelso 1997, 24) in that much of the Hobbs Land settlement leadership and Central Management, outside of one prominent female character, are male—a condition that does not change over the course of the novel. While it is possible that some of the "Topmen" are women, the use of a gendered job title hides this possibility.

More nebulous, perhaps, is Tepper's utopic vision of the family because we can read it in at least two different ways in the text. First, a matrilineal society that saddles women with sole responsibility for the care of their children with no expected support from their fathers seems similar to the stereotype of the 1950s housewife. However, the women on Hobbs Land appear to work in agricultural production in some capacity. Each settlement has a community crèche staffed by retired workers that frees up women with children who have not yet reached school age to do work outside of the home. The state of motherhood does not seem to hold women back from pursuing their career goals. For example, Africa has five children, ranging from a toddler through age 14, and being a mother seems to have had no negative effect on her advancement to Team Leader or Central Management's recognition that she is the best Team Leader in the ten settlements. Africa is obviously "Topman" material and should be leading her own settlement, indicating the location of the glass ceiling at the very top tier of settlement career opportunities. While women have sole responsibility for their children, they have communal and societal support—to a point—that allows for some semblance of balance with work outside the home, the kind of support feminists have called for in American society for generations. Despite the matrilineal custom on Hobbs Land, China Wilm calls her third child, "Sam's baby," much to her sister Africa's disapproval: "The baby could not be called Sam's baby, not in any well-managed society, but Africa did not take time to argue" (Tepper 1990, 429).

Herein lie the two different ways of reading Tepper's argument about families: on the one hand, it seems that Tepper might be re-inscribing the paradigm of the nuclear family—a paradigm that Hobbs Land had gotten away from—by China naming Sam as the father of her child and indicating an expectation that Sam will be an acknowledged part of her baby daughter's life. On the other hand, however, given the intense nature of the text's argument against patriarchal inheritance and critique of the father-son relationship through Sam's misadventures, Tepper seems to argue for a new definition of what constitutes a family. The model of the nuclear family as well as Hobbs Land's custom of women bearing sole responsibility for their children both have their disadvantages. Ultimately, the text seems to subtly call for a new pattern of family, or perhaps just a more flexible way of constituting who makes up a family. The text does not offer a model of what such a flexible pattern would look like, and this absence is perhaps the most compelling feminist argument: each family should define itself in whatever ways suit its members' needs. This ideological move, combined with the eco-feminism, interconnectedness, and peaceful resistance to warfare, constitute the metaphorical warfare that *Raising the Stones* performs in the War on Women.

"Their fear was their weakness": Power and Asymmetric Warfare in Feminist Dystopian Writing

Aside from the war-like conditions discussed in *Les Guérillères* and *The Female Man*, which are generally thought of as utopian texts despite their hybridity, some feminist dystopian texts, such as Louise Marley's *The Terrorists of Irustan*, Sheri S. Tepper's *The Gate to Women's Country* (1989), and Pamela Sargent's *The Shore of Women* (1986), portray women waging war against men. Unlike the gender-role reversals that Larbalestier and Russ have categorized, the women waging war in these texts do not demonstrate that women should not have access to power, but rather that power itself is the problem. This concept is also evident in Marge Piercy's *He, She and It*.

In *The Terrorists of Irustan*, the titular terrorists are women. The violence that the fundamentalist regime that controls Irustan, a space colony originally populated by a Muslim-like sect from Earth, and the boundary policing Irustani society exerts against women, their agency, and their bodily autonomy seems to spawn a cycle of multiplying abuses. The text raises the question of who are the real terrorists: women who act to protect themselves, their children, and subaltern Others, or the men whose cruelty and privilege keep women living in terror on a daily basis? After years of patching up battered women and sending them back to their husbands and feeling constricted by the rigid laws of her society that restrict her movement and even how she dresses in the privacy of her home, the protagonist Zahra takes action: she uses her medical knowledge to manufacture a poison that will be virtually undetected in order to kill to kill men who abuse women and children. As Zahra relates, "the women of Irustan have tolerated the abuses of such men. No matter how many sons we bear, how much work we do, how faithful we are in our prayers, we have no power, no control over our lives, no way to protect ourselves or our children or our sisters" (Marley 2000, 180). Yet Zahra and her friends do not embark on the path of murder and terrorism for themselves; like battered women who finally leave their batterers, they do so for the sake of their children (Pharr 1988, 9). Irustani women, it would seem, have enough to fear in their daily lives from the fundamentalist structure of their society; thus Zahra spares women from further terror and seeks vengeance. Significantly, Zahra chooses a malady that only affects men: she wants men to be fearful because "their fear was their weakness" (Marley 2000, 153) and she fully manipulates male fear to produce terror in the general populace.

In view of the agency denied women by the kyriarchal misogyny in Irustani society, Zahra and her accomplices certainly exercise their agency—an agency bred to violence from violence and which they view as the only means of resistance open to them. Moreover, Zahra takes incredible risks to incite fear in Irustani men; however, she wants their terrorist actions to mean something and not be dismissed as coincidence or a run of bad luck (Marley 2000, 207). As Amina Wadud observes, "[p]atriarchal control over what it means to be human robs females of their God-given agency and full humanity" (Wadud 2006, 255). Ultimately, Zahra does become a martyr, sacrificing herself in order to protect the complicity of her circle friends and her household in a final act of agency.

In some ways, Zahra and her friends' terrorism presents the perfect type of warfare: they judiciously select their targets and only harm men who have repeatedly harmed and terrorized others. Yet they do so outside of a judicial system. The physical warfare is effective in exposing, in Irustani men's distaste for bodily functions, the ideological warfare in which the text engages. The novel demonstrates Marley's deft understanding of some of the ramifications of specifically kyriocentric practices meant to shame women or imply that they are somehow impure and therefore lesser beings—an ideological stance that feminism rejects and continually struggles against.

The women's communities, inhabiting technologically advanced cities, in *The Shore of Women*, engage in limited physical warfare against men—limited primarily because the women have superior weapons, like lasers and the aircraft to deploy such weapons, while the men have bows and arrows and spears. In the text, whenever the nomadic and tribal-like men attempt to organize agrarian and herding communities, the women destroy the group and scatter the survivors to keep them in hunter-gatherer-style existences with no technological benefits. The women believe that "[m]en had used their power for evil, and the world had been devastated and poisoned in ancient times by the weapons men had controlled" (Sargent 1986, 95). The women fear that men will rise up and destroy the society of empowered women that they have built over generations, restoring men to kyriarchal power and reducing women to subservience. Men are present in this futuristic world that resembles some of the lesbian separatist utopian texts of the 1970s, rather than removed from it, but the question again arises of how to deal with aggression, violence, and the distribution of power. In other words, the women in this text legitimately fear becoming victimized by a resurrection of the War on Women.

Sargent does present a kind of gender-role-reversal story—men are associated with nature, women are associated with technology—and women do abuse their power by keeping men from developing their own civilization beyond primitive survival while also exploiting the unwitting men for their sperm in order to perpetuate humanity. However, unlike the texts that Larbalestier and Russ examine, *The Shore of Women* does not ultimately conclude that women should not have social, political, legal, or economic power. Rather, the plot follows Birana, a woman exiled from her city, and Arvil, a man who lives in the wild, and their building of a relationship free from social constructions of gender. They find equality with each other and generate an egalitarian relationship by overcoming their own pre-conceived notions about gender and by living completely removed from other social influences that would privilege one gender over the other. The text's ideological argument calls for the re-negotiation of equality free from traditional social constructions of gender and matriarchal control. Any kind of biological essentialism reproduces kyriarchal inequalities through extremism.

Physical warfare is present in *The Gate to Women's Country*, which is some way is also the most gender essentializing in ascribing violence solely to men. In the novel, Sherri S. Tepper presents a gender-segregated post-nuclear holocaust society that encourages male aggression and allows a cult of militarism to ostensibly flourish. The women's communities each have a garrison compound outside their gates for the alleged purposes of defending the women from other garrisons or marauders. However, the women's Councils manufacture wars for the garrisons to participate in, despite trade agreements and open communications between the cities, in order to further decrease the warrior population and to demonstrate to the warriors the consequences of violence and perpetuating a military cult of masculinity. As one character observes, "Warriors can't have doctors. And they must fight at close range, not at a distance. And they must see their own blood and the blood of their fellows, and they must care for their own dying and see their pain. It's part of the choice they have to make" (Tepper 1989, 128). The Councils ensure that the men in the garrisons know the costs of engaging in physical warfare, though the men do not always seem to internalize or understand this knowledge.

Yet the threat of physical warfare resides not only among garrisons warring with each other: the warriors, despite having all of their basic needs provided for them by the women's communities, periodically make plans to attack the women they are sworn to protect and take them over for the sake of comfort and so that they will be able to pursue their sexual "amusements" whenever they wish, not just during the semi-annual carnivals when the warriors are allowed into the cities for what they believe are procreative purposes. For this reason, the Councils ensure that the women and "servitors," men who have chosen to live within the women's communities and eschew violence, outnumber the men in the garrisons at all times. The physical warfare of the text presents very real threats and revolves around the tension between the garrisons and the cities to outmaneuver and outwit each other. One character remarks, "How many rebellions do you think there have been? Every decade, every score of years there is a rebellion. Some faction in a garrison begins to feel aggrieved. Some group of women begin to play the fool. Rebellions! They begin like a boil, swelling and pustulent, and we let them grow until they come to a head" (Tepper 1989, 290). The Councils set the garrisons against each other with made up grievances in order to reduce the garrison populations, and in one case in the narrative, utterly destroy every last man in a garrison that has repeatedly tried to threaten the women's community that provides for them.

The text demonstrates that the women's Councils decidedly have the upper hand and are aware of the warriors' plotting, but the warriors, blinded by assumptions about their own superiority and the supposed powerlessness of the women, repeatedly fail to recognize the futility of their situation. The men in the garrison have no concept of the ideological warfare that the women wage against them. In contrast, ideological warfare seems largely waged among the women of Women's Country and the Councils who lead them. The women undergo, unwittingly, a test of their own ideological beliefs: whether they learn to identify the difference between the swaggering, bullying warriors, with their lip service to ideals of honor and duty and their behavior indicative of the reverse, versus the unobtrusive yet thoughtful servitors who are the actual fathers of all the children in the women's communities. The women who pay attention to their upbringing and their education, like the protagonist Stavia, eventually overcome the ideas of romances with brave warriors that fill their heads, and learn to value and respect the servitors, possibly earning themselves places on the Council of their city. The women who develop the ability to see past the social constructs under which they are all brought up also retain their reproductive rights and can plan their families with servitors they choose rather than whomever the Council chooses for them.

The Councils and the servitors are working toward an egalitarian, utopian vision of the future; they are doing so, however, by selectively breeding for the kind of masculinity the women perceive as non-threatening, rather than learning to socialize men and women differently than in their history. Their eugenics program, despite its impulse toward utopian ideology, has created an elite social class of women and servitors who continue to force their agenda on an uninformed populace in a decidedly dictatorial manner. What makes the eugenics program and the Councils' actions problematic, in addition to the lack of reproductive choice for most of the community, is that those in the upper strata of hierarchical organizations rarely voluntarily give up or share their power with the lower strata, no matter how compelling the reasons, in much the same way that many men have balked at the idea of equality for women. As a result, the text itself ideologically challenges extremes of biological essentialism, much like *The Shore of Women*, and makes an argument for equality rather than reproductions of kyriarchal control in the form of a war on men or a War on Women.

He, She and It (1993) challenges biological essentialism in another way: the main plotline concerns determining whether an android, who is a sentient being, is a person, albeit, not a human person. The physical warfare in this novel is largely limited to the terrorist act of Yod, the android, undertaking a suicide mission to destroy the headquarters and top personnel of a multi-national conglomerate. Yod also destroys his maker, Avram, and Avram's records, so that no one can recreate androids and enslave them to the will of humans as Avram enslaved Yod. This physical warfare, sometimes taking place in virtual reality in the text, is less a gender war than a class war, since it pits huge multi-national conglomerates against the free-towns and the unorganized workers of the Glop. One of the characters is an information pirate who "liberates" information from the multis and makes it available to everyone for the good of humankind. However, the text also delves into social constructions of gender where ideological warfare becomes more apparent.

Piercy's text smashes through the masculine/feminine binary perpetuated in Western thought and culture and any insistence upon "natural" gender roles for men and women. Yod's unrelenting egalitarianism and resistance to exemplifying a masculine gender role and a cloned woman's resistance to a feminine gender role challenge tenets of biological essentialism: when men and women refuse to fill these roles, the roles themselves break down and show themselves to be arbitrary rather than based on biological imperatives. This challenge to "tradition" for men and women's roles in society also undermines the necessity for controlling women, and by extension, undermines justification for kyriarchal systems of power. In this respect, Piercy continues the argument she advanced in *Woman on the Edge of Time* that favors androgyny—in personality, if not appearance.

In the 1980s, Second and Third Wave feminist movements distanced themselves from 1970s advocacy of androgyny, yet Piercy persists in celebrating difference but also valuing human beings who integrate both traditionally masculine and feminine traits into their behaviors and characters. Perhaps the more salient argument of these texts and the ideology they advocate lies in Piercy's valorization of gender mainstreaming and neutrality, and the fact that all humans are capable of taking on both traditional masculine and feminine traits. Rather than putting forward an argument for androgyny, every character in both texts is readily identifiable as biologically female or male apart from their gender identity. Like most human beings, and unlike the gender binaries enforced and naturalized by kyriarchal constructions of gender, Yod presents a mixture of both "masculine" and "feminine" traits. Unlike most human beings, Yod's qualities skew toward exhibiting the more desirable traits in both "masculine" and "feminine" categories. I would argue that Yod's personality traits are not "feminine" so much as exemplifying the best *human* qualities such as compassion for and connection to others.

The War on Women

Perhaps the two novels which most ably capture the War on Women do so through an absence of physical warfare altogether, focusing only on the ideological warfare that the texts themselves wage against misogyny. *Native Tongue* (1984) and *Judas Rose: Native Tongue II* (1987)[12] by Suzette Haden Elgin and the more recent *When She Woke* (2011) by Hillary Jordan both explore the logical extremes of the War on Women when the government rolls back the legal gains of the 1970s Second Wave feminist movement.

Elgin's novel, like Atwood's, depicts a dystopian society in which women have been relegated to lower-class status, subsequent to a revocation of their rights as American citizens. In this dystopian future, the 19th Amendment is repealed and a new Amendment enacted that explicitly states that women are inferior beings and cannot hold office, work in certain professions or at all without express written permission, and the like. Without an Equal Rights Amendment or other Constitutional protection, women's status thus reverts to the same as minor children under the control of male family members: husbands, fathers, or other (male) biological relatives. Their few remaining "rights" tend to be characterized by a perceived need for women's protection as the physically, mentally, and emotionally "weaker" sex.

The main plotline of *Native Tongue* seemingly has more to do with a family of inter-galactic translators, upon whose skills the Earth's trade with alien planets depends. The Chornyak family needs every family member's contributions to translation so the idea of the female family members staying at home and not working is an absurd one. However, the women in the family are overburdened with carework responsibilities in addition to their work in the public sector as translators. The family desperately needs to produce linguistically talented children and thus treats women like brood mares, forcing them to produce a child every three years from the age of 16 until the onset of menopause. The protagonist, Nazareth, anxiously awaits her "retirement" to the Barren House, the confines of women no longer useful to the family for public or domestic work, where ostensibly she can knit, gossip, and relax for the remainder of her years. Yet the real work of the women in the Barren House is the creation of a woman-centered language that captures the essences of women's experiences and feelings and makes them communicable.

Through this new language, the female linguists believe that they can end male oppression of women—an oppression only too explicit in a political and cultural milieu where women have no rights or bodily autonomy other than what their closest male relatives permit them to have. Elgin's application of the Sapir-Whorf theory of language—that linguistic structure influences thought processes and, in turn, behavior—makes clear that kyriarchal language centered around a white, heterosexual, able-bodied, cis-gendered, wealthy man as the universal representation of the human is inherently oppressive to women, people of color, queer persons, the impoverished, and the differently-abled. The non-physical war that the women linguists engage in is, at once, ideological and metaphorical: ideological as a defense against the War on Women played out in the novel's pages; and metaphorical as a rhetorical strategy that exposes the limits to women's freedoms without an Equal Rights Amendment.

Hillary Jordan's *When She Woke* also engages in ideological warfare against the War on Women and examines the extremity to which that war is currently headed. A pandemic that causes infertility among women causes deeply harms the world's population growth, to the point that the future of humanity is in jeopardy. In the United States, the "Scourge" is the catalyst for a series of "Sanctity of Life" laws that make abortion illegal with no exceptions and generate mandatory health screenings for those within child-bearing age (Jordan 2011, 36–7). Unlike other countries, the U.S. stops short of harvesting eggs from young women and/or forcing them into pregnancy with artificially inseminated zygotes due to the advent of some drugs that cure the Scourge.

Although Hannah, the protagonist, joins a resistance movement after having obtained an illegal abortion and been convicted of her "crime," the extent of any type of physical warfare is limited to moving criminalized women to Canada, reversing their "punishment" of having their skin turned a bright red color, and continuing to provide abortion services to women who need them. The ideological war that the text engages as a defense against the War on Women–run-amok, is much more significant: women who do not want to carry pregnancies to term will always seek ways of ending those pregnancies regardless of risk or legality. The War on Women's goal of restricting women's control over the management of their own fertility and to determine whether to carry any pregnancy to term is perhaps the most meaningful social issue of our time. Without recognition of women's bodily autonomy, kyriarchal societies will never recognize the full humanity of half the population and we will live under the conditions of *Native Tongue*, with women relegated to the status of minors, in reality, if not constitutionally mandated.

Conclusion

I have surveyed a plethora of feminist utopian and dystopian texts in order to examine whether Russ's observation of physical warfare being distant and peripheral has held up over time and across the genre. While physical warfare seems much more prevalent in the dystopian texts published after Russ's essay, her argument is still valuable for the study and criticism of feminist utopian and dystopian writing for one primary reason: the physical warfare carried out in the texts pales in comparison to the metaphorical warfare being waged on ideological levels. This metaphorical warfare not only takes place in the texts with different societies and cultures "battling" each other as the way of the future, but expands into reality in that the texts themselves are waging ideological warfare on contemporary American society and its kyriarchal institutions. Feminist utopian and dystopian writing provide metaphorical blueprints of egalitarian futures that then serve to subvert and defend against the war, the assault, on women and women's rights. The War on Women is far from over, yet feminist utopian and dystopian writing presents progressive possibilities for combating misogyny in tangible and ideological modes. These novels form the vanguard, waging metaphorical war on the kyriarchal misogyny of the War on Women.

NOTES

1. The views expressed in this essay are those of the author and do not reflect the official policy or position of the Department of the Army or the Department of Defense.
2. See Frances Bartkowski's *Feminist Utopias*.
3. See also Dworkin 1997, 105 and Cranny-Francis 1990, 142.
4. See Potok and Schlatter; Menzies; Solinger; and Dunphy.
5. See the National Women's Law Center, Nash et al, and the Guttmacher Institute's "Monthly State Update" for discussion and tabulation of bills introduced that reduce women's access to abortion and/or birth control, and restrict or attempt to make abortion illegal.
6. However, crime shows with women crime-fighters depicted about half of the murderers as female, successfully challenging the image of passive, sweet, docile femininity so prevalent then.
7. B. J. Salterberg, *The Outlander: Quest*, Unpublished ms. Salterberg's unpublished sequel delves more acutely into ideological warfare when Konnor discovers another, more egalitarian and technologically advanced society that sends him to psychotherapy.
8. emphasis in original
9. Incidentally, the Valans eventually effect their own liberation from their militarism and greed and become a peaceful interplanetary federation. See Slonczewski's *Daughter of Elysium* (1993).
10. emphasis in original
11. emphasis in original
12. The third book in the trilogy, *Earthsong: Native Tongue III* (1993), moves away from Elgin's original concept to an extent, so I do not include it here.

WORKS CITED

Atwood, Margaret. 1985. *The Handmaid's Tale*. New York: Ballantine.
Bartkowski, Frances. 1989. *Feminist Utopias*. Lincoln: University of Nebraska Press.

Beck, John, and Mark Dorrian. "Postcatastrophic Utopias." *Cultural Politics* 10.2 (2014): 132–50.

Bowman, Barbara. 1984. qtd in Natalie M. Rosinsky, *Feminist Futures: Contemporary Women's Science Fiction.* Ann Arbor, MI: UMI Research Press, 79.

Burdekin, Katharine. 1993. *Swastika Night.* New York: The Feminist Press at CUNY.

Charnas, Suzy McKee. 1994. *The Furies.* New York: Tor.

_____. 1999. *The Conqueror's Child.* New York: Tom Doherty Associates.

_____. 1999. *The Slave and the Free: Books 1 and 2 of "The Holdfast Chronicles": Walk to the End of the World" and "Motherlines."* New York: Tor.

Cranny-Francis, Anne. 1990. *Feminist Fiction: Feminist Uses of Generic Fiction.* Cambridge: Polity Press.

Davis, Jamie. "Utopia in Blood: Monique Wittig's *Les Guérillères.*" *West Virginia University Philological Papers* (Fall 2002): 27–35.

Delaney, Samuel R. 1996 *Trouble on Triton: An Ambiguous Heterotopia.* New York: Wesleyan. Reprint edition.

Dunphy, Richard. 2000. "Ideologies of Masculinity and Femininity: The Critique of 'Men's Studies' and Feminism." *Sexual Politics: An Introduction.* Edinburgh: Edinburgh University Press. 83–99.

Dworkin, Andrea. 1997. *Life and Death: Unapologetic Writings on the Continuing War Against Women.* New York: Free Press.

Elgin, Suzette Haden. 1984. *Native Tongue.* New York: Daw Books.

_____.2002. *Earthsong: Native Tongue III.* The Feminist Press at CUNY. Reprint edition.

_____. 2002. *The Judas Rose: Native Tongue II.* New York: The Feminist Press at CUNY. Reprint edition.

Faludi, Susan. 1991. *Backlash: The Undeclared War Against American Women.* New York: Crown.

Fitting, Peter. 1990. "The Turn from Utopia in Recent Feminist Fiction." *Feminism, Utopia, and Narrative.* Ed. Libby Falk Jones and Sarah W. Goodwin. Knoxville: University of Tennessee Press. 141–58.

Fowler, Gene, Jr. *I Married a Monster from Outerspace.* Paramount Pictures, 1958.

Gearhart, Sally Miller. 1976. *The Wanderground: Stories of the Hill Women.* Watertown, MA: Persephone Press.

Guttmacher Institute. March 1, 2015. "Monthly State Update: Major Developments in 2015." Accessed March 10, 2015, https://www.guttmacher.org/state-policy

_____. March 1, 2015. "State Policies in Brief: Requirements for Ultrasound." Accessed March 31, 2015, https://www.guttmacher.org/state-policy

Jordan, Hillary. 2011. *When She Woke.* Toronto: HarperCollins Canada.

Kelso, Sylvia. 1997. *A Glance from Nowhere: Sheri S. Tepper's Fantasy and Science Fiction.* London: Nimrod Publications.

Larbalestier, Justine. 2002. *The Battle of the Sexes in Science Fiction.* Middletown, CT: Wesleyan.

Lees, Susan H. 1984. "Motherhood in Feminist Utopias." *Women in Search of Utopia: Mavericks and Mythmakers.* Ed. Elaine Hoffman Baruch and Ruby Rohrlich. New York: Shocken Books. 219–32.

Marley, Louise. 2000. *The Terrorists of Irustan.* New York: Ace.

Menzies, Robert. 2007. *"Virtual Backlash: Representation of Men's 'Rights' and Feminist 'Wrongs' in Cyberspace." Reaction and Resistance: Feminism, Law, and Social Change. Ed. Susan B. Boyd. Vancouver: University of British Columbia Press. 65–97.*

Mercer, Naomi R. "Utopia and Dystopia as Process in Feminist Science Fiction." Paper presented at the Northeast Modern Language Association Annual Conference. Toronto, ON, April 30, 2015.

Mohr, Dunja M. 2005. *Worlds Apart: Dualism and Transgression in Contemporary Female Dystopias.* Jefferson, NC: McFarland.

National Women's Law Center. January 2015. "2014 State Level Abortion Restrictions: An Extreme Overreach Into Women's Reproductive Health Care." *nwlc.org.* Accessed March 31, 2015, https://www.nwlc.org/wp-content/uploads/2015/08/2014_state_abortion_legislation_factsheet_1.22.15v2.pdf

Pharr, Suzanne. 1988. *Homophobia, a Weapon of Sexism.* Inverness, CA: Chardon Press.

Piercy, Marge. 1976. *Woman on the Edge of Time.* New York: Knopf.

_____. 1993. *He, She, and It.* New York: Fawcett Crest.

Potok, Mark, and Evelyn Schlatter. March 1, 2012. "Men's Rights Movement Spreads False Claims About Women." Accessed February 4, 2016, https://www.splcenter.org/fighting-hate/intelligence-report/2012/men%E2 %80%99s-rights-movement-spreads-false-claims-about-women

Rosinsky, Natalie M. 1984. *Feminist Futures: Contemporary Women's Science Fiction.* Ann Arbor, MI: UMI Research Press.

Russ, Joanna. 1980. "*Amor Vincit Foeminam*: The Battle of the Sexes in Science Fiction." *Science-Fiction Studies* 7.1: 2–15.

_____. 2000. *The Female Man.* Boston: Beacon Press. Reprint edition.

_____. 2000. "Recent Feminist Utopias." *Future Females, the Next Generation: New Voices and Velocities in Feminist Science Fiction Criticism.* Ed. Marleen S. Barr. Lanham, MD: Rowman & Littlefield. Reprint edition.

Salterberg, B.J. 1989. *The Outlander: Captivity.* Tucson: Harbinger House.

_____. n.p. *The Outlander: Quest.* Unpublished ms. Personal Collection of Naomi R. Mercer.

Sargent, Pamela. 1986. *The Shore of Women.* New York: Crown Publishers.

Schwartz, Pepper. 1995. *Love Between Equals: How Peer Marriage Really Works.* New York: Touchstone.

Slonczewski, Joan. 1986. *A Door Into Ocean.* New York: Arbor House.

_____. 1993. *Daughter of Elysium.* New York: William Morrow.

Solinger, Rickie. 2013. "Men and Reproductive Politics." *Reproductive Politics: What Everyone Needs to Know.* Oxford: Oxford University Press. 141–44.

Starhawk. 1993. *The Fifth Sacred Thing.* New York: Bantam Books.

Tarico, Valerie. October 26, 2015. "The 'war on Women' Is Not a War—it's an Assault." Accessed November 3, 2015, http://churchandstate.org.uk/2017/03/the-war-on-women-is-not-a-war-its-an-assault/

Tepper, Sheri S. 1989. *The Gate to Women's Country.* New York: Bantam.

_____. 1990. *Raising the Stones.* New York: Doubleday.

Wadud, Amina. 2006. *Inside the Gender Jihad: Women's Reform in Islam.* Oxford: Oneworld.

Wittig, Monique. 1971. *Les Guérillères.* Trans. David Le Vay. New York: Viking.

A Call to Arms

Star Wars, Star Trek *and the Science Fiction of the German Democratic Republic*

THOMAS P. DAVID

On 25 June 1983, a citizen of the German Democratic Republic [GDR] wrote a letter to the Cultural and Educational Section of the Central Committee of the Socialist Unity Party of Germany (*ZK SED, Abteilung Kulturpolitik*). The letter is several pages long and densely written in the voice of a citizen, concerned with the state of his nation vis-à-vis the United States of America. He expresses his concern about works of science fiction that do not adequately depict the inherent dangers of capitalism and imperialism in "the contemporary stage of the worsening class struggle with the mortal enemy"[1] (Scheibe 1983, 71). He expounds on his understanding of this popular genre and how it must necessarily reflect and address the issues confronting its society. And he argues that GDR SF must adhere to the dictum that "the weaker imperialism becomes, the more aggressively and unpredictably it behaves" (Scheibe 1983, 72).

This essay examines GDR SF from this period of the class struggle in which the mortal enemy showed itself to be more aggressive during the last decade of the Cold War. It specifically analyzes Horst Ansorge's novel *Raumkundschafter Katman* (*Space Scout Katman*, 1987) and Wolfgang Kellner's short story "Tödlicher Irrtum" (*Fatal Mistake*, 1985) that depict hostile confrontations with alien civilizations which necessitate armed and ready vigilance in the face of an existential threat: They do this despite the usual convention of GDR SF that alien creatures, capable of interstellar flight and communication, by and large, would necessarily represent a higher stage of development and would accordingly be inherently peaceful. There was to be no bloody clash of civilizations in the pages of GDR SF.

With Ronald Reagan's "Address to the Nation on Defense and National Security" on 23 March 1983, though, such a violent confrontation became a really-existing possibility. Speaking from the Oval Office for slightly longer than 29 minutes, Reagan outlined his reasons for the necessity of increased military spending and the steps he had undertaken to make America great again. Most importantly, he announced his intention to fund the construction of a defensive missile shield that would be partially based in space and that could theoretically destroy incoming nuclear missiles from the Soviet Union.

From the perspective of the GDR, this proposal was a thinly veiled attempt to militarize space and thus to tip the balance of the Cold War's equilibrium—as mad, though effective, as it may have been—in favor of the United States. As such, it posed a clear and imminent danger to the socialist world to which the GDR belonged and for which it was a militarily strong bulwark. This, perhaps, was reason enough for a concerned citizen to put pen to paper three months later and demand an adequate, albeit literary, ideological response.

This speech is more popularly known today by its science-fictional namesake: the "Star Wars" Speech. Domestic opponents of Reagan's proposal quickly gave it this moniker in an attempt to disparage his plan to build a space shield. In doing so, they were utilizing the same impulses of contemporary popular culture that Reagan was employing, but as a rhetorical counter narrative to this initiative that seemed to be wildly expensive, grandly other-worldly, and practically impossible—that is, the stuff of which science-fictional dreams are made.

Star Wars (George Lucas) was very much part and parcel of the popular imagination of the times. The term itself embodies much more than the title of the original film that was released on 25 May 1977 to the American public on a mere 35 screens across the nation. It represents a franchise, and to a certain extent, a universe of its own that has undergone, and continues to undergo, expansions and amendments. To many fans, it even became a way of life.

The original *Star Wars* film quickly became not only a Hollywood "blockbuster," but also a global phenomenon. Its success caught many people, even its creator, by surprise. Its resonance in the popular imagination, and perhaps even its universal appeal, might well be due to the simplicity of its story in which good battles evil on a galactic scale and a lowly orphan rises to become a space-age knight in the cause of peace, justice, and perhaps even, the "American Way" of life, ideologically devoted to the individual's crusade for recognition in a hostile world.

By the time of Reagan's speech, the original film had been re-released several times in conjunction with the subsequent films that constitute the original trilogy, such that they served as a backdrop to Reagan's speech and a ready-made stockpile of imagery for both the opponents and proponents of his strategic initiative. The last decade of the Cold War was shaped by the renewed arms race between the United States and the Soviet Union for which Reagan's speech served as a hallmark and a battle-cry. Yet, one would do well to recall that the end of the Cold War and the demise of the GDR were by no means apparent or inevitable at the time, when these two seemingly alien civilizations stood in armed opposition to one another.

The encounter with the alien is a standard feature of SF. Occasionally friendly, often aggressive, the alien is always the other of humanity that reflects the best and worst sides of human nature—frequently, though, in a fusion of both. In the canon of SF fiction, H.G. Wells' *War of the Worlds* (1898) serves as the template for the belligerent alien race that is determined to conquer and colonize Earth. This trope, though, was largely absent from GDR SF, and this essay looks at two examples from the last decade of the Cold War in which the alien does appear as the aggressor, the proverbial space invader of SF, as a representative of its ideological and geopolitical opponent.

This essay explores how Ansorge's *Raumkundschafter Katman* and Kellner's "Tödlicher Irrtum" simultaneously invoke and restyle an accepted convention of GDR SF—that of the advanced, inherently peaceful alien— in order to re-present the perceived threat of Reagan's "Star Wars" visions. It situates these stories in the context of GDR SF. And it places them in conversation with their Anglo-American counterparts—most notably and manifestly *Star Wars*, but also with its most well-known competitor and concurrent in the universes of SF, *Star Trek*—in order to discuss the affinities between SF in the East and the West as a genre inherent to and innate in any society that depends on science and technology for its path forward into the possibilities of the future.

> The official cosmic science has taught for centuries that there is no threat from the universe. The first few contacts with alien civilizations confirmed this too. The cosmic civilizations that were discovered at their early stages of development remained objects of research that were handled with the utmost caution. And the only group contacted so far with a biologically completely different, but technologically, very highly developed civilization was indeed a deeply humanistic social order. The theory that technologically superior civilizations could only exist in highly developed social orders was raised to a space truth of the first degree [Ansorge 1987, 30–1].

The Chairman of the World Security Agency (*Weltsicherheitsbehörde*) is lecturing space scout Katman on the history of space exploration and the official dogma that guides it and has been proven correct by it. Katman does not need to be reminded of this. He is a highly decorated and honored member of the Space Agency (*Weltraumbehörde*), and his service has been grounded in this system of belief.

Katman has a problem, though. He is the only survivor of an

encounter with alien beings on the planet Yoga 9 in the year 2439. And no one believes his story that his companion was killed and his ship destroyed immediately on sight by creatures that did not make the slightest attempt at communication.

The problem is that his story goes against this official dogma: Technological progress entails the progress of society to a more enlightened stage of history. This sentiment at the heart of the Chairman's words is also an encapsulation of the generic attitude, the unwritten, but generally acknowledged convention of GDR SF that one might call the "Cosmic Law." The novel, *Raumkundschafter Katman*, challenges this convention in its deployment of a technologically sophisticated, alien civilization that is uninterested in communication and concerned only with the eventual colonization of Earth.

The novel first appeared in the GDR in 1987. It was published by the *Verlag Das Neue* Berlin in its *SF-Utopia* series. The *Verlag Das Neue* Berlin was one of the largest publishing houses in the GDR with a special concentration in the genres of detective and SF. It also published the literary-theoretical "fantastic almanac" *Lichtjahr* (*Lightyear*) in which Kellner's short story appeared. This series' six volumes, published in the last decade of the GDR, included essays about the genre and SF short stories by well-known authors and critics from the GDR and beyond in an oversized, hardcover format.

The *SF-Utopia* series published forty-four works of modern and vintage SF by GDR and foreign authors from 1980 to 1990, which belonged both to the canon of international SF as well as that of the GDR. It began publication with a re-issue of *Der Mann vom Anti* (*The Man from Anti*), originally published in 1975, an anthology of GDR authors who, as the back cover states, "disprove the view that the utopian story has no home in the GDR." And it ended with Karl Čapek's *Das Absolutum* (*The Absolute at Large*) from 1922. It included, among others, Shelley's *Frankenstein* and the Strugazky brothers' *Der ferne Regenbogen* (*Far Rainbow*). It was the "only book series of the GDR that [was] specialized in SF" (Simon and Spittel 1988, 76). Consistent with the series' parameters, *Raumkundschafter Katman* was published in a paper-back format and had an initial run of 100,000 copies.

The computers of Katman's world tell a different story than his. They reckon the probability of his veracity at less than one percent. It is more likely, as they inform the Chairman, that he was the victim of a far-reaching terrorist attack by those members of the underground who are dissatisfied with the progress that his future Earth has attained. His world is indeed one in which a semblance of unity has been achieved, but problems persist. Drugs, boredom, and dissatisfaction remain, and a "gray market" has arisen to take advantage of these fissures in the utopian system of a unified Earth that has moved beyond its terrestrial boundaries and into the stars.

The world of Katman is never fully explained in the pages of the novel. It is a globalized world, in the best sense of the word, where the petty wars of nation-states, and the imperialistic dominance of one over the other, are things of the past, at the same time that it is a world in which the all too real human problems of existence persist. How does one come to terms with a perfection of technology that allows humanity to live without the existential apprehension that has been a hallmark of its development? There is always an irreducible remainder that does not want to be part of the whole. And so it is with Katman's world. It is a utopia in the same sense of More's coinage of the term: a possibility that is a futuristic no-place.

In this sense, the novel attempts to depict a realistic portrayal of a possible future. As Michael Szameit writes in the last anthology of new GDR SF writers, *Der lange Weg zum Blauen Stern* (*The Long Way to the Blue Star*) in 1990: "It is the most noble tradition of the utopia to utilize the resolution of the nowhere and the never in the anywhere and the anywhen in order to examine closely and critically contemporary issues of the present through the confrontation of ideal with reality" (Szameit 1990, 216). This is the defining characteristic of the SF genre that goes beyond its stereo-typical markers of robots and computers, aliens and space. It is a genre that actively explores the potentialities of human development. This is the same principle at the heart of the work by Western theorists, such as Darko Suvin and Fredric Jameson, who emphasize SF's critical capacity to comment on contemporary conditions through the technique of spatial and temporal estrangement.[2] And Szameit makes it clear in his introduction that the stories in the anthology, as SF, fundamentally examine the human condition as it exists on the "blue star" of planet Earth.

Katman's Earth has sent out a ship to investigate his encounter on Yoga 9. All contact has been lost with this ship suddenly and mysteriously. Few, though, are willing to give Katman's story any credence, if only because the computers deal in facts. And the facts of the case, such as they are known, are not enough to overcome a logic that is based on the "Cosmic Law." Some even consider his story to be the result of hallucinations brought on by environmental conditions, so far fetched does it seem to claim that ten humanoid creatures, dressed in identical spacesuits and acting in unison, unexpectedly appeared on the planet's surface and vaporized his companion without the slightest hesitation.

Nevertheless, a second mission to the Yoga star system is prepared, and Katman is asked to take part. His request that it be armed is rejected. Weapons are part of Earth's past. To even carry weapons is considered to be a sign of aggression, and thus entirely inappropriate for a mission that is meant to open up the channels of communication. It is during this mission that the crew has the opportunity for extended discussions on the nature and validity of the "Cosmic Law."

This law functions in much the same way as the "Prime Directive" in *Star Trek*, debatably the most well-known work of SF in the Anglo-American tradition after (or before, depending on one's perspective) *Star Wars*. Gene Roddenberry's *Star Trek* first aired on NBC from 1966 to 1969. Despite its cancellation, it too became a franchise in the same sense as *Star Wars*. Complete with on-going spin-offs, sequels, and re-vamps, it also spawned a universe of its own.

Star Trek also aired in the Federal Republic of Germany and was thus also available to viewers in the GDR who could receive television signals from the West (Fritzsche 2006, 377–78). Hesse cites a figure of 80 percent for GDR households that regularly followed broadcasts from the FRG (Hesse 1990, 358). For the purposes of this essay, though, it is not necessary to establish exact figures for the audience of *Star Trek* in the GDR, even if that were possible; rather, this essay seeks to establish correlations and correspondences between GDR and Anglo-American SF that result from their systemic, generic affiliations.

Star Wars, for that matter, was never released in the GDR, although it did find its way onto the screens of several other members of the Socialist Bloc (and of course those of the FRG). Given its nature as a global phenomenon, though, it can be inferred that *Star Wars* was, indeed, a known quantity in the GDR—otherwise, it would have made little sense to publish articles and books, such as those analyzed later in this essay, if their readers would have been unaware of their subject matter. Science fiction authors, as members of a literary community that was accorded a privileged position within the GDR, would certainly have been familiar with both *Star Wars* and *Star Trek*.

The correlation between these two franchises is not just one of creating constantly expanding, albeit competing, universes for their respective fan bases, but also one of mutually reinforced success. *Star Trek's* popularity served as a prototype for *Star Wars* by showcasing a new type of SF in the popular format of television. At the same time, it benefited from *Star Wars'* monumental success that helped to make SF present in the popular imagination that in turn led to *Star Trek's* own revival and subsequent return to the large and small screens. The two franchises represent opposite poles on the continuum of SF, though, with *Star Trek* on the one side as a representative of the genre's critical capacity and *Star Wars* on the other as its much more stereo-typical, science—fantastical *Doppelgänger*.

Star Trek depicts a possible direction in humanity's progress to a higher stage of development, one in which the "Cosmic Law" would seem to be applicable, at least for the human race and its humanoid allies. It obliquely confronts contemporary issues, such as racism, sexism, and economic inequality through its depiction of a semi-utopian future. Despite any of its failings, all too obvious at times and too numerous to discuss here adequately, *Star Trek* does address the possibilities and the problems that are intrinsic to a society that is dependent on technology for its evolution.

Star Wars, on the other hand, does little to address the relationship of humanity to technology—the essential function of the SF genre in a world increasingly governed by the logics and rationalities of technological dependence. To be sure, technology is ever-present, and the sheer awesomeness of its deployment in the likes of the Death Star, for example, could be associated with the destructiveness of nuclear weapons in the semblance of a warning. More often than not, though, technology is a mere effect meant to enhance the science-fictionalized aspects of a fairy tale presented on the grand scale of a space opera.

Indeed, the opening words of the film make this clear to the viewer: "A long time ago in a galaxy far, far away...." The cadence and the meaning are a cosmic rewording of the stereo-typical beginning of any fairy tale, the elements of which the film provides in space-age packaging: a beautiful princess, her hero, his sometimes faithful companion, a good wizard to guide him, and an evil one to rule them all from a seemingly impregnable fortress. "With one sentence, the 'rules of the game' are given [...]" (Gakow 1985, 50). And the film accordingly follows through true to its preordained form.

The story is one of good versus evil, and of how one man, the proverbial "Great Man" of history, overcomes the odds and meets the challenges to emerge triumphant and reborn in the mold of an individual savior. In this sense, the story is proto-typically American and is a reinterpretation of the American ideal of individuality. As such, it can all too easily be fitted into Reagan's rhetoric of a renewed American Manifest Destiny, replete with overtures of the Wild West and the conquest of space.

In times of crisis, and the 1970s were certainly one for the U.S., see, for example, Michael Harrington's *The Twilight of Capitalism*,[3] the reaction is often to look for appropriate models in the past, to reinvent oneself according to some mythical, and thus heroic, past golden age. George Lucas may have intended his film to provide an unambiguous champion of the good at a time when many felt that the U.S. had lost its moral compass in the wake of Vietnam, but he "[s]inglehandedly [...] revived the romantic notion of military adventures after a period in American history when war had become synonymous with all that was wrong with the U.S. political system" (Jamilla 2012, 154). His intention may have been to re-tell the story of Nixon's corruption of the American Republic on an intergalactic scale, but the action of the film is dictated by the opening "rules of the game" that can be interpreted as "Don't bother trying to figure out the relationship between what you're about to see and your own Earthbound reality, because there isn't one" (Taylor 2015, 166).

This sentiment, so boldly proclaimed at the outset, undercuts *a priori* any critical capacity that might be found in the film. It is an inversion of the fundamental principle of SF that asks, if not demands, that its reader (or viewer, as the case might be) make critical connections between the text and his/her surroundings. "Made with all the features of SF […], the film uses these elements to efface and deny the utopian possibilities inherent in such impressive technical and technological developments" (Fitting 1980, 290). And it is the technical prowess of the film that gives it its command of the popular imagination. Light sabers and space blasters, spaceships in hyper-space and space stations in orbit, aliens in the neighborhood bar and androids at the ready, all these stereo-typical conventions of SF serve to reinvent a space-age myth that comes pre-packaged in the quasi-mystical "Force."

The religious overtones are unmistakable. The Force simply exists, "an energy field created by all living things," in the words of Obi Wan Kenobi, an old and venerable, but completely fictional Jedi Knight whose quite obviously alien and foreign sounding name does not cause the least problem for a modern word-processing program—a clear indication of the acceptance of the film into the general vernacular of contemporary society. As such, the Force can be utilized either for good or for evil if one is seduced by the temptations of its "Dark Side." It is a trademark of *Star Wars*, in other words, a re-invocation of some quasi-religious power, akin to the Holy Ghost, that guides and serves a humanity that has been displaced into the far reaches of a galaxy, a long time ago.

The Prime Directive is a hallmark of the *Star Trek* franchise. Its name implies its meaning and importance as the basis for space exploration by the Star Fleet of a future United Federation of Planets, of which a united and peaceful Earth is a founding member. It forbids interference in the internal affairs of others. On the one hand, it has a benevolent intention. It does not allow Star Fleet to influence the development of any alien society. Every society should have the right to develop and evolve on its own accord and at its own pace—a lesson from Earth's history in which the more technologically advanced society has often decimated those of less sophisticated ones.

On the other, the Prime Directive has a practical function too. It keeps Star Fleet from becoming involved in (un)necessarily messy, alien engagements in which it has no standing. It is meant to prevent exactly those misunderstandings that can all too easily arise when foreign cultures encounter one another—encounters that can unexpectedly and unpredictably prove fatal to either one or both of the involved sides.

This is exactly the reason why a painting called "Fatal Mistake" hangs in the office of the Chief Communicator in the Cosmic Council, Holan Vorwiet, in Kellner's story by the same name. The painting depicts a white explorer walking towards a group of darker-skinned people who are clad in loincloths. The explorer has his hands raised in what he thinks is a demonstration of his peaceful intentions. For the "children of nature," though, his gesture is a declaration of his hostility. And they defend themselves accordingly with a poisoned arrow.

The painting is meant to remind the Chief Communicator of the danger inherent in contact between beings whose cultural codes are unfamiliar and unknown to one another. This is a danger which he hopes to avoid should the time arrive when humanity makes first contact with an alien civilization. Although he has spent most of his life preparing for this task, he has had no opportunity to put his training to use.

He has, though, prepared a mathematical program of welcome. In the absence of a universal language, mathematics are construed in the SF genre as a universal constant that provides a basis for communication between species that cannot speak the same *literal* language. It is, in other words, a universal language of its own. Numbers are, by all accounts, neutral by nature.

The mathematical program of the First Communicator is meant to demonstrate humanity's technological progress to any alien society and allow for communication that is unbiased by cultural prejudices. That is the plan, at least, until a sphere arrives on Earth that shows no reaction to and has no regard for this program. The First Communicator must enter this sphere physically and communicate with it *verbally*—in an ironic inversion of the painted (fore)warning on his office wall.

When he does so, his conduct and his expectations are governed by the same "Cosmic Law," as in *Raumkundschafter Katman*, namely that "whoever crosses the cosmos interstellarly or intergalactically, lives in a highly developed, and for that reason, peaceful society" (Kellner 1985, 142). He encounters, though, an unknown entity that speaks of the need to be given "homage." The feudal nature of this demand is not lost on the members of the Cosmic Council who represent a humanity that has advanced to a higher stage of social progress, a unified Earth that has overcome the hostilities of early eras to become one.

Whether the words of the sphere are perchance a mistranslation or perhaps a misunderstanding, they are the source of the Council members' debates about the nature of this seemingly mechanical and emotionless visitor. Nevertheless, the "Cosmic Law" serves as their basis of interpretation—indeed, it is the only way in which they can make sense of the reality of their situation. It is their "prime directive" through which they view their own world and the universe around them.

In the *Star Trek* universe, the Prime Directive is often invoked, frequently discussed, and at times conveniently ignored, and alien races supply ready-made, and stereo-typical, templates of terrestrial cultures. *Star Trek* is clearly an Anglo-American product, where the Klingons are the Russians of the Cold War Soviet Union and the Romulans imperialistic, space-age Romans—or perhaps they are all stand-ins for the Germans of the Second World War? The alien races of *Star Trek* are often construed in such a way that each race could be said to signify one particular, usually negative aspect of an overly generalized human psyche. They thus function as a means for the critical viewer to reflect upon human nature. Be that as it may, Star Fleet stands ready to fulfill its exploratory mission "to boldly go where no man has gone before," fully armed and ready to defeat any enemy, domestic or foreign, that it might encounter.

The Prime Directive is the basis for space exploration in *Star Trek*, as is the "Cosmic Law" in *Raumkundschafter Katman* and "Tödlicher Irrtum." This law, though, is a part of an accepted code of belief that does not allow for the same nuances (and loopholes) that the members of Star Fleet take advantage of. It is an absolute. Time and time again, the other members of the Cosmic Council refuse to hear Vorwiet's pleas to consider the possibility that the sphere could actually want the entirety of humanity to pay it "homage" and, in the absence of knowing what this really means, that this demand could well imply a threat.

Time and time again, over the course of the novel, the crew members of the second mission to the Yoga system remind themselves that there can be no exception to the accepted fact that technological progress entails a corresponding evolution of society into a non-violent social order. Unlike Star Fleet, though, they are without armaments, and thus seemingly ill-equipped to engage an unknown entity. They do not even have the depot of antiquated weaponry to which the First Communicator still has access. In the case of a violent encounter with an alien civilization, they will have to make do with improvised weapons that must be modified from the peaceful tools of planetary exploration.

Their faith, nevertheless, remains constant until their fatal encounter with an enemy that is simply inconceivable to their *Weltanschauung*. It may be out of place to describe the "Cosmic Law" as a matter of faith, especially in a world that is at least partially governed by the impersonal logic of computers. In a future without religion, though, it serves as a secular substitute, a means through which they can make sense of their universe and their place in it.

This law then functions very much as a belief. Unlike a religious tenet, though, it has been formed and formulated on the basis of rational, human deliberation. The ironic result of this is that people cling to it with a sort of religious fervor. The possibility that it may not be universally true provokes heated discussions among the crew. In their debates, a characteristic of the socialist tradition of a democratic collective of which the novel is an example, another, linguistic convention of GDR SF is fractured, at least, if not broken—that of Russian as the language of the future. If the question of a global language is by and large ignored in Anglo-American SF, it is usually because the assumption, practical as well as ideological, is that English will accordingly be the common language of the world in the future.

In GDR SF, Russian is, not unexpectedly, sometimes portrayed as a global language of the future. In Manfred Küchler's *Der Planet ohne Sonne* (*The Planet without Sun*), for example, the international crew of *Kosmonauten* is surprised and shocked to be addressed in the English language when "the whole world can speak Russian" (Küchler 1990, 41). This is in keeping with the logic of SF both as a genre of the future and as genre that reflects its contemporary conditions of production. The use of Russian as an international lingua franca expresses confidence in the ultimate victory of the October Revolution on a global scale and recognizes the Soviet Union's role as the leader of the socialist *Gemeinschaft*.

Russia does hold a privileged position in the projected futures of GDR SF, and a place is often held in reserve for the model Soviet citizen. "As Michael Szameit once said: [W]ith me, the space commander is always a Soviet citizen, and then everything is okay."[4] The reader, though, is at times just as likely to encounter the Anglo-American *Astronauten* as the Russian *Kosmonauten* to describe the space travelers of the future—sometimes even in the same text. The forty-year formal history of GDR SF is not a monolingual discourse, but, as with any genre in any national literary canon, a multivocal dialogue between texts and the world surrounding them that evolved over time.

Over the course of the GDR's history, its authors produced more than 150 SF novels. This number does not include children's books and the numerous short stories published in magazines, anthologies, and collections, or those published in single-story paperback booklets, such as those from the *Das neue Abenteuer* (*The New Adventure*) series that had initial printings of over 100,000. It also does not include works by authors from other socialist states and international works that belong to the genre's canon.

Science fiction was a popular genre in the GDR, and most of its works quickly sold out. Many were re-released due to popular demand. The first work of GDR SF was published in 1949, Ludwik Turek's *Die goldene Kugel* (*The Golden Sphere*). The novel tells the story of how peace-loving aliens from Venus come to Earth to stop the U.S. from an atomic first-strike and put the Earth on the path to a peaceful and socialist future.

Despite this thrilling inauguration, SF in the GDR moved away from the merely inspirational as it progressed. To be sure, works of GDR SF often had to display a certain degree of *Parteilichkeit*, or conformity to the Party line, in order to be published, such as including a model Soviet citizen among the crew as Szameit's comment shows. And one can ascribe a certain amount of, perhaps retrospectively, naïve and overt optimism in their depictions of the future, possibly best encapsulated in the Steinmüllers' history of the genre in the GDR, *Vorgriff auf das Lichte Morgen* (*Anticipation of the Bright Tomorrow*).

Science fiction in the GDR was customarily categorized as "scientific-fantastic" (*wissenschaftlich-phantastik*) literature, borrowing from the Russian designation for the genre. The use of this term has its origins in the 1962 German Writers' Union Conference on Literature of the Future. Partially an attempt to distinguish the manifestation of the genre in the GDR from its West German counterpart, dominated as it was by the influence of the Anglo-American tradition and the flood of such works into the West German market, the scientific-fantastic was defined as "a finer East German socialist SF, which used its fantastic qualities not to escape contemporary problems, but to aid scientifically in their rational solution, along the same ideological vector designated by the term 'novel of the future'" (Fritzsche 2001, 108).

Other designations included *Utopischer Roman* (utopian novel), *Zukunftsroman* (novel of the future), or the equivalent for short stories. These designations were never applied with enough consistency to arrive at a reliable explanation for how they were determined for any particular work. The term "science fiction" did not appear as an officially sanctioned label on the front cover of a work by a GDR author until 1984, with the publication of the short story anthology, *Windschiefe Geraden* (*Crooked Straight Lines*), by Angela and Karlheinz Steinmüller, two of the most popular SF authors in the GDR. The Steinmüllers were not told at the time that their book would receive this appellation and still do not know why they were selected to receive this distinction.[5]

The term "science fiction," nevertheless, was in widespread use among fans of the genre, and was used by editors at the publishing houses in internal documents and by literary theorists and critics in the titles and within the pages of essays on the genre. Indeed, the Verlag Das Neue Berlin published a brochure entitled *Science-fiction in der DDR: Personalia zu einem Genre*, edited by Erik Simon and Olaf R. Spittel in 1982. This brochure, though, was not intended for distribution within the GDR, but was meant for distribution at writers' congresses abroad (Steinmüller 1995, 58).

And of course, the term did appear in abbreviated form in the title of the SF-*Utopia* series in which *Raumkundschafter Katman* was published. The novel's inclusion in this prominent series points to the significance that it was accorded at the time. The publishing approval protocols of the Verlag Das Neue Berlin (*Druckgenehmigungsverfahren*) ascribe to it a contemporary relevance. "The most important realization that the reader takes is that one must not face aggressiveness unarmed, if one wants to claim to be a humane being" (Kracht n.d., 521–22). The seemingly paradoxical moral of the story is that humanity can only be maintained by being militarily prepared.

The Cold War could easily have become the reality of a third world war with nuclear implications, especially given the rhetoric of Reagan. The GDR stood on the frontline of any possible conflict and maintained the second strongest army in the Warsaw Pact to meet the demands of such a contingency. And the National People's Army (*die Nationale Volksarmee*, or NVA) readily demonstrated its preparedness in the annual May Day parades through the center of Berlin.

These demonstrations were naturally formulated in terms of the defense of socialism. The GDR presented itself as the "First Workers' and Peasants' State on German Soil," as a "really existing" socialism that needed to be defended from the capitalist, imperialist powers that would seek to take away what it had achieved by force if necessary. The NVA were the ready defenders of this state that represented itself as the "victor of history," a higher, more humane stage of the inevitable evolution of human society.

In the 1980s, Reagan's rhetoric was an easy source by which to portray the threat that the U.S. posed to the GDR and the socialist system to which it belonged—made all the more real by the continued heavy presence of the U.S. military in West Germany that included the deployment of tactical short-range conventional missiles. In the face of this threat, the GDR's ruling party, the Socialist Unity Party of Germany (*die Sozialistische Einheitspartei Deutschlands*, or SED), "began a campaign designed to further incite youths to join the military and develop a willingness to defend the GDR" (Bickford 2011, 62). Resurrected from the ruins (as its national anthem declared) of the Third Reich, the GDR proclaimed itself to be the better Germany that had learned the lessons of history and was the natural champion of peace. The preservation of this peace, though, necessitated the maintenance of a strong and heavily armed, though nominally defensive, force to serve and protect it—the same rhetoric that Reagan utilized in his speech on defense and national security.

In a similar sense, the GDR needed its young people to choose careers in the fields of science and technology. This was an absolute necessity for a state, theoretically based on an inherently rational, socialist order and practically in need of those workers who could build it. From the state's perspective SF could help to inspire its readers to make this choice to build a future that was often "prophesized" in the stories of its "scientific-fantastic." The historical trajectory of global progress from primitive accumulation to the finality of communism was extrapolated onto a universal scale.

Despite the proclivities of publication in the GDR, and the perhaps muted and subtle attempts to differentiate socialist works of the genre from their Western counterparts, SF in the GDR must be understood to be just that—science fiction—in both the best and worst senses of the term, a genre that attempts to deal in the possibilities and potential futures of a socialist society for which the scientific-technical revolution (the *wissentschaftlich-technische Revolution*, or *WTR*, as it was known in the GDR) was *the* path forward. It is, therefore, employed in this essay to describe works from the GDR, regardless of their designation at the time. GDR SF is one national variant of this most modern and international genre that is inherently universal in its scope.

The usual stereo-type is that the East is always an imitation of the West. In terms of SF, the literary theories about the genre converge as might well be expected from systems of human civilization for which scientific-technical innovation was the means forward for society's evolution. This is clear in Szameit's answer to the question about the similarities between the theories of SF in East and West:

> [Y]es, there are amazing correspondences. These "theories," though, were for us the result of our own thinking, were much more the product of practical work. And in countless discussions with one another during private get-togethers and at events of the publishing houses and the Writers' Union. [...] In a certain sense, we invented the bicycle for a second time. It is only that we constructed it, rather than designing a blueprint beforehand.[6]

Science fiction can be said to arise from the same fundamental desire and need, in East and West, to identify and comprehend a present temporality that has been increasingly conditioned by the technological transformations of the Industrial Revolution.

The qualities, and the quality, of GDR SF evolved in the fullness of time in much the same way as in the West. From overtly optimistic prognostications of an achieved (socialist) future to cautionary tales of the hazards of overreliance and overdependence on the technological, the development of GDR SF mirrors that of the current, quite obviously, dominant Anglo-American model. Quantitatively, more SF was published in the GDR during the 1970s than in the 20 preceding years of the GDR (Förster 1980, 32). And qualitatively, an increasing, and welcomed, diversity was ascribed to the SF genre in both its thematic content and formal conventions (Heidt-mann 1982, 157). In the first dissertation on the genre, published 28 years after the GDR's founding, Alfred Sckerl remarks that GDR SF "has now as well taken up with consequence the versatile possibilities that have already been acquired in the development of this world-literature genre. It has attained the level of international developments" (Sckerl 1977, 183–84).

Over the course of the GDR's history, the authors of the genre increasingly came to make use of the fantastic elements implied by its GDR designation in order to critique the system—not to change it outright, but to reform it from within. The satirical, the grotesque, and the tragic-comic elements were utilized in place of a "vulgar Marxist supported description of the future" (Steinmüller 1992, 167) in order to make the points of their critiques pertinent. By the 1980s, the "scientific-fantastic" showed a marked trend towards portraying the individual's responsibility in society and assuming the function of "warning" its readers to problems before it would be too late for a solution.

In the case of *Raumkundschafter Katman*, the international crew members of the second mission engage in a heated debate about possible candidates for a "unified earthly language." This is not an issue in "Tödlicher Irrtum," where such a language already exists. While the Russian first officer argues for her native language, the commander opts for English, because "this language is already spoken in various parts of the world. Besides which it is constructed simply and is being further simplified by linguists that it is already understood as the second language in half the world. While Russian has even kept the Cyrillic letters" (Ansorge 1987, 100).[7] This questioning of Russian for very practical and realistic reasons is noteworthy in a novel that also directly questions the propriety of the "Cosmic Law." It is a nuanced view of the future that avoids the overly and overtly propagandistic picture of an enemy that has nothing positive to offer.

The depicted future is one in which the petty rivalries of nation-states have been overcome. Terrestrial solidarity is reflected in the internationality of names—a common practice on the science-fictional terrain. The commander is perchance a native of Holland with the telling family name, Dutch. The chief medical officer is Chinese and uses Latin adages (all of which are helpfully translated for the reader in footnotes) to add rhetorical force to his utterances. And such is the influence of the "Cosmic Law" that he commits suicide when he realizes that the Yoga civilization is the exception that negates the rule. The hero, Katman, is conceivably German, but his first name, Salek, has a decidedly foreign shade to it, while his girlfriend's name is the clearly foreign, all too American Cindy. And the head of the World Security Agency has a Scottish surname.

While a security agency may seem out of place on this world, its existence is explained by the imperfections of the depicted utopia that have given rise to terrorism related to a militant drug scene. The Earth is a unified whole, though, peaceful and ostensibly socialist. It stands as proof of the veracity of the "Cosmic Law," an example of the way forward for humanity.

At the core of this law stands the dynamic interplay between the evolution of technology and the society that develops, deploys, and employs it. The exploration of the cosmos requires immense resources, those of an entire planet. In the words of the First Communicator: "A civilization, capable of interstellar or even intergalactic undertakings, must be peaceful, because the capacity of a society can either be used for murderous wars or the discovery of the cosmos. The energies are not sufficient for both" (Kellner 1985, 150). Only a society that does not squander its wealth on warfare can ever hope to acquire and develop such resources—even as history has often shown that technological leaps forward have been driven by the necessities of war.

This law remains valid until the second mission encounters the deadly exception to this rule: the Yoga civilization. This civilization is not interested in communication; it is only interested in one particular commodity: water. It is not that dissimilar to the aliens of *Independence Day* (Roland Emmerich, 1996) or any number of other invaders from the pages and scripts of Anglo-American SF that seek to colonize Earth for its resources. And the Yoga civilization communicates only by way of demands. No room for negotiation or accommodation—not to speak of cooperation—is given—and confrontation is the order of the day.

This law maintains, though, that there is a tipping point is on the scale of development. The capital of technology is either re-invested in an enhanced lethality of better and bigger guns, or in the advancement of true social progress. As the Russian first officer emphatically states about the Yoga civilization: "Otherwise this civilization, an empire of darkness, would have destroyed itself long ago" (Ansorge 1987, 93).

In the curious context of the Cold War, her words are an inversion of Reagan's indictment of the Soviet Union as an "Evil Empire." Ironically enough, neither this "Evil Empire" nor that "empire of darkness" had suffered self-destruction and continued to pose a very real, existential threat, militarily and/or ideologically, to its counterpart. And the Yoga civilization is a *Doppelgänger* for the U.S., only interested in conquest and colonization. In the Manichean universe that *Star Wars* made spectacularly popular, good and evil are in a universal struggle with one another. In the practical realities of the Cold War, each side rhetorically presented itself to be on that of the "good" and proceeded to define this ambiguous quality according to its own particular best interests.

In a speech to the National Association of Evangelicals on 8 March 1983, Reagan famously called the Soviet Union "an Evil Empire." Given the venue, it is not all that surprising that he should choose such a figuratively loaded adjective with religious overtones to describe an all-too earthly foe. His oratorical style was often characterized by salutary invocations of superficial appeals to metaphysical Christian ideals, but his rhetorical approach was a clear echo of the popular environment created by the success of *Star Wars*.[8] It was also a foreshadowing of his subsequent announcement two weeks later of the "Strategic Defense Initiative," as it was officially designated a year later, or simply "Star Wars," as it is still commonly known—a legacy that has yet to meet its promised guarantees of security.

In the aftermath of the *Star Wars'* success, two sequels followed in three-year intervals: *The Empire Strikes Back* (Irvin Kershner) in May of 1980 and *The Return of the Jedi* (Richard Marquand) in May of 1983. The original film was accompanied by a mass marketing and merchandising campaign. This included comic books and novelizations, action figures and toys, commercial tie-ins and clothing, so that its grand exploits could be re-materialized, re-capitalized, and re-enacted on the scale of the everyday.

This continued with the release of each sequel. In order to renew and fuel the public's interest and enthusiasm, the original film was re-released in theaters prior to each sequel. It was also shown on Pay-per-view television and made available in the relatively new format of the VHS tape, so that its spectacle could be enjoyed in domestic comfort. When it was released on VHS in April of 1981, it was henceforth given the subtitle, "Episode IV, A New Hope," and was by this point clearly part of an on-going modern saga for the space age. By the time of Reagan's "Address to the Nation on Defense and National Security," *Star Wars* was, in a sense, everywhere and on—or very much in—everyone's minds. It was, by all accounts, a presence in the popular imagination that "had popularized the notion of space-based systems" (Kramer 1999, 44).

In *cosmic secret: Testfall SDI—Mythen und Szenarien* (*cosmic secret: Test Case SDI—Myths and Scenarios*), Horst Hoffman traces the development of the Strategic Defense Initiative and investigates the connections between the American military-industrial complex and the entertainment industry.[9] The book appeared with an initial run of 50,000 copies in the *nl-konkret* series of affordably-priced paperbacks that was intended to introduce adolescent and young adult readers to important political topics of the day. In his estimation, the SDI program is meant to appease and enrich the American military-industrial complex. It is also a means to keep the members of NATO and Japan dependent on the U.S. economically and to possibly bankrupt the Soviet Union through the exorbitant expenditures of a renewed arms race.

Hoffman sees the popularity of *Star Wars* as a vehicle through which to normalize space as an appropriate arena for the continuation of earthly warfare. The films' merchandising and commercial tie-ins are apparent parts of a concerted propaganda campaign that serve this aim of militarizing the space around the Earth. Even the made-for-TV film, *The Day After*, broadcast on the major television network ABC on 20 November 1983, which was presented to the public at the time as an accurate depiction of the horrors of a nuclear war and thus as an absolute danger to be avoided at all costs, is in his opinion part of a commercialized polemic meant to show the necessity of the SDI program.

The stated aim of the SDI program was to gain the ability to shoot down incoming nuclear missiles from the Soviet Union. If it proved to be feasible, then the doctrine of "Mutually Assured Destruction," or MAD, that had served to keep the peace between the opposing sides of the Cold War, in which any attack by one side on the other would immediately result in its own destruction, would no longer pertain. The U.S. would have the ability to prevent a retaliatory strike and could thus theoretically win a nuclear war.

This possibility also found its ways onto the pages of GDR SF. The letter writer to the *ZK SED*, *Abteilung Kulturpolitik*, for example, cites Peter Lorenz's *Homunkuli* as the best work of GDR SF to address the threat that the U.S. poses to world peace in his complaint about Szameit's novel *Alarm im Tunnel Transterra* and its trivialization of the danger posed by the last capitalist state on what is otherwise a unified and socialist Earth. Part of a loosely connected trilogy that "takes up the best traditions of the 'space opera'" (Simon and Spittel 1988, 251–52), the grand scope of Szameit's novel and trilogy does not depict battles on a lavish scale, as might be expected in the Anglo-American model, but rather shows the personal and collective struggles that arise from the efforts to understand the relics of a vanished alien civilization.

Lorenz's novel was originally published in 1978 by the Verlag Neues Leben in its long-running BASAR series. Set in the 21st century, it tells the story of a microbiologist who unknowingly becomes involved in a secret U.S. program to produce clones. These clones are meant to rebuild the world after a purportedly preventative nuclear first strike against the United Communist States. In the end, these clones become self-aware and prove themselves to be the better human beings. They rebel before the plan can be put into effect. And the leaders are arrested and charged with war crimes.

Reinhold Kriese's *Eden City, die Stadt des Vergessens* (*Eden City—the City of Oblivion*), which was also published by the Verlag Neues Leben in the same BASAR series first in 1985 and again in 1987, tells a similar story.

Members of the American military-industrial complex attempt a nuclear first-strike and hide themselves away in a bunker to await the time when the Earth can sustain human life again. When the human clones that have been produced to serve them revolt and break out onto the planet's surface, they find that the first strike never happened—a people's uprising at the last minute prevented the execution of their plan and a socialist world has been constructed in its aftermath.

Star Wars, though, is set in the spatial and temporal dimensions of "a long time ago in a galaxy far, far away." Its action, nevertheless, contains many elements borrowed from the battles of the Second World War—the last war that the U.S. waged in the officially legal use of the term and the last "good" war in American history, if only because the U.S. victory was unmistakable. The opposing sides of the Second World War were clearly delineated into those of good and evil. If the GDR presented itself as the *a priori* "victor of history," because it was socialist in name, then the U.S. presented itself as the champion of the "good," because it defeated Imperialist Japan and Nazi Germany, if only due to its use of the first atomic bomb and its alliance with the Soviet Union.

The dogfights between the Tie-fighters of the Empire and the X-Wing fighters of the Rebel Alliance are modeled on those of the Second World War, or more tellingly, on their depictions in popular films of the 1950s that stoked and maintained the feeling of victory after the fact. The large-scale galactic warfare of the film is entirely reminiscent of the battle scenarios of the Second World War. The Imperial star cruisers appear as the direct descendants of WWII aircraft carriers in the blackness of space. And the troops of the Empire are called "Stormtroopers" in a direct reference to the Nazi paramilitary organization.

The uniforms of the Empire's officer corps resemble those of the Nazi Army, and by extension, perhaps unintentionally, but paradoxically, of the defenders of the GDR, the NVA. The style of NVA uniforms was chosen "to show that while the NVA was a 'new' type of German military, a military based on Marxist-Leninist principles, it was still a 'German' army, linked to German military traditions and prowess" (Bickford 2011, 44). The totalitarian overtones of this choice were an unintended consequence which was only strengthened by the retention of the Prussian goose step. The officers of the Empire wear the same type of jack boots so commonly associated in the Anglo-American mind with its authoritarian enemies. And the helmets of the Empire's human officers and non-coms are unmistakably the same type as those of the NVA.

All of these elements serve to reinforce the malevolently tyrannical nature of the Empire that the viewer first sees in the descriptive words of the opening crawl: "the evil Galactic Empire." In the victorious haze of post–WWII America, the figure of the unfeeling, coldly-calculating German represented the ultimate face of evil in the world. This association was all too effortlessly, and conveniently, displaced onto the new Cold War enemy of the Soviet Union and its ally, the GDR—a connection made all too easy by the outward similarities in the militaristic stylings of these Cold War adversaries.

The parameters of the story that are established in the opening crawl are dichotomous in nature with freedom-loving Rebels on the one side and an evil Galactic Empire on the other. There is no middle ground for compromise in such a struggle. The monolithic way in which the Empire is described emphasizes the all-encompassing nature of its power. Its supremacy is even illustrated typographically by the use of all capital letters to describe its "ultimate weapon, the DEATH STAR." It is a totality that reigns over life and death—its armored space station, an anti-sun of annihilation.

The very notion of Rebels that are engaged in a struggle against an evil empire invokes the spirit of the American Revolution, the bicentennial of which had been grandly celebrated the year prior to the film's release. The crawl proclaims that "it is a period of civil war," and the American Revolution was to a certain extent also one within the British Empire of the time. And the rebels of the film occupy the same position as those of the Revolution, that of an underdog that must struggle against overwhelming odds—a favorite trope of the American historical imagination and cult of individuality.

This is the same rhetoric that Reagan made use of in his speech (Reagan 1983). In an invocation drawn directly, whether intentionally or not, from the revised opening crawl of *Star Wars*, he proclaims that he is offering "a new hope for our children in the 21st century." It is a proclamation of science-fictional proportions in its *spatio*-temporal displacement—that is, the extrapolation of future possibilities based on current conditions, the underlying formula of the science-fictional text. And indeed, the future is the final destination that can never be reached for any utopian project—American or otherwise.

In this "Star Wars" Speech, Reagan recites a short history of the Cold War. He places the U.S. in the position of the weaker military power in the face of an overwhelming Soviet threat. And he emphasizes this threat through a detailed accounting of the expansion of Soviet capabilities and the perceived escalation of existential danger that this entails for the U.S.

While speaking of the possibilities of war, though, Reagan constantly invokes the notion of peace and maintains that peace is his ultimate concern. The words "peace" and "strength" occur no less than 14 times in combination with one another over the course of his speech. The peace that he proposes to preserve, though, is one that must be attained and sustained by strength—a strength that can only be arrived at and derived from superior American armament.

The only means to achieve this is to implement and deploy a program of space weaponry that can defend the American people and their allies from the totalitarian reaches of the Soviet Union. Although formulated in the rhetoric of open-handed negotiation, reminiscent of the fatally misunderstood explorer in the painting from "Tödlicher Irrtum," Reagan is proposing that the U.S. gain the upper hand militarily over its ideological adversary for fundamentally terrestrial, power-political reasons. Two civilizations, nominally communist and capitalist, stand in opposition to one another, as if they were from different worlds, although both have their basis in the possibilities and capabilities of the Industrial Revolution and the Enlightenment.

Technologically advanced, both represent possible pathways for the evolution of human society. The proverbial law of the jungle, supposedly left behind at an early stage of development, but always part of the American ideal of the individual, still applies. And another law is invoked—that of might makes right.

In this sense and for this reason, the First Communicator enters the sphere for one last time. In his hand, he holds a remnant of Earth's violent history, a museum piece on the pacified surface of the globe, a small spherical grenade that has the destructive force to destroy the larger sphere. As a communicator, he has failed twice-over. He has not been able to establish meaningful communication with the alien entity of the sphere. And he has not been able to communicate to his peers that this entity's demand for homage is not a simple mistranslation, but an accurate description of its hostile intentions. He knows that the "Cosmic Law" has been broken and that this first encounter with an alien civilization must be the last. He consequently, and with consequence, activates the grenade's countdown.

On Katman's Earth, the countdown has already begun. The second mission to the Yoga system has ended in failure and destruction. In a last act of service, Katman has sacrificed himself and destroyed his ship to impede the Yoga ships on their path to Earth. The Yoga civilization has made its demands known—unequivocally and in English no less. It is not the exception that proves the rule, but the one that breaks the "Cosmic Law" and the system of belief it upheld. In an epilogue to Katman's story, the High Council sees that it has no other choice but to order the necessary military preparations for the defense of Earth.

On 9 November 1989, the so-called "anti-fascist defense wall" (*anti-faschistischer Schutzwall*), more popularly known in the West as the Berlin Wall, was opened for citizens of the GDR. It had stood for slightly over

28 years, separating East from West at the heart of the Cold War. Not a shot was fired by the NVA. Less than a year later, on 3 October 1990, the GDR, four days shy of the forty-first anniversary of its founding, ceased to exist— its class struggle finished in the heavens of its SF as it was on Earth, it was incorporated, bodily, into its Western *Doppelgänger*.

NOTES

1. Unless otherwise noted, all translations from the German are my own.

2. See, for example, Darko Suvin's *Metamorphoses of Science Fiction: On the Poetics and History of a Literary Genre* (New Haven: Yale University Press, 1979) and Fredric Jameson's "Progress Versus Utopia; or, Can We Imagine the Future?" (*Science Fiction Studies* 9.2 [1982]: 147–158).

3. See Michael Harrington. 1976. *The Twilight of Capitalism*. New York: Simon and Schuster.

4. Erik Simon in an interview, quoted in Angela Steinmüller and Karlheinz Steinmüller. 1996. "Die befohlene Zukunft: DDR-Science Fiction zwischen Wunschtraum und (Selbst-) Zensur," in *Hier Zensur—wer dort? Zensur und Selbstzensur in der Literatur.* Eds. Peter Brock-meier and Gerhard R. Kaiser. Würzburg: Königshausen und Neumann. 275–288, 284.

5. See Personal Interview, 3 January 2008.

6. See E-mail from the author, 7 March 2008. Although Szameit emphasizes the daily praxis of writing in his answer, there were also numerous theoretical discussions in the GDR about the genre, where SF is posited as a genre that deals with the problems of the present through its deployment of a projected future along the same analytical lines of Suvin and Jameson. See, for example, the protocols from the *Kulturbund* of the GDR in the *Bundesar-chiv*, DY 27/3535 *Gespräch über utopisch-phantastische Literatur in Berlin am 20.6.1973* and DY 27/4902 *Wochenendgespraech der Bezirksleitung Suhl zum Thema "Jules Verne" am 14. und 15.4.1978 in Suhl.*

7. World governance gives rise to orthographic problems, just as the National Socialist regime discovered that fraktur does not work well to rule an empire, on Earth or in the heavens: "[...] the real reason for the abolition of *fraktur* was power politics. In 1941, Hitler's armies were victorious on every front. The future world power had to adapt to the 'world type' (Roman) in order to exercise its power." See H.P. Willberg. 1998. "Fraktur and Nation-alism." *Blackletter: Type and National Identity.* Eds. P. Bain and P. Shaw. New York: Princeton Architectural Press, 49.

8. See Peter Kramer. 1999. "Star Wars." *History Today* 49.3: 41–47.

9. See Horst Hoffman. 1988. *cosmic secret: Testfall SDI—Mythen und Szenarien.* Berlin: Verlag Neues Leben.

WORKS CITED

Ansorge, Horst. 1987. *Raumkundschafter Katman.* Berlin: Verlag Das Neue Berlin.

Bickford, Andrew. 2011. *Fallen Elites: The Military Other in Post-Unification Germany.* Stan-ford: Stanford University Press.

Fitting, Peter. 1980. "The Second Alien." In "Symposium on 'Alien.'" *Science Fiction Studies* 7.3: 278–304.

Förster, Werner. 1980. *Realität und Entwurf: Zur einigen Aspekten des Genres Phantas-tik in der DDR-Literatur der siebziger Jahre.* Dissertation zur Promotion A. Leipzig: Karl-Marx-Universität.

Fritzsche, Sonja. 2001. *Alternate Worlds, Alternate Visions: Cultural Politics and Socialist Cri-tique in East German Science Fiction.* Ann Arbor: UMI Dissertation Services.

_____. 2006. "East Germany's 'Werkstatt Zukunft': Futurology and the Science Fiction of 'defa-futurum.'" *German Studies Review* 29.2: 367–386.

Gakow, Wl. (Michail Kowaltschuk). 1985. "Die Sternstunde des Science-fiction-Films." In *Lichtjahr 4*. Berlin: Verlag Das Neue Berlin. 41–63.

Gespräch über utopisch-phantastische Literatur in Berlin am 20.6.1073. BArch 27 / 3535.

Harrington, Michael. 1976. *The Twilight of Capitalism*. New York: Simon & Schuster.

Heidtmann, Horst. 1982. *Utopisch-phantastische Literatur in der DDR: Untersuchungen zur Entwicklung eines unterhaltungsliterarischen Genres von 1945–1979*. München: Wilhelm Fink Verlag.

Hesse, Kurt R. 1990. "Cross-Border Mass Communication from West to East Germany." *European Journal of Communications* 5: 355–371.

Hoffman, Horst. 1988. *cosmic secret: Testfall SDI—Mythen und Szenarien*. Berlin: Verlag Neues Leben.

Independence Day. Film. Directed by Roland Emmerich. Los Angeles: Twentieth Century Fox, 1996.

Jameson, Fredric. "Progress Versus Utopia; Or, Can We Imagine the Future?" *Science Fiction Studies* 9.2 (1982): 147–158.

Jamilla, Nick. 2012. "Defining the Jedi Order: Star Wars' Narrative and the Real World." In *Sex, Politics, and Religion in Star Wars. an Anthology*. Eds. Douglas Brode and Leah Deyneka. London: Scarecrow Press. 147–163.

Kellner, Wolfgang. 1985. "Tödlicher Irrtum." In *Lichtjahr 4*. Berlin: Verlag Das Neue Berlin. 137–159.

Kracht, Horst. *Review of Raumkundschafter Katman*. BArch DR 1 / 3634a. 519–522.

Kramer, Peter. 1999. "Star Wars." *History Today* 49.3: 41–47.

Kriese, Reinhard. 1987. *Eden City, die Stadt des Vergessens*. Berlin: Verlag Neues Leben.

Küchler, Manfred. 1990. *Der Planet ohne Sonne*. Berlin: Verlag Neues Leben.

Lorenz, Peter. 1978. *Homunkuli*. Berlin: Verlag Neues Leben.

Reagan, Ronald. "Address to the Nation on Defense and National Security." reaganlibrary. archives.gov/archives/speeches/1983/32383d.htm

Scheibe, Detlef. *Letter to the ZK der SED, Abteilung Kulturpolitik, regarding Szameit's Alarm im Tunnel Transterra (25 June 1983)*. BArch DR 1 / 5440. 71–73.

Sckerl, Alfred. 1977. *Wissenschaftlich-phantastische Literatur: Überlegungen zu einem literarischen Genre und Anmerkungen zu seiner Entwicklung in der DDR*. Dissertation. Berlin: Humboldt-Universität zu Berlin.

Simon, Erik and Olaf R. Spittel. 1988. "Die Entwicklung der Science-fiction Literatur der DDR." In *Die Science-fiction der DDR: Autoren und Werke*. Eds. Erik Simon and Olaf R. Spittel. Berlin: Verlag Das Neue Berlin. 11–90.

Star Trek. Television Series. 1966–1969. Created by Gene Roddenberry. Aired on NBC.

Star Wars. Film. 1977. Directed by George Lucas. Los Angeles: Twentieth Century Fox.

Star Wars: Episode V—The Empire Strikes Back. Film. 1980. Directed by Irvin Kershner. Los Angeles: Twentieth Century Fox.

Star Wars: Episode VI—Return of the Jedi. Film. 1983. Directed by Richard Marquand. Los Angeles: Twentieth Century Fox.

Steinmüller, Angela, and Karlheinz Steinmüller. 1995. *Vorgriff auf das Lichte Morgen: Studien zur DDR-Science-Fiction mit einer Bibliographie von Hans-Peter Neumann*. Passau: Erster Deutscher Fantasy Club e.V.

_____. 1996. "Die befohlene Zukunft: DDR-Science Fiction zwischen Wunschtraum und (Selbst-) Zensur." In *Hier Zensur—wer dort? Zensur und Selbstzensur in der Literatur*. Eds. Peter Brockmeier and Gerhard R. Kaiser. Würzburg: Königshausen und Neumann. 275–288.

_____. 2008. Personal Interview. 3 January.

Steinmüller, Karlheinz. 1992. "Das Ende der Utopischen Literatur: Ein Themengeschichtlicher Nachruf auf die DDR-Science-fiction." *The Germanic Review* 67.4: 166–173.

Suvin, Darko. 1979. *Metamorphoses of Science Fiction: On the Poetics and History of a Literary Genre*. New Haven: Yale University Press.

Szameit, Michael. 1982. *Alarm im Tunnel Transterra*. Berlin: Verlag Neues Leben.

_____. 1983. *Im Glanz der Sonne Zaurak.* Berlin: Verlag Neues Leben.

_____. 1984. *Das Geheimnis der Sonnensteine.* Berlin: Verlag Neues Leben.

_____. 1990. "Nachwort." In *Der lange Weg zum Blauen Stern.* Ed. M. Szameit. Berlin: Verlag Neues Leben. 214–220.

_____. 2008. E-mail from the Author. 7 March.

Taylor, Chris. 2015. *How Star Wars Conquered the Universe.* London: Head of Zeus Ltd.

Willberg, H.P. 1998. "Fraktur and Nationalism." In *Blackletter: Type and National Identity.* Eds. P. Bain and P. Shaw. New York: Princeton Architectural Press.

Wochenendgespräch der Bezirksleitung Suhl zum Thema 'Jules Verne' am 14. und 15.4.1978 in Suhl. BArch 27 / 4902.

Love and Death in Two Nuclear Defense Films

Doug Davis

Atomic Cyborg Love Stories

It takes an especially inventive Hollywood film to make nuclear escalation look appealing. For that matter, it takes an equally inventive Hollywood film to make nuclear defense look unappealing. In this essay I show how two major Cold War Hollywood films rewrite the reality of the nuclear weapons state in a science fictional way to build political consensus for and against the policy of nuclear deterrence. Anthony Mann's Air Force public relations film, *Strategic Air Command* (1955), and Stanley Kubrick's black comedy, *Dr. Strangelove: Or, How I Learned to Stop Worrying and Love the Bomb* (1964), both demonstrate what most Cold War filmmakers and theatergoers already, if unconsciously, knew. Some of Hollywood's most celebrated films about the bomb aren't really about the bomb at all. What they are really about is love.

Mann's and Kubrick's films are the two most prominent examples of a form of Cold War narrative invention that rewrites America's strategy of nuclear deterrence as a fiction of atomic love rather than war. Developed in the early 1950s, nuclear deterrence is the terrifying strategy in which the military uses a show of nuclear force to prevent enemy states, in particular the Soviet Union, from attacking the nation or its allies. The result of this strategy was an escalation in the stockpile of American nuclear weapons from about 1000 warheads in 1953 to nearly 18,000 strategic, tactical, and air-defense warheads by 1961, and American nuclear war plans best described as "overkill" (Rosenberg 1960, 133). *Strategic Air Command* and *Dr. Strangelove* each build political consensus around the Cold War American strategy of nuclear deterrence by distracting their audiences from the conflicted politics of nuclear defense itself. To their martial Cold War plots these films appended a none-too-subtle and far more personal and familiar subtext: the allure of wartime service. While working to completely opposite political ends, *Strategic Air Command* and *Dr. Strangelove* each tell an atomic cyborg love story, producing consent or dissent for American nuclear policy through scenes of beautiful, strange, and unnatural posthuman romance.

In the canon of what has come to be called "nuclear films"—that loose conglomeration of films that deal with the effects of all forms of nuclear energy[1]—these peculiar love stories of man-machine couplings occupy a special place.[2] They are rare instances when Hollywood showed its audiences something they otherwise would never get to see in the Cold War security state: the top-secret world of nuclear defense in action. The longing gaze these films cast on the posthuman world of nuclear defense has a sublimating effect within the Cold War's conflicted political discourse of nuclear defense, transforming the secret, troubling spaces of national security into thinly veiled boudoirs wherein military service is presented as a labor of love. Hollywood thus plays one of the oldest and most manipulative tricks in its book, pinning the morality of nuclear defense on its audiences' taste for its cinematic love affairs.

Although the term "cyborg" was coined only in 1960 (Clynes and Kline 1995), cyborgs themselves have a long history both in the military and in narrative. As Sydney Perkowitz discusses in *Digital People*, human bodies augmented by such technologies as artificial limbs can be found in histories and myths dating back thousands of years (Perkowitz 2004, 87). The history of the cyborg dovetails with the long history of prostheses in particular. "Much of the impetus to make artificial limbs that actually work," Perkowitz notes, "has come from the needs of injured warriors and soldiers" (Perkowitz 2004, 88). The most common kind of cyborgs found in both ancient and modern cultures are wounded soldiers whose lost limbs have been replaced by artificial ones.

As the technology of warfare developed over the past millennia, so too did the science of prosthetics. During the Second World War, the "man-machine system was institutionalized through operations research and scientific management practices" (Gray 2001, 58). Scientists working in the new field of cybernetics designed weapon control systems that integrated human bodies closely with the technology of fighting machines. This new military technology then informed the design of new prostheses. In the decades following the war, as David Serlin documents in *Replaceable You: Engineering the Body in Postwar America*, "new biomechanical principles and cybernetic control systems had begun to be applied to the operation of artificial arms and legs" (Serlin 2004, 26), thus creating the world's first truly cybernetic organisms.

The prosthetic cyborg technologies developed after the war were products of culture as much as they were of science and engineering, for they "expressed postwar culture's need to reengineer the physical body to accommodate the social mandates of the era" (Serlin 2004, 16). As N. Katherine Hayles observes in *How We Became Posthuman: Virtual Bodies in Cybernetics, Literature, and Informatics*, the new science of cybernetics demonstrated "that the boundaries of the human subject are constructed rather than given" (Hayles 1999, 84). The cyborg became a model in both science and culture for a new kind of subject purpose-built for the postmodern era. The postwar cyborg swiftly transcended its military and prosthetic ancestry, becoming "simultaneously entities and metaphors, living beings and narrative constructions" (Hayles 1999, 114). While real cyborgs such as people who wear pacemakers now make up a substantial minority of the world's population, metaphoric and narrative cyborgs abound throughout postmodern culture anywhere subjectivity, science, and technology intersect (Hayles 1999, 115). Indeed, as film scholar Sue Short argues, cyborgs have become such a common fixture in postmodern culture that they have inspired their own sub-genre of popular filmmaking featuring characters that are literally part human and part machine, "cyborg cinema" (Short 2005).

Writing during one of the heights of the Cold War in the 1980s in her influential "Cyborg Manifesto," Donna Haraway identifies the cyborg as an ideal image for a postmodern kind of subjectivity "intimately restructured through the social relations of science and technology" (Haraway 1991, 165). The cyborg's literal embodied technologies serve Haraway as a metaphor that describes the whole lived experience of the Cold War and contemporary capitalism, denoting not merely modern humanity's dependence on electronics, but every individuals' constitution as a subject of multiple sciences and technologies in a permanent war economy. In an age of electronic surveillance, biotechnology, and total war, Haraway argues, identity is best thought of as the multiple, partial, and often contradictory expressions of the scientific, technological, and even cultural "integrated circuits" in which one lives and through which one's money, labor, and even desire flows. Haraway's hope is that those oppressed in the integrated circuits of multinational capital who are increasingly unable to find common ground in the old political categories of identity—race, class, gender—can still organize around their many affinities as dispersed subjects of local and global high-tech society. For Haraway, the cyborg is a way to raise consciousness about one's relationship to others in a coded, fragmented, technologically mediated and multiply targeted world.

We stand before two cyborg futures, Haraway contends, one of which threatens to be an ossification of the Cold War while the other holds out hope for radical new political alignments, from one perspective, a cyborg world is about the final imposition of a grid of control on the planet, about the final abstraction embodied in a Star Wars apocalypse waged in the name of defense, about the final appropriation of women's bodies in a masculinist orgy of war.... From another perspective, a cyborg world might be about lived social and bodily realities in which people are not afraid of their joint kinship with animals and machines, not afraid of permanently partial identities and contradictory standpoints [Haraway 1991, 154].

Both perspectives describe our common postmodern world; either we will surrender to "the awful apocalyptic telos of the 'West's' escalating dominations of abstract individuation" and embrace the alienated condition of "an ultimate self untied at last from all dependency, a man in space," or we will start to recognize our deep and contingent interrelations with each other in our wired world (Haraway 1991, 150–151).

Hollywood tends to tell stories about men in space rather than Haraway's more hopeful, globally connected cyborgs when it represents the business of nuclear defense. While they may value it differently, Hollywood's atomic cyborg love stories dive right into the "masculinist orgy" of nuclear defense, an orgy that does not include women. "As soldiers become more like cyborgs" over the 20th century, Chris Hables Gray observes in *Cyborg Citizen*, "their gender identify shifts." Because soldiers like the Cold War's nuclear bomber pilots serve primarily as operators of machines, a "new 'masculine' identity of soldiers is constructed more around mechanization—fixing machines and working with machines—than the traditional masculine identity of the user of physical force, easy access to violence, and the direct subjugation of other men and all women" (Gray 2001, 58). The machinery of nuclear defense accordingly appropriates the social and the biological functions of women's bodies in *Strategic Air Command* and *Dr. Strangelove*, both figuratively and literally.

Atomic cyborg love stories are populated almost entirely by lovingly depicted machines and chilly men in space, some of whom really are in space: pilots, bombardiers, generals, politicians, and strategists all integrated into the circuits of nuclear deterrence. These films depict the practice of nuclear defense from the inside, offering viewers rare visions of the soldiers, scientists, and statesmen who are passionately committed to the *techne* of nuclear defense. They do not dwell on the effects of nuclear war to take a stand on the bomb for they are neither war films nor post-apocalyptic films. Rather, they spend all of their screen time on the inner workings of the technological system of nuclear defense. Whatever the viewer thinks about America's strategic commitment to the bomb in films such as *Dr. Strangelove* and *Strategic Air Command* has entirely to do with how they value their characters' passionate commitments to the inner workings of nuclear deterrence.

Both *Strategic Air Command* and *Dr. Strangelove* are laden with contradictions that they do not resolve. While made with the full support of the Air Force, *Strategic Air Command* isn't blustery propaganda about the Strategic Air Command's (SAC's) nuclear warfighting prowess. It presents SAC as a worried war machine, lacking funds and public support and never sure if its bases are secure or even if its boys are up to the job. *Dr. Strangelove*, on the other hand, has complete faith in SAC's destructive reliability. Kubrick's bombers, bases, and doomsday machines work all too well once set in motion, even when done so accidentally. The situations these films present would appear to be working at cross purposes: Mann's Air Force PR film is raising doubts about the nuclear striking force's effectiveness as a war machine while Kubrick settles all of Mann's doubts by delivering technologically slick visions of the nuclear war machine working even better than advertised, even when run by buffoons.

Yet rather than paradoxically build or undermine America's faith in its nuclear defenses, Hollywood's atomic cyborg love stories step away from the political and focus, instead, on the personal side of nuclear defense. As the film historian Robert Ray observes in his study of the technical and thematic procedures of classic Hollywood film, Hollywood has a special ability to assuage the "troubling inconsistencies" of American society by converting "all political, sociological, and economic dilemmas into personal melodramas" (Ray 1985, 57). This "certain tendency" is particularly apparent in atomic cyborg love stories, which operate much like Hollywood's combat films of World War II. "Despite their reliance on realistic *mise en scénes*," Ray notes, "the combat pictures were essentially romances that magically resolved the tensions created by contradictory needs" (Ray 1985, 113). The magic Ray has in mind here can best be described as a disappearing act. Faced with situations that seemingly demanded a choice between irreconcilable needs, a focus on individual desire makes choice between the two a non-issue. With its focus on the fulfillment of fleeting individual desires, what matters most in classic Hollywood film is a protagonist's personal satisfaction. Hollywood films offer small and temporary fixes that make cases for a personal course of action—such as enlisting in the Air Force or scorning nuclear defense—but that leave all underlying social dilemmas unsettled. Taking sides in a political debate is strictly a matter of temporarily rooting for or against a character's personal happiness.

Ray doesn't extend his analysis of combat pictures to the realm of posthuman affairs, but his analysis applies just as well to cyborg melodramas set in the Cold War, for atomic cyborg love stories just as neatly side-step the contradictions and uncertainties behind the nation's permanent nuclear mobilization. *Strategic Air Command* studiously avoids resolving the contradictions present in its plot. Instead, it makes emotional cases for a life of nuclear defense by displacing all concerns about national security onto evaluations of the strange attraction that binds people and machines together in nuclear defense. *Dr. Strangelove*, in turn, stylistically foregrounds the narrative device, the story of nuclear attraction, at work in Air Force PR films such as *Strategic Air Command*. Nuclear defense is revealed in Kubrick's film not so much as a mad strategy but as a *physical space* for the fulfillment of its characters' posthuman desire for intimate coupling with the engines of total war. Yet even *Dr. Strangelove* remains a Hollywood film (generously financed by Columbia Pictures) as it doesn't resolve the contradiction present in its own loving, costly representation of the nuclear war machine in efficient, deterring action. It does, however, bury its cinematic celebration of nuclear-defense-in-action by making nuclear defense's bond between man and machine an object of derisive laughter.

Ultimately, genres rather than planes are the delivery systems of Hollywood's atomic cyborgs. Hollywood's atomic cyborg love stories deal their visions of the war machine in action to audiences in distinct genres, and it is through their choice of genre that these films actually make their cases for or against the bomb. Their acceptance or rejection of their unnatural loves serves as tacit judgment on the policy of nuclear defense. Popular films made in support of the nuclear defense, such as *Strategic Air Command*, make nuclear deterrence mainly a matter of the heart's fulfillment in a wartime romance. Films that challenge the morality of nuclear defense work in genres that undercut that romantic narrative's realism, turning its posthuman unions into objects of comic horror. *Strategic Air Command*'s wartime romance between man and flying machine becomes awkward and pornographic when dealt to us in the comedy of *Dr. Strangelove*. So, pro or con, Hollywood films contribute to the political discourse of nuclear defense by presenting cinematic discourses in genre on—yes—strange love.

Lost in Space: *Strategic Air Command*

Director Anthony Mann's 1955 celebration of America's airborne nuclear fleet, *Strategic Air Command*, is a lavish Air Force public relations vehicle that announces its political intentions in its opening credits. As the names of cast and crew dissolve over the service crest of the Strategic Air Command (a gauntlet reaching into the sky holding a lightning bolt and an olive branch), a choir intones a rousing march penned for the occasion, "The Air Force Takes Command." Dedicated in its opening credits to all the young men in the audience poised to enlist in the Air Force, *Strategic Air Command* premiered in the Spring of 1955 at the Paramount Theater in Times Square in a national extravaganza sponsored by the Air Force

Association. Searchlights swept above a parade of 3500 invited guests, a decorated spectacle of senators, starlets, and captains of industry rubbing elbows with Air Force brass on the red carpet. Arthur Godfrey served as moderator for the night's proceedings and broadcast celebrity interviews for his own national program from the Paramount's lobby. The night was capstoned with the presentation of a special citation of honor by the Major General of the Air Force Association to the film's male lead, the real-life World War II bomber pilot Jimmy Stewart, which noted the actor and veteran's "distinguished public service and outstanding artistic achievement" in the present film (Crowther 1955).

However, as the lights dim on our Air Force parade, its celebrity guests may very well start to wonder what all the fuss is about. As the drama unfolds, it becomes clear that the wide blue yonder stretches over a valley where not bombs but mostly tears rain down. Stewart plays Dutch Holland,[3] a third baseman for the St. Louis Cardinals who is forced to trade his red pinstripes for Air Force blues. Dutch is a distinctly American mythopoetic figure, a ball player who gladly served in World War II and returned home to set RBI records. Yet this gentile version of the real-life baseball-star-turned-war-hero, the World War II anti-tank gunner and Detroit slugger Hank Greenberg, is also an Air Force reservist, a former bomber pilot who flew missions over Tokyo and whose eyes still linger skywards as huge B-36 nuclear bombers thunder over the Cardinals' spring training camp at altitudes low enough to catch pop flies in their blazing props.

Dutch is on screen less than three minutes before he is forced by the Air Force to abandon his $70,000-a-year baseball contract and sign on for 21 months of active service in SAC at military scale wages. As soon as he arrives on a SAC base, Dutch witnesses a sneak attack drill that exposes SAC's lack of preparedness and vulnerability. Dutch's fellow reactivated reservists grumble about never seeing their families and losing their civilian careers, beginning with his own navigator, who lost his "nice TV business" along with the house he had just bought for his family. When not flying for his nation, Dutch spends what little time he has at home in the kitchen fighting with his wife, who is in agony every time her absentee husband risks his neck in the air for no immediate benefit. "The job is big," SAC's commander General Hawks (Frank Lovejoy) explains, "and the pay is small." Nevertheless, Dutch decides to stay on for a lifetime career in SAC, at the cost of his baseball career and perhaps even his new family.

With home, family, baseball, and TV threatened, it seems SAC is already delivering a deadly blow to American culture. *Strategic Air Command*'s plot hardly seems the stuff of good public relations or good deterrent politics. Yet the Air Force, which paid for all of the film's aerial scenes with hundreds of thousands of dollars of taxpayer money, was pleased with *Strategic Air Command* (Suid 1979, 221–2). And for those who had just seen the film's premier this should hardly be surprising, for what the Air Force enjoyed in *Strategic Air Command* was nothing less than the film's longing images of its own mighty planes in action.

By the time of *Strategic Air Command*'s release, the potential for movies about military flying to serve as public relations tools capable of boosting morale for the service and maybe even enlistment had been long recognized by military commanders. Hap Arnold, the Commander of the Army Air Force throughout World War II, had even once worked as a Hollywood flyer while serving as a young officer in the U.S. Army Signal Corps, showing off his biplane in the 1911 film *Military Scout* (Suid 1983, 14). In times both of peace and war, the Air Force and the rest of the armed services have regularly enjoyed the support of Hollywood producers eager to demonstrate their patriotism in scores of films about military life and combat. In return for a favorable portrayal, military commanders would offer filmmakers the use of genuine military equipment, locations, and manpower for nominal fees, a mode of public relations that has continued, not without some controversy, throughout the Cold War and to the present day.[4]

Strategic Air Command boosts the nation's morale for an airborne nuclear defense fleet at a time when the Air Force has just gotten a huge boost from the federal government. The film premiered just as the Strategic Air Command—newly armed with thermonuclear weapons—was becoming America's first line of defense under Eisenhower's economizing "New Look" for the military, which shifted the burden of national defense from costly standing troops to more affordable nuclear weapons. Anthony Mann's nuclear bombers further enlist the nation's desire for the New Look's combat-ready nuclear fleet by being the sexiest things on the silver screen. The personal and social crises that result from SAC's permanent military mobilization are displaced through the film's longing gaze upon the higher marriage of man and flying machine.

Strategic Air Command is so confident in its own melodramatic manipulations that it foregrounds not one but two crises of nuclear defense in its plot—SAC's disruption of the domestic economy and its own potential weakness and vulnerability—while utterly ignoring a third: the terrifying, world-destructive power of the bombs its planes are carrying. *Strategic Air Command* does not solve any of the crises it raises. Rather, the film deflects our attention onto the personal relationship Dutch shares with his planes. Staying in SAC ultimately isn't a rational choice or a patriotic duty, but a matter of one man following his heart.

Generously filmed on location at MacDill Air Force Base in Florida with full support from SAC and shot with Paramount's new VistaVision cameras (Suid 1979, 221)—the IMAX system of the day that ran film horizontally through the camera in order to double negative size and produce positive prints that exhibited unprecedented clarity and vibrant color—*Strategic Air Command* makes the flight of its true-to-life bombers its sole objects of desire. There isn't a miniature model to be found in the ten minutes devoted to the film's richly orchestrated and glamorous aerial sequences, scenes that would be especially extraordinary if seen in one of Paramount's flagship theaters equipped with horizontal VistaVision projectors. During Dutch's first flight in the B-36 long-range bomber, the film draws the audience's attention to the technical workings of the plane itself. Mann's camera cannot get enough of the B-36. Before takeoff, the camera surrounds the plane amidst technical chatter and the rising roar of engines, offering the audience the best views possible of the plane's six props and then cutting to rear views of tail flaps flapping and close-ups of auxiliary jets revving up. The engine roar dominates the soundtrack from the start of the scene until takeoff. The camera follows the plane down the runway and, to the viewer's amazement, takes off with it into an intensely blue sky. The camera zooms in on the B-36's retracting wheels as the engine roar gives way to the smooth swoon of romantic strings. Dutch spends the whole night inside the B-36, the passage of time marked as the audience follows the bomber through a tremendous sunset, the score still swooning over pink contrails and clouds turned the color of roses.

The exterior shots of Dutch's plane during his maiden flight with SAC present the film's first true joy. Airborne is where both the viewer and the B-36 want to be, carrying nuclear bombs away from all the problems on the ground. The camera is remarkably stable and controlled while flying through the air. Everything is in extremely sharp and deep focus. The confident, lingering shots of the B-36 in flight stall the narrative, constituting it as an object of beauty and desire independent of the crises of its combat readiness. At these moments in *Strategic Air Command*, the B-36 serves as much the same kind of spectacle as the figure of a women often does in narrative film: "her visual presence tends to work against the development of a story-line, to freeze the flow of action in moments of erotic contemplation" (Mulvey 1989, 19). The B-36 may be the albatross of the Air Force with its hybrid jet-prop configuration and sprawling design, but it looks complacent and luxurious in several front and rear shots featuring it plowing through the gulf coast's puffy white clouds, its giant props stirring each nimbus like cream. A bearer of nuclear bombs, the B-36 cannot remain in such a passive state, and it does not as soon as it goes off screen. In its margins *Strategic Air Command* reminds us what it is this plane actually does, occasionally intercutting its aerial footage with shots set in command centers where huge maps labeled China and U.S.S.R. loom, although the terms "nuclear weapons" and "the atomic bomb" are each mentioned only once in the film.[5]

For the boyish Dutch, a career in SAC begins as a surprisingly innocent and irresistible treat. *Strategic Air Command* makes good on its aero-erotics soon enough, though, when it introduces Dutch to the B-47, the Air Force's new swept-wing jet bomber. Dutch had just crashed his old B-36 into Greenland and is waiting to hitch a ride back to Texas with SAC's commander, General Hawks. Planes and bodies broke alike during Dutch's emergency landing, yet Dutch's growing desire to stay in SAC leads him to deny the seriousness of his injury. While they're waiting for the General's plane, Hawks—who with cigar firmly planted in mouth is the spitting image of real-life SAC commander Curtis LeMay—gives Dutch a peek at a B-47 laid out in a quiet private hanger as dimly lit as a bedroom.

It is love at first sight. The two Cold Warriors have to duck through a tiny door to get inside and see the new bomber. The ensuing high-angle long-shots can hardly contain the plane. The B-47 juts out of the screen, embracing the two onlookers in the crook of its wing and fuselage. Dutch's desire is hard to miss as he whispers "so this is the B-47, huh? Why she's the most beautiful thing I've ever seen in my life, General. Why just look at her, look at her. Oh I sure would like to get my hands on one of these" (Mann 1955).

Dutch has the time of his posthuman life flying the B-47. Once he commits himself to a lifetime in SAC, he consummates his career by performing the in-flight refueling technique that will allow the B-47 to stay permanently aloft. Accompanied by muffled technical voiceover set amid now-familiar swelling romantic music, a determined Dutch nuzzles the nose of his B-47 ever closer to an aerial fuel tanker's descending pipe while flying over snow-peaked mountains. The score reaches a climax as he makes contact, the two planes joining like mating whales magically flying over mountains. A look of satisfaction and relief washes over Dutch's helmeted face once he finishes the job. (Small wonder that Stanley Kubrick chose to mock this particular scene in the opening credits of *Dr. Strangelove*, setting stock footage of a B-52 refueling to the tune, "Try a Little Tenderness.")

The presence of sexual imagery in films such as *Strategic Air Command* has been much commented on by critics of Cold War cinema who interpret Air Force jargon as erotic innuendo, a symptom of the Air Force's Freudian unconscious running at flat-out death drive. There is much symbolism to rake. General Hawks compulsively fiddles and gestures with his cigar. Dutch's injured arm goes limp during a long flight, signifying his impotence as a fighting man (Biskind 1983, 68). Even when limp, Dutch's landing at Kadena Air Force Base sounds like a heavy date turned serious, although it is amusingly translated into the technical praxis of "immediate jet penetration" as Ground Control initially wards off Dutch's advance:

> GROUND CONTROL: Advise you hold east of the outer marker.
> DUTCH: Negative, negative, Kadena. I can't hold. I'm committed. I don't have enough fuel to go around. Go on now and bring me on in.
> GROUND CONTROL: Affirmative, continue your penetration [Mann 1955].

The sexually loaded language hovering just below the surface of consciousness in *Strategic Air Command* works in the service of the film's cyborg romance by defining the healthy new posthuman condition of Air Force life. The film's humanized and sexualized technical jargon is only one of the more obvious signs of the discursive process by which SAC mobilizes human bodies in the hybrid network of the war machine. Just as planes are sexualized and new nuclear weapons are referred to as "a new family," humans are machined and weaponized. "All staff officers are pilots first and desk jockeys second," Dutch is told when he reports to duty. SAC's officers are parts of a flying machine, not a bureaucracy. "All sharp tools," Dutch's flight engineer dubs his crew. As we learn in the film's first scene from Dutch's old flying buddy, the aptly named General Rusty Castle (Bruce Bennett), SAC relies on a steady infusion of new talent to keep its fortifications sharp. Sent to collect Dutch from the Cardinals, Rusty tells the Cardinals' coach how, above all, SAC needs Dutch's motor-skills. Reactivated to become part of a machine, Dutch is desired for his component parts, his "judgment and coordination" and the "old hands" (Mann 1955) of combat experience fine-tuned while firebombing Japan.

The discursive construction of SAC as a cyborg lifeworld turns even human babies into spare parts of the war machine. Integrated into SAC's flying machine, Dutch and his fellow SAC fathers come to refer to their own children in aeronautic terms. SAC is a fertile machine, Dutch tells Sally, its base hospitals delivering 1500 babies every month. Dutch himself "met the stork at 40,000 feet," and his engineer proudly tells him of how he has "one on the ramp, one in the hanger." Before leaving on his ill-fated B-36 mission, Dutch tries to console Sally, who is expecting their first baby, by telling her, "I kind of have a feeling the little fellow's not going to report in for about two weeks." And when handed his daughter for the first time, his first instinct is to protest, "Well I'm not checked out on this" (Mann 1955).

Strategic Air Command's posthuman melodrama values the machinery of nuclear defense over the sanctity of the nuclear family. As Dutch become an ever more lovable cyborg, his wife, Sally, bears the brunt of the film's scorn as a bothersome—and all too human—wife. Mann's film drives a wedge between man and (human) wife from the very first scene where the newly-drafted Dutch arrives on base for his physical. This humorous scene merits a very close look for it illustrates how propaganda for the New Look of American nuclear defense hinges on the fine details of casting, costume, and editing.

Dutch changes over the course of the film from that "nice guy who played third base for the Cardinals" to a man in space dressed in a pressure suit who is almost indistinguishable from his cockpit and who has neither the time nor the desire to be with his wife. The scene of Dutch's physical exam begins this process of change. It plays out in the large as a comedy of errors as Sally tries to wrest her man from the military through repeated acts of passive aggression over a telephone. In its details, though, the scene is doing much more, for under its laughs it is winning audience support for American nuclear policy.

Dutch is at first enraged when his reserve status is suddenly activated and he is ordered to serve in the Strategic Air Command. He is plucked from the pinnacle of his career, driven away from the fine new Florida home he shares with Sally, and deposited in concrete officers' barracks far away in Fort Worth, Texas. His wife Sally, of course, will have none of it. Unfortunately, despite the fact that she is played by an actress who has been Stewart's longtime screen wife, Sally doesn't have a chance. As soon as SAC gets its hands on Dutch—literally during his initial physical exam—both he and the film start to turn against her.

This scene proves to be pivotal for the film, for as it wins its chuckles at Sally's expense something very interesting happens to the viewer's sympathies both for Sally and for the life of nuclear defense. A military bureaucracy is stealing Dutch away from his wife and, to compound it all, his job as a baseball player, yet the viewer does not resent it. Rather, the viewer resents Sally, played by June Allyson as a breathy, helpless, clingy, ignorant, needling spouse.

When Dutch begins his physical, the shot/counter-shot editing of his first conversation with his wife treats the two as equals. Newly arrived on base and now seated in a sterile optometrist's office, Dutch is reading letters aloud through an eye exam machine when a phone rings. He keeps on reading as the optometrist answers for he doesn't expect to be disturbed, but surprisingly it is a call for him:

DUTCH: Colonel Holland. Sally! W'how are you? Where are you? [Mann 1955].

Cut to Sally in a mid-shot, standing before a window with planes taxiing behind her. Already, she is an incongruous figure, wearing a chaste white housedress buttoned up to a big beige scarf. With her efficient figure tucked under a spunky blond pageboy, she looks like a cross between a grade-schooler and a nun, not an inhabitant of a SAC base.

So far, Sally and Dutch are still treated as partners as the ensuing dialog plays out in shot/counter-shot:

SALLY: I'm at the airport.
DUTCH: What airport? Here in Fort Worth? W'What are you doing here?
SALLY: Well what do you think I'm doing? I came to be with you. Mmmm. Oh, I've missed you. I'm your bride of five months, remember me?
DUTCH: Yes dear I know, but….
SALLY: Well I just didn't see any sense in sitting around and waiting so here I am. Don't you want me?
DUTCH: Well honey of course I want you but we don't have any quarters yet… [Mann 1955].

As this conversation comes to a close, though, Dutch and Sally begin to disconnect, both in the film's narrative and in its editing. Dutch tells Sally to check into a hotel and wait for him, but Sally doesn't go to the hotel he recommends. Rather, as we dissolve into the next, nearly identical shot, Dutch is seated with his tongue sticking out at another doctor and saying "ahhh"—and the phone rings.

DOCTOR: Captain Johnson. It's for you, Colonel.
DUTCH: Colonel Holland. (Voice rises, shocked) You're at the main gate!? [Mann 1955].

This time there is no shot/counter-shot editing. Sally is kept entirely off screen. She is no longer Dutch's partner in dialogue and the communication between them starts to break down:

DUTCH: Get someone to take you over to the officer's club. I'll come over as soon as I'm finished. Well I have no idea dear uh they go over your head to foot, they're just down to my throat now. What? Well, this one says I don't have any adenoids. Adenoids! Bye dear [Mann 1955].

By now Dutch is becoming exasperated with his wife and for that matter so is the audience. The scene dissolves to a new setting in which Sally cannot even speak directly to her husband. A major in a blue Air Force uniform stands before a row of flyboys wearing helmets and breathers seated on a bench in a training pressure tank. "We're going to take you up to 45,000 feet," the major explains as he closes a huge metal door on them and bolts it shut. Back in the control booth, the major is seated before an observation window, monitoring responses closely—and his phone rings.

MAJOR: Major Flemming. Colonel Holland can't come to the phone right now. (Addressing Dutch through the window, still deadpan) It's your wife, Colonel Holland. She says it's urgent. (Mann 1955)

This time the shot/counter-shot editing cuts between Dutch and the major, treating the two as partners in the expert technical practice of depressurization. By now, Dutch has traded the support of his wife for the support of the breathing machine that is keeping him alive in the depressurized training tank. His voice is drowned out by hissing air and muffled by his breathing mask. His mouth is obscured by his mask for the entire scene, and the major's is obscured by the phone throughout his whole exchange with Sally. Both voices sound oddly filtered and disembodied, quite different from ordinary human tones.

> DUTCH: Well, uh, tell her I'll call her back.
> MAJOR: He says he'll call you back. He's up to 45,000 feet [Mann 1955].

Here Sally stops talking like a wife and starts talking like a figure of ridicule. We cut briefly to her in a phone booth as she leans out the door and looks up at the sky, perplexed.

> SALLY: I don't see him.
> MAJOR: No no, in the training tank, Mrs. Holland. (Puts phone down and speaks to Dutch) Mrs. Holland is in your quarters. She says to meet her there [Mann 1955].

Now Dutch truly is exasperated, for it turns out that Sally has no idea of the one thing she should know: where their new home actually is. Jimmy Stewart has to work hard to show emotion through all his flight gear, throwing his hands up and rolling his eyes.

Sally knows that there is much more at stake in Dutch's physical than her family's future livelihood. She is losing her man, but not in the way one would expect. Dutch isn't being dragged away to join an intimate brotherhood of well-oiled Spartan fighting men in the Cold War Republic—that's the *least* of Sally's worries. Service in *Strategic Air Command* is far stranger, for it entails entering into a sacred, deeply personal union with the very machinery of nuclear defense.

During his physical, Dutch has been increasingly isolated not only from his wife, but from his fellow airmen as well, made anonymous behind his gear and finally linked to them only by communications and air pressure. As each shot dissolves into the next over the course of his physical, he is transformed into a being of the Cold War, a creature of technology and technique, a man in space. Progressively losing contact with his wife, Dutch becomes more intimately connected to the machines and the military institution that sustain him as a flyer. In the language of Anthony Mann's film, this self-sustaining relationship between man and machine is more intimate and desirable than marriage. Sally has every reason to be jealous, for as the film progresses it becomes clear that Dutch wants to be inside an airplane as much as he wants to be with her. As long as Dutch serves in SAC, Sally will have to share him with his new love, the B-47 nuclear bomber. *Strategic Air Command* may have premiered as an Air Force PR film, but it is the record of the man in space's journey through the emotional highs and lows of Cold War polygamy. And if it wins the audience's sympathy for

Dutch's strange threesome, the film garners its tacit support for the foreign policy of strategic nuclear deterrence that got him there.

The crisis of the Cold War's permanent military mobilization is writ small in Dutch and Sally's bedroom. It is not just that the reactivated Dutch does not have the time to put his wife first, but rather that he no longer desires to do so. Sally intuits this fact soon after his first flight as a new officer of the Strategic Air Command, a scene where Dutch also informs her that he has just spoken to the base doctor and found out that she is pregnant. "Well all I can say is we're mighty lucky it happened before you had to report to duty," Sally tells him as she clings to his flight suit in their last happy embrace for the remainder of the film, then adding: "judging from my short experience in the Air Force it couldn't very well have happened after that" (Mann 1955). Sally had eagerly waited for Dutch on the airfield as he returns to base after his maiden flight, but at this point SAC won't let go of him before his "steam bath and massage in the physical conditioning room" (Mann 1955), and Sally is sent home alone. One flight down and SAC has already insinuated itself bodily between man and wife.

Halfway through his stint in SAC, Dutch finally gets to meet his newborn daughter, Hope, but what should be good news for Sally quickly turns to bad as Dutch gushes over his new assignment to a B-47 wing in terms that Sally expects should have been reserved for his newborn:

SALLY: Well now you say goodbye to your father.
(SALLY HANDS HOPE OFF TO A NURSE.)
DUTCH: Goodbye, Hope. I'll, uh, I guess I'll be seeing you around. That was sort of a silly thing to say.
(SALLY LAUGHS THROATILY.)
DUTCH: I think she's gonna like it in Florida. Florida, ooh, I forgot to tell ya.' We're gonna move.
SALLY: When?
DUTCH: In about two weeks. I've been transferred to MacDill. We're going back to our old house.
SALLY: Oh that's wonderful. We'll be there just in time to watch the spring training. How'd that happen?
DUTCH: Yeah, yeah—They're setting up a new B-47 wing. General Hawks gave me a chance to get in on the ground floor.
SALLY: General Hawks….
DUTCH: Uh huh.
SALLY: What's a B-47?
DUTCH: It's a new jet bomber and it's the most beautiful, wonderful airplane you've ever see in your whole life. Sally, this is the most wonderful thing you could ever imagine [Mann 1955].

Not even his new baby can distract Dutch from SAC's allure.

Sally is permitted one moment to step out of her helpless character and confront the other woman on equal terms. Having wooed Dutch away from her with the new B-47 wing, General Hawks finally pays Sally a visit at the ballpark while she is watching the Cardinals warm up.

> HAWKS: It's a real pleasure, Mrs. Holland. I've been looking forward to meeting you.
> SALLY: Same here. Only I'm a little disappointed. I thought you'd be breathing fire.
> HAWKS: Well I usually do. I just had a flame-out [Mann 1955].

It is an awkwardly formal meeting that soon becomes a sparring match between Sally and Hawks, made all the funnier because the characters nimbly step into and out of each other's gender roles. Despite Hawks' blustery attempts to represent himself as a dangerous part of the war machine, all of a sudden he finds himself in an unmistakably reversed gender role as the Other Woman:

> DOYLE [COACH OF THE CARDINALS]: So you're the man that stole my third baseman?
> HAWKS: I wish we could keep him too.
> SALLY: Hmmm, I bet you do.
> HAWKS: So you're on Mr. Doyle's side, eh?
> SALLY: Yes I am.
> HAWKS: Well we've got a job to do, Mrs. Holland, and getting men like your husband isn't easy.
> SALLY: Well, hah, don't tell me your little problems, General. I'm only interested in results.
> HAWKS: (small laugh) Touché [Mann 1955].

Lest their catty behavior cast too much doubt on a General's manhood, Hawks quickly shoves a cigar in his mouth and points it at Sally's head as they exchange a final look.

A *deus ex machina* ultimately saves Dutch and Sally's marriage when Dutch's body breaks, leaving him unfit for flight (but, fortunately, not for baseball). Just as General Hawks frees the heartbroken flyer from military service to return to the Cardinals, a chagrined Sally bursts into Hawks' office finally willing to *sally* forth for the war effort and share her husband. No matter now, for "he's all yours" Hawks brusquely tells her (Mann 1955). As the reunited couple stands with Hawks before a window, their embrace is disrupted—much as it has been throughout the film—by the roar of the new B-47 wing taking off. Sally's gaze falls on Dutch, but Dutch still looks to the sky where his gaze triangulates not with his wife's but with that of General Hawks, who is also watching the planes take off.

Strategic Air Command's story of atomic love's labors lost pulls off a neat trick. The crises of the Air Force's disruptions of the homefront and troubles in the sky are not so much addressed as they are absolved by Dutch's unconditional love of flying. *Strategic Air Command*'s cyborg romance of Cold-Wartime service makes the audience, like Sally, in the final instant regret Dutch's return to the Cardinals. In channeling Dutch's and the viewers' desire towards its flying total war machines, by making a story about the needs of nuclear defense become a cyborg romance about one man's needs, the film makes an emotional case for nuclear deterrence without ever settling any doubts about nuclear weapons or policy at all.

Nuclear Misfits: Dr. Strangelove: Or, How I Learned to Stop Worrying and Love the Bomb

Stanley Kubrick's *Dr. Strangelove* entertains no doubts whatsoever about the inhumanity of the policy of nuclear defense. Kubrick rewrites all of the characters who play a part in the nation's nuclear defense from its flyers to its strategists, turning them, much as Mann does, into cyborgs more attached to machines than their fellow human beings. Behind the comic machinations of its plot, *Dr. Strangelove* is ultimately concerned with the same thing that *Strategic Air Command* is: what life has become in an age of nuclear defense. But rather than representing that cyborg life as an object of desire, *Dr. Strangelove* makes life in the cyborg world of nuclear defense a grotesque object of parody.

In a piece of advance publicity for his film, Kubrick writes that in adapting Peter George's all-too-serious 1958 novel about an accidental nuclear war, *Red Alert*, for the screen, the business of nuclear defense turned amusing by default:

> I found that in trying to put meat on the bones and to imagine the scenes fully one had to keep leaving things out of it which were either absurd of paradoxical, in order to keep it from being funny, and these things seemed to be very real. Then I decided that the perfect tone to adopt for the film would be what I now call nightmare comedy, but it most truthfully presents the picture [Kubrick 1963, 12].

In figuring out the truth of nightmare comedy, Kubrick hit upon a subversive Cold War filmmaking strategy: to take the formula of the atomic cyborg love story and stand it on its head.

Dr. Strangelove is a far more complex and fragmented atomic cyborg love story than *Strategic Air Command*, for it is composed of three interleaved storylines that represent different nodes in nuclear defense's cybernetic network of communication, command, and control. The film's plot—which stems from the wild coincidence of an insane SAC base commander launching his wing against Russia at the exact same time that the Soviet Union has secretly activated one of nuclear strategy's fantasy gadgets, an automatic global doomsday machine—is a device, an excuse to give the audience not one but three separate views of the interior life of nuclear defense in action.

Dr. Strangelove spends very little time at all representing dooms-day. Rather, like *Strategic Air Command*, it offers a series of family por-traits of nuclear defense in action. Kubrick treats his star, Peter Sellers, just like Anthony Mann's SAC treats Dutch, as a component capable of being plugged into any leading part. Kubrick originally assigned Sellers four com-pletely different roles to play spread throughout the film's three storylines (Minoff 1963): nuclear strategist Dr. Strangelove and American President Merken Muffley, two denizens of the underground Pentagon war room; group captain Lionel Mandrake at Burpleson Air Force Base, who spends most of the film trying to persuade his mad base commander to recall the planes he has sent to attack the Soviet Union; and Major Kong, the lone B-52 captain who makes it all the way through to the Soviet Union and whose heroic efforts trigger the end of the world (illness and exhaustion eventually forced Sellers to deed the role of Kong to Slim Pickens). Unlike Jimmy Stewart, though, who melts effortlessly into character when reca-pitulating his real-life role as a bomber pilot and inspirational war hero, Sellers-the-actor is visible throughout his roles.

Dr. Strangelove does not mock the actual practice of American nuclear defense policy. Its war machines work all too well. Rather, the film mocks the narrative conventions that had previously been mustered in support of the military and of nuclear defense, foremost among them the romance of the atomic cyborg. *Dr. Strangelove* makes visible all the men in space who had been made invisible in the Cold War cinema. The film is a self-reflexive montage of homages to past war films, and in particular to Anthony Mann's *Strategic Air Command*, whose invisible cyborg romance Kubrick makes plain in his very title. The "I" of *Dr. Strangelove*'s enigmatic subtitle, *How I Learned to Stop Worrying and Love the Bomb*, is none other than the "eye" of the camera itself, the process of cinematic narration that had been used to make nuclear deterrence a matter of personal human fulfillment. The eye that loves the bomb is the eye of all the directors like Anthony Mann who worked for the Air Force's Hollywood and who made the unnatural cou-plings and deadly strategies of nuclear defense a family affair.

Anthony Mann had to work hard at the dawn of the Cold War to pro-duce desire for the unnatural life of nuclear defense. Nine years later, life with the bomb is an accomplished fact and Kubrick has to work hard to critique its unnatural settlements. *Dr. Strangelove* lays bare the narrative devices that naturalize nuclear defense by setting the words and deeds of its Cold Warriors within the strikingly high-tech world of nuclear warfighting, and in the process makes blatant clichés out of what had been invisible con-ventions. The metaphoric cyborg affair of Strategic Air Command is literal-ized in *Dr. Strangelove* as a whole way of life, an integrated life marked by its characters' locations in space and physical attachments to the war machine.

The film is populated entirely with atomic cyborgs: soldiers and statesmen who live the practice of nuclear defense so naturally that they are finally unable to do anything other than live with it to the end.

Kubrick's filmmaking shows how humanity itself does not belong in SAC's high-tech spaces. Kubrick express the madness of nuclear defense by making the coupling of man and machine in the spaces of nuclear defense a comic mismatch. *Dr. Strangelove*'s men in space utter words and act in ways that are inappropriate to the high-tech flow of events on screen. The conventional imagery and heroics of not only *Strategic Air Command* but of all World War II air combat films become *outré* when put into the bodies that inhabit the brave new world of nuclear deterrence. Likewise, the Cold War discourses of nationalism and paranoia prove to be laughable and ultimately self-destructive when applied to the posthuman settlements of the nuclear weapons state.

Dr. Strangelove has a strikingly familiar air despite the fact that much of its action takes place in an underground Pentagon war room that the United States government never even acknowledge to exist and that the hydrogen bombs it features have never been seen by unclassified eyes (Minoff 1963). Watching its bombers in flight and bases under assault, the audience gets the clear impression that it has seen and heard all of the film's events before, even though this film is about a kind of war that has never happened at all. Each of the film's three storylines is filmed in its own distinct yet familiar camera style and aspect ratio (Kagan 1972, 138–9). For instance, the exterior scenes of Burpleson Air Force Base—from which the mad SAC General Jack Ripper (Sterling Hayden) has ordered his bombers to attack the Soviet Union—are shot with a jerky 16mm handheld camera. General Ripper closes off the base and orders his troops to defend it to the death from Communist troops disguised as Americans, but of course those troops really are Americans too. The battle to recapture Burpleson has the grainy look and sound of genuine footage from Korea or World War II (Walker 1999, 136). As with most combat newsreel footage, the viewer is never sure precisely what is going on. The camera hides behind bushes and offers the viewer quick glimpses of fallen bodies and smoke. Gunfire rings out at random over the barely-heard cries of soldiers. Intercut with the documentary-style footage, Kubrick adds shots that could have been plucked from any number of Hollywood combat pictures. As an army convoy approaches the base, a machine gunner tosses his cigarette and grimly pulls the bolt back on his mounted machine gun. "Gee those trucks sure look like the real thing," he muses as he takes the convoy in his sights (Kubrick 2016 [1964]).

The film's central storyline, the flight of the B-52 that accomplishes its bombing run, likewise echoes Hollywood's World War II combat films. The crew of the B-52 is a hallmark of Hollywood, a cross section of America with an aw-shucks-slinging wild-west Major, a Jewish radioman named Goldy who speaks with a Brooklyn accent, a few other anonymous fresh-faced Midwestern boys and also, as a sign of the new times, an African American, assembled just as if they were on a mission to Tokyo. The camerawork for the B-52's bombing run is nearly identical to the camerawork in a World War II film about the first American bomber attack on Japan, the Doolittle raid on Tokyo as dramatized in Mervyn LeRoy's *Thirty Seconds Over Tokyo* (1944). Kong's B-52 performs the same spectacular low-altitude "hedgehopping" maneuvers that LeRoy's bomber fleet performs on its own run over Tokyo harbor, hopping this time over icebergs instead of Japanese trawlers.

Kubrick plays up the generic quality of the B-52's bombing run to the hilt. As a choir hums "Johnny Comes Marching Home," Major Kong dons a cowboy hat and offers some captainly words to his crew just as LeRoy's captains offered their crews. "Heck I reckon you wouldn't even be human beings if you didn't have some pretty strong personal feelings about nuclear combat," Kong confides, but then gently reminds his crew:

> that folks back home is a counting on ya and by golly we ain't about to let them down. Tell ya something else. This thing turns out to be half as important as I figure it just might be, I'd say that you're all in line for some important promotions and personal citations when this thing's over with. That goes for every last one of you, regardless of your race, your color, or your creed [Kubrick 2016 (1964)].

The viewer cannot believe she is hearing this despite the fact that she has heard similar sentiments expressed time and again in war films.

Dr. Strangelove takes pains to represent the practice of nuclear defense with an eye for intricate technical detail. Most of the film's action takes place within meticulously designed space-age sets: bomber, war room, air base. Loaded with food—particularly the GI staple, chewing gum—the cyborg habitats sustain their occupants. They mediate their inhabitants' access to the outside world through vast banks of instruments, huge tactical displays, and omnipresent telephones.

The film's two nonstudio location shots in particular work to turn the film's soldiers into men in space. The background air sequences filmed over the Arctic—an echo of *Strategic Air Command*'s own wintery aerial footage—place the B-52 and its crew in a lifeless, stratospheric environment in which the bomber figures as both a weapon and a kind of home away from home. The first scene of the film that actually features a human being, set at Burpleson Air Base, was actually filmed at the London office of IBM. Group Captain Lionel Mandrake makes his debut shuffling the printout of IBM's giant Computer 7090, the same machine used to calculate the orbit of astronaut John Glenn's flight around the Earth (Minoff 1963). Computer

7090 is a room in itself, framing Mandrake within its spinning tape wheels as he talks with General Ripper and puts Burpleson on red alert.

The underground Pentagon war room, presented in carefully composed static long shots, is a cathedral of technology that comes complete with its own buffet spread. Everybody is a man in space inside the war room. Cold Warriors sit at a great, empty round table under a ring of artificial lights. Voices echo off of giant tactical screens canted like windows onto an alien, cybernetic world. The tactical displays increasingly envelop the President and his generals as the film progresses and the dotted lines of bombers move ever closer to Russia. When Dr. Strangelove finally makes his appearance, he rolls about each scene as if a literal extension of war machines past and future, his head full of nuclear strategic thought and his one gloved arm hardwired to fire a Nazi salute. A true cyborg fighter of the next war, the lenses of Strangelove's glasses and the chrome on his wheelchair mirror the edgy light of the war room's tactical displays. Resting his head upon his gloved hand, he becomes a grotesque posthuman amalgam of Auguste Rodin's Thinker and Fritz Lang's mad scientist Rotwang.

The B-52 cockpit, designed from a single unclassified picture clipped from a British aviation magazine, is a maze of dials, wires, screens, and controls. The relatively small set itself cost the then-impressive sum of $100,000 to build, and each shot of the B-52 in flight cost about $6,000 to produce, again quite a large sum spent for the sake of realism ("Direct Hit" 1964, 79). It's all business in the B-52. The final bombing run is a portrait of the integrated circuit in action, filmed in quickly cut close-ups that echo *Strategic Air Command's* imagery, fragmenting the bodies of the aviators and merging them with their machines so that only their eyes remain showing. The bomber speaks to its crew in mechanical chunks, flashing lights, and alphanumeric symbols. Human voices, given a tinny tone by the plane's internal communication system, calmly read off coordinates even as an anti-aircraft missile closes in. Voices finally blur with the machines as the missile hits and the B-52 erupts into flashes of light and roars in pain. Major Kong aside, the crew is remarkable for its calm and precision. The members of the crew spend most of their time reading off checklists and adjusting machines as they arm their plane for the bombing run, review the contents of their survival packs, and finally zero in on their target. They are competent professionals to the end. If only it weren't for the fact that they are going to destroy the world, they would make patriotic American viewers proud.

Set in motion, nuclear defense's war machine works perfectly fine all on its own, which is precisely the problem in *Dr. Strangelove*: the cyborg nature of modern war itself. The blurring of the natural boundaries of man and machine in the posthuman space of national defense is what is truly responsible for the world's doom in *Dr. Strangelove*, a point only partially intimated in the film's treatment of food as swept up in the flow of the war machine. Up until the end of the film, the cyborg orgy of World War III is mirrored in a food orgy the audience continually witness on screen. Food becomes progressively more violent and unhealthy over the course of the film, finally turning into a weapon in its own right.

At first, food is merely as excessive as the defense budget. Everybody is eating on the B-52 when the viewer first meets them; in fact, Goldy is eating so fast that he spits food into his headset as he talks to Kong. In the war room, General Buck Turgidson shovels piece after piece of gum into his mouth as he briefs President Muffley on General Ripper's actions. Russian Ambassador De Sodesky walks the length of a glutinous buffet spread out in the war room and quibbles over the lack of fresh fish.

Once the fighting starts in the skies, the lines between food and war machinery blur. Food stops going into people and starts going into guns. During the assault on Burpleson base, General Ripper pulls a huge machine gun from his golf bag along with a long bandoleer. "Feed me this belt, boy!" he demands of the cowering Captain Mandrake, who has been fidgeting with a piece of unwrapped chewing gum throughout the entire scene (Kubrick 2016 [1964]). Ripper eventually eats his own bullet and then food itself starts fighting back. Mandrake does not have enough change in his pocket to call the President and give him Ripper's recall code, so he asks one of the soldiers who has just retaken the base to shoot a Coca Cola machine open for him. The machine then dutifully shoots cola into the soldier's face.

The culmination of this slapstick theme was ultimately left on the cutting room floor at the director's behest. The first cut of *Dr. Strangelove* did not end with a montage of nuclear explosions set to Vera Lynne's wistful "We'll Meet Again." That was added only later, following the film's preliminary test screening. *Dr. Strangelove* originally ended in a massive food fight replete with custard pies hurled between all the Cold Warriors assembled in the war room (Kubrick 1970, 309). (Why else spread a lavish buffet in a war room?) Turning their own food against themselves, the viewer gets the point that man may be just as unfit to handle the other things that sustain him deep underground and flying high at 45,000 feet and in the end will only turn them against himself.

Pie fights aside, Kubrick critiques the posthuman state of nuclear deterrence by setting a number of conventional discourses and normal human behaviors within its cyborg lifeworld, in the process making them seem alien and absurd. Major Kong's rousing World War II–era speech rings hollow when directed to his cyborg crew, especially when the audience knows that the only home they will ever return to will be a smoking, radiated ruin. Laughing at the misfit between the film's words and deeds, the viewer soon realizes that man himself does not properly fit within *Dr. Strangelove*'s elegantly designed cyborg spaces. Major Kong's "dangerous anachronism" (Maland 1964, 200) of a gung-ho speech is only the beginning of a series of inappropriate discourse conventions.

As *Dr. Strangelove* darts from camera style to camera style and aspect ratio to aspect ratio, the viewer sees that even film itself is unfit to represent this strange new world in a coherent manner. The film's abrupt editing between each of its three parallel narratives disrupts any continuity of mood. The cinematic conventions that have been used to film America's past wars now look like blatant devices themselves when thrown together in a collage that can't figure out how to represent the cyborg orgy the audience is seeing on screen.

Just as film is unfit to contain the practice of nuclear defense, the discourses of everyday life should not be uttered within the cyborg space of the war machine. Everything normal becomes laughable. "Most of the humor in *Strangelove* arises from the depiction of everyday human behavior in a nightmarish situation," Kubrick tells Joseph Gelmis in a 1969 interview (Kubrick 1970, 308). Yet everyday human behavior is funny in *Dr. Strangelove* even before the film's situation turns nightmarish. The crew of the B-52 is introduced to the audience doing the normal stuff that soldiers do when not fighting, such as napping, playing cards, and reading *Playboy*, all of which provokes giggles when set amidst the latest high-tech gadgets of America's nuclear defense.

When war breaks out, the film does not adjust: the dialogue and the props remain those of every normal day, except that now all of it is strange and laughable. "This is your attack profile," Major Kong tells his crew once he receives the order to begin his bombing run, speaking in tones as if here were a captain of a commercial airliner describing the day's flight to Dallas, except that he is talking about jamming enemy transmissions and dropping 30 megaton atomic bombs (Kubrick 2016 [1964]). The crew is issued survival packets, each of which contain, among other necessities of life while traveling abroad, a miniature combination Bible and Russian phrasebook that is ludicrously dwarfed by a crewmember's massive, helmeted head. Back in the war room, President Muffley telephones Soviet Premier Kissoff in order to inform him that the U.S. has accidentally started World War III, and in the process turns the Cold War's battle of wills into a battle of whines as each leader insists on maintaining the niceties of everyday conversation and attempts to express a greater degree of sorrow over the coming nuclear apocalypse. Kong's hat waving and rebel yell as he rides a nuclear bomb down onto its target of course properly belongs on a bronco, or at least in a pickup truck. Even fighting itself doesn't belong in the Pentagon's war room. Scolding Soviet Ambassador De Sodesky and General Turgidson for grappling with one another over a tiny spy camera that De Sodesky has smuggled into the Pentagon, Muffley delivers one of the film's ironic punch-lines: "Gentlemen, you can't fight in here, this is the War Room!" (Kubrick 2016 [1964]).

Everyday sayings and behaviors appear in amusing contradiction to the technical praxis of nuclear defense. For that matter, so do the names of all the characters. The symbolic names given to the film's characters foreground how just how unfit the film's cyborg world really is, much as the symbolic names given *Strategic Air Command*'s characters underscored the gravity of that film's plot. The characters' names—Generals Buck Turgidson and Jack Ripper, President Merkin Muffley and Premier Dimitri Kissoff, etc.—are all satiric labels that do not name people but rather blatantly announce their place in the symbolic economy of the film's narrative. Named by their function in a nuclear narrative, the audience struggles to treat the major players in *Dr. Strangelove* as real or serious people.

Nor can the audience take the cyborg coupling of man and machine in nuclear defense seriously. *Dr. Strangelove* makes the invisible romantic theme of the atomic cyborg explicitly erotic. *Strategic Air Command*'s aerial refueling scene becomes pornographic in *Dr. Strangelove*'s opening credits, as Kubrick employs similar shots of a B-52 refueling as featured in Mann's PR film about the B-47. Rather than being the climax of an invisible cyborg romance, here the refueling is presented before the plot as an act in itself, with the same two-minute length and repetitive editing between mid-shots and close-ups as an 8mm blue film.

But the audience especially cannot take cyborg coupling seriously when it is embodied in the figure of Air Force Chief of Staff General Buck Turgidson. While Dr. Strangelove may bear the film's title, Turgidson is the most sexually coded atomic cyborg in the film, as becomes clear through the affair he has with his secretary, Miss Scott (whom, it turns out, viewers have already seen in the *Playboy* centerfold aboard Kong's B-52). Here *Dr. Strangelove* once again makes reference to *Strategic Air Command*, specifically the scene in which Sally keeps calling Dutch during his physical examinations. Turgidson's integration into the circuit of nuclear defense becomes a bad marriage once Miss Scott starts calling him at work. No sooner has Turgidson briefed President Muffley on Ripper's having launched his wing against Russia when the phone on his desk unexpectedly buzzes.

> BUCK: Hello? I told you never to call me here. Don't you know where I am? Well look, baby, I can—I can't talk to you now, my President needs me [Kubrick 2016 (1964)].

Even more than Sally Holland, Miss Scott doesn't have a chance. Held off screen, she suffers the patronizing discourse of a married man to his mistress:

> BUCK: Of course Bucky wants to be there with you. Of course it isn't only physical. I deeply respect you as a human being. Some day I'm gonna make you Mrs. Buck Turgidson. Oh, listen, ah, you, you go back to sleep, hon. Bucky'll be back there just as soon as he can. (Buck moves to hang up but has an afterthought.) Listen, shug, don't forget to say your prayers [Kubrick 2016 (1964)].

This pleading offscreen mistress hardly seems like the same secretary who was so visible earlier, clad in a bikini but officiously going about her business. When the audience first sees her, the film's lone woman is also presented as a military professional, even when on display wearing a bathing suit and high heels. She is a secretary in space, a sexed communications filter that lives in the artificial hardened environment of military command. Yet once Turgidson leaves the bedroom they share at the beginning of the film and goes to work defending the nation, she is pushed off screen. She is no longer in space but on the phone, another woman left behind.

As Turgidson acts like a husband on the sneak, the nuclear attraction that binds him to his post begins to look increasingly suspect. *Dr. Strangelove* makes a comic object out of the Air Force's manipulative cyborg romance, for what is truly amusing here—and strange—is that Buck acts guilty at all. Anthony Mann's wartime romance had finally made Cold War viewers accept the fact that the ordinary business of American family life no longer applies to the Cold War's men in space. Kubrick's black comedy, in turn, brings the man in space firmly back down to Earth. As embodied in General Turgidson, the fit between man and war machine is both awkward and dishonest.

George C. Scott plays Turgidson as a clown whose body explodes into motion. Turgidson is so integrated in the circuit of nuclear defense that he actually becomes a plane at the culmination of Major Kong's bombing run. Framed in a two-shot with a row of grim Generals standing in silhouette behind him, Turgidson's excitement grows uncontrollably as he explains to Muffley how the B-52 operates, finally crouching down and spreading his arms as if he were a flying plane himself:

> TURGIDSON: Well, uh, sir, uh, if a pilot's good, see, I mean if he's really sharp, he can barrel that baby in so low, he he, you outta see it some time, it's a sight, a big plane like a 52, VROOM, with jet exhaust frying chickens in the barnyard!
> MUFFLEY (HYSTERICAL): Yeah, but has he got a chance?
> TURGIDSON: Has he got a chance? Hell yea—, (stopping himself) yuh… [Kubrick 2016 (1964)]

The union of man and plane turns bleak as even Turgidson realizes the inappropriateness of his glee.

Laughter at the misfit between *Dr. Strangelove's* conventional words and high-tech deeds leads directly away from any sympathy for the film's harried men in space and to the realization that the only thing that is inappropriate here—the thing that remains, finally, unspeakable without the accompaniment of nervous laughter—is the practice of nuclear defense. It is simply too inhuman—posthuman—to take seriously. The common discourses of Cold War America are not only inappropriate when uttered within the space of nuclear defense, but their misfit is ultimately self-destructive.

The action at the heart of *Strategic Air Command* and *Dr. Strangelove* does not revolve around the strategic relationship between the United States and its enemies, but around the personal relationship between man and fighting machine. *Strategic Air Command* uses classic Hollywood's invisible style to relate that action as an invisible cyborg romance. *Dr. Strangelove,* in turn, foregrounds the technical *and* narrative devices behind nuclear defense's posthuman settlements, turning the atomic cyborgs of Cold War Hollywood into openly misfit couplings of man and war machine. The same kind of fantasy underscores both supportive and critical approaches to nuclear policy in this class of Hollywood film: whether the audience supports American nuclear policy depends on what it thinks of, and how seriously it take, Hollywood's atomic love affairs.

NOTES

1. The wide net of this conglomeration is summed up in the subtitle of Mick Broderick's exhaustive, year-by-year compendia of nuclear films in his 1991 study, *Nuclear Movies: A Critical Analysis and Filmography of International Feature Length Films Dealing with Experimentation, Aliens, Terrorism, Holocaust and Other Disaster Scenarios, 1914–1989* (Jefferson, NC: McFarland).

2. While I focus on two films in this essay, my argument can be extended to other Cold War films about nuclear deterrence such as *A Gathering of Eagles* (1963), *Fail-Safe* (1964), and *Colossus: The Forbin Project* (1970) as well. Each of these three films also features an emotionally charged relationship between man and nuclear war machine that is much like the kind of cyborg relationship I analyze in *Strategic Air Command* and *Dr. Strangelove.*

3. Character names in *Strategic Air Command* as well as in *Dr. Strangelove* have obvious symbolic meanings. For instance, Dutch Holland is named—doubly so—after a neutral country that was nevertheless overrun in World War II. Where *Strategic Air Command* symbolically militarizes its characters by giving them names such as Major Rusty Castle and General Hawks, *Dr. Strangelove* turns around and overtly sexualizes them with names such as Major Kong and General Buck Turgidson.

4. A number of historians have documented the military's relationship with Hollywood. Lawrence H. Suid's *Guts and Glory: Great American War Movies* (New York: Addison-Wesley, 1979) does a particularly helpful job discussing the institutional history of this relationship over the course of the Cold War. Thomas Doherty's *Projections of War: Hollywood, American Culture, and World War II* (New York: Columbia University Press, 1993) and Clayton R. Koppes and Gregory D. Black's *Hollywood Goes to War: How Politics, Profits and Propaganda Shaped World War II Movies* (Berkeley: University of California Press, 1987) each focus on

how military pressures shaped the content of Hollywood films, particularly during World War II.

5. In one of the film's more unsettling asides, the audience is even told that SAC's favorite pastime is to target heartland USA. "We've been bombing cities every day and every night all over the U.S.," a well-pressed duty officer proudly tells us in a darkened bunker during a practice run, "only people never know it."

Works Cited

Biskind, Peter. 1983. *Seeing Is Believing: How Hollywood Taught Us to Stop Worrying and Love the Fifties*. New York: Pantheon.

Broderick, Mick. 1991. *Nuclear Movies: A Critical Analysis and Filmography of International Feature Length Films Dealing with Experimentation, Aliens, Terrorism, Holocaust, and Other Disaster Scenarios*. Jefferson, NC: McFarland.

Clynes, Manfred E., and Nathan S. Kline. 1995 (1960). "Cyborgs and Space." In *The Cyborg Handbook*. Edited by Chris Hables Gray. New York: Routledge.

Crowther, Bosley. 1955. Review of *Strategic Air Command. New York Times.* New York, NY, 21 April.

"Direct Hit." 1964. *Newsweek*, 3 February.

Doherty, Thomas. 1993. *Projections of War: Hollywood, American Culture, and World War II.* New York: Columbia University Press.

Haraway, Donna J. 1991. "A Cyborg Manifesto: Science, Technology, and Socialist-Feminism in the Late Twentieth Century." In *Simians, Cyborgs, and Women: The Reinvention of Nature.* New York: Routledge.

Kagan, Norman. 1972. *The Cinema of Stanley Kubrick.* New York: Holt, Rinehart and Winston.

Koppes, Clayton R., and Gregory D. Black. 1987. *Hollywood Goes to War: How Politics, Profits and Propaganda Shaped World War II Movies.* Berkeley: University of California Press.

Kubrick, Stanley. 1963. "How I Learned to Stop Worrying." *Films and Filming.* June, 12–13.

_____. 1970. *The Film Director as Superstar.* By Joseph Gelmis. New York: Doubleday.

_____. 2016. *1964 Director of Dr. Strangelove: Or, How I Learned to Stop Worrying and Love the Bomb.* New York: Criterion, Blu-ray.

Maland, Charles. 1983. "*Dr. Strangelove*: 1964 Nightmare Comedy and the Ideology of Liberal Consensus." In *Hollywood as Historian: American Film in a Cultural Context*, edited by Peter C. Rollins. Lexington: University Press of Kentucky.

Mann, Anthony, dir. 1955. *Strategic Air Command.*; Chicago: Olive Films, 2016. Blu-ray.

Minoff, Leon. 1963. "'Nerve Center' for a Nuclear Nightmare." *New York Times.* New York, NY, April 21.

Mulvey, Laura. 1989. "Visual Pleasure and Narrative Cinema." In *Visual and Other Pleasures.* Bloomington: Indiana University Press.

Perkowitz, Sidney. 2004. *Digital People: From Bionic Humans to Androids.* Washington, D.C.: Joseph Henry Press.

Ray, Robert B. 1985. *A Certain Tendency of the Hollywood Cinema, 1930–1980.* Princeton, NJ: Princeton University Press.

Rosenberg, David Alan. 1983. "The Origins of Overkill: Nuclear Weapons and American Strategy, 1945–1960." *International Security* 7, no. 4 (Spring): 113–181.

Short, Sue. 2005. *Cyborg Cinema and Contemporary Subjectivity.* New York: Palgrave Macmillan.

Suid, Lawrence H. 1979. *Guts and Glory: Great American War Movies.* New York: Addison–Wesley.

_____. 1983. "Mythmaking for the War Effort." In *Air Force.* Madison: University of Wisconsin Press.

Walker, Alexander. 1999. *Stanley Kubrick, Director.* New York: W.W. Norton and Company.

About the Contributors

Emrah **Atasoy** is an assistant professor in the Department of English Language and Literature, the Faculty of Humanities at Cappadocia University, Turkey. He wrote his dissertation on 20th-century dystopian fiction with a specific focus on Katharine Burdekin, Anthony Burgess and P.D. James. His areas of interest include speculative fiction, twentieth-century literature, dystopia, utopia, science fiction and Turkish utopianism.

Ruy **Burgos-Lovece** was born in Chile in 1957. He obtained a high school physics teacher degree from a Venezuelan university in 1980, and an MA in French from the University of Arkansas in 1987. In 1994, he became a freelance translator. By 2001, he had a Ph.D. in French literature from UNC–Chapel Hill. His research interests include the ontology of the self through science fiction and the resonance of the Algerian War on contemporaneous French science-fiction.

AmyLea **Clemons** is an associate professor of English at Francis Marion University in South Carolina. Her work explores the intersections of rhetoric and literature, with particular attention to the rhetorical strategies involved in the writing and reading of dystopian, fantasy, and SF texts. Primarily a Kenneth Burke scholar, she explores a wide range of "literatures" with Burke's flexible theories, from the early novel to current fan-produced texts.

Thomas P. **David**, Ph.D. in Germanic studies, is a lecturer in the Department of Cultural Studies and Comparative Literature at the University of Minnesota. His dissertation examines how the science fiction of the German Democratic Republic addresses the nature of the technologically advanced society that has emerged since the end of the Cold War and the concomitant economic, social, and political processes that today are collectively designated by the concept of globalization.

Doug **Davis** is a professor of English at Gordon State College in Barnesville, Georgia, where he teaches literature and writing. His scholarly interests include science fiction, Cold War culture, and the literature of the American south. He has published several essays that explore the intersection of military strategy, literature, and film, as well as many more on his favorite southern author, Flannery O'Connor.

Julie **Hugonny** earned her Ph.D. in French literature from New York University in 2014. Her dissertation tackles disasters, epidemics, devolution and the end of the world. Her research interests include science fiction from its origin to present times, and depictions of monsters in literature and film. She is a visiting assistant professor at Georgia Tech.

Annette M. **Magid**, Ph.D., is a professor affiliated with SUNY Erie Community College in Buffalo. Her areas of expertise include American/British utopian literature and film, theater, science fiction literature and film, as well as children's literature. Her publications include *Quintessential Wilde* (2017); *Apocalyptic Projections* (2015); *Wilde's Wiles* (2013); and a volume of poetry, *Tunnel of Stone* (2002). In addition, she has published articles in a variety of journals and monographs.

Naomi R. **Mercer** is an independent scholar and diversity, equity, and inclusion specialist. She recently retired from a 25-year career in the United States Army. She specializes in feminist dystopian and utopian writing and 20th century literature. Her publications include *Toward Utopia* (2015); "Masculine Expansions of Other-mothering in Toni Morrison's *Beloved*, *Jazz*, and *A Mercy*"; and "Malkah, Aging, and Jewish Identity in Marge Piercy's *He, She and It*."

Erin M. **Roll** received her MA in English from Montclair State University in Montclair, New Jersey, in 2018. Her master's thesis concentrated on memory loss and cultural amnesia in the novels of Ursula K. Le Guin. She has presented her research at the 2016 NeMLA conference and the 2016 GradCon. Outside of her academic work, she has worked as a journalist, editor and photographer.

Index

243